CASEBOOKS PUBLISHE

Austen: *Emma* DAVID LODGE
Austen: *'Northanger Abbey' & 'Persuasion'* B. C. SOUTHAM
Austen: *'Sense and Sensibility', 'Pride and Prejudice' & 'Mansfield Park'* B. C. SOUTHAM
Blake: *Songs of Innocence and Experience* MARGARET BOTTRALL
Charlotte Brontë: *'Jane Eyre' & 'Villette'* MIRIAM ALLOTT
Emily Brontë: *Wuthering Heights* MIRIAM ALLOTT
Browning: *'Men and Women' & Other Poems* J. R. WATSON
Bunyan: *Pilgrim's Progress* ROGER SHARROCK
Byron: *'Childe Harold's Pilgrimage' & 'Don Juan'* JOHN JUMP
Chaucer: *Canterbury Tales* J. J. ANDERSON
Coleridge: *'The Ancient Mariner' & Other Poems* ALUN R. JONES & WILLIAM TYDEMAN
Congreve: *Comedies* PATRICK LYONS
Conrad: *'Heart of Darkness', 'Nostromo' & 'Under Western Eyes'* C. B. COX
Conrad: *The Secret Agent* IAN WATT
Dickens: *Bleak House* A. E. DYSON
Dickens: *'Hard Times', 'Great Expectations' & 'Our Mutual Friend'* NORMAN PAGE
Donne: *Songs and Sonets* JULIAN LOVELOCK
George Eliot: *Middlemarch* PATRICK SWINDEN
George Eliot: *'The Mill on the Floss' & 'Silas Marner'* R. P. DRAPER
T. S. Eliot: *Four Quartets* BERNARD BERGONZI
T. S. Eliot: *'Prufrock', 'Gerontion', 'Ash Wednesday' & Other Shorter Poems* B. C. SOUTHAM
T. S. Eliot: *The Waste Land* C. B. COX & ARNOLD P. HINCHLIFFE
Farquhar: *'The Recruiting Officer' & 'The Beaux' Stratagem'* RAYMOND A. ANSELMENT
Fielding: *Tom Jones* NEIL COMPTON
Forster: *A Passage to India* MALCOLM BRADBURY
Hardy: *The Tragic Novels* R. P. DRAPER
Hardy: *Poems* JAMES GIBSON & TREVOR JOHNSON
Hopkins: *Poems* MARGARET BOTTRALL
James: *'Washington Square' & 'The Portrait of a Lady'* ALAN SHELSTON
Jonson: *'Every Man in his Humour' & 'The Alchemist'* R. V. HOLDSWORTH
Jonson: *Volpone* JONAS A. BARISH
Joyce: *'Dubliners' & 'A Portrait of the Artist as a Young Man'* MORRIS BEJA
Keats: *Narrative Poems* JOHN SPENCER HILL
Keats: *Odes* G. S. FRASER
D. H. Lawrence: *Sons and Lovers* GAMINI SALGADO
D. H. Lawrence: *'The Rainbow' & 'Women in Love'* COLIN CLARKE
Marlowe: *Doctor Faustus* JOHN JUMP
Marlowe: *'Tamburlaine the Great', 'Edward the Second' & 'The Jew of Malta'* JOHN RUSSELL BROWN
Marvell: *Poems* ARTHUR POLLARD
Milton: *'Comus' & 'Samson Agonistes'* JULIAN LOVELOCK
Milton: *Paradise Lost* A. E. DYSON & JULIAN LOVELOCK
Osborne: *Look Back in Anger* JOHN RUSSELL TAYLOR
Peacock: *The Satirical Novesl* LORNA SAGE
Pope: *The Rape of the Lock* JOHN DIXON HUNT
Shakespeare: *A Midsummer Night's Dream* ANTONY W. PRICE
Shakespeare: *Antony and Cleopatra* JOHN RUSSELL BROWN
Shakespeare: *Coriolanus* B. A. BROCKMAN
Shakespeare: *Hamlet* JOHN JUMP
Shakespeare: *Henry IV Parts I and II* G. K. HUNTER
Shakespeare: *Henry V* MICHAEL QUINN

Shakespeare: *Julius Caesar* PETER URE
Shakespeare: *King Lear* FRANK KERMODE
Shakespeare: *Macbeth* JOHN WAIN
Shakespeare: *Measure for Measure* G. K. STEAD
Shakespeare: *The Merchant of Venice* JOHN WILDERS
Shakespeare: *'Much Ado About Nothing' & 'As You Like It'* JOHN RUSSELL BROWN
Shakespeare: *Othello* JOHN WAIN
Shakespeare: *Richard II* NICHOLAS BROOKE
Shakespeare: *The Sonnets* PETER JONES
Shakespeare: *The Tempest* D. J. PALMER
Shakespeare: *Troilus and Cressida* PRISCILLA MARTIN
Shakespeare: *Twelfth Night* D. J. PALMER
Shakespeare: *The Winter's Tale* KENNETH MUIR
Shelley: *Shorter Poems & Lyrics* PATRICK SWINDEN
Spenser: *The Faerie Queene* PETER BAYLEY
Swift: *Gulliver's Travels* RICHARD GRAVIL
Tennyson: *In Memoriam* JOHN DIXON HUNT
Thackeray: *Vanity Fair* ARTHUR POLLARD
Trollope: *The Barsetshire Novels* T. BAREHAM
Webster: *'The White Devil' & 'The Duchess of Malfi'* R. V. HOLDSWORTH
Wilde: *Comedies* WILLIAM TYDEMAN
Woolf: *To the Lighthouse* MORRIS BEJA
Wordsworth: *Lyrical Ballads* ALUN R. JONES & WILLIAM TYDEMAN
Wordsworth: *The Prelude* W. J. HARVEY & RICHARD GRAVIL
Years: *Poems, 1919–35* ELIZABETH CULLINGFORD
Yeats: *Last Poems* JON STALLWORTHY

The Metaphysical Poets GERALD HAMMOND
Poetry of the First World War DOMINIC HIBBERD
Thirties Poets: 'The Auden Group' RONALD CARTER
Comedy: Developments in Criticism D. J. PALMER
Drama Criticism: Developments since Ibsen ARNOLD P. HINCHLIFFE
The Pastoral Mode BRYAN LOUGHREY
Tragedy: Developments in Criticism R. P. DRAPER
The English Novel: Developments in Criticism since Henry James STEPHEN HAZELL
The Language of Literature NORMAN PAGE
The Romantic Imagination JOHN SPENCER HILL

CASEBOOKS IN PREPARATION

Beckett: *'Waiting for Godot' & Other Plays* JOHN RUSSELL BROWN
Defoe: *'Robinson Crusoe' & 'Moll Flanders'* PATRICK LYONS
Dickens: *'Dombey and Son' & 'Little Dorrit'* ALAN SHELSTON
T. S. Eliot: *Plays* ARNOLD P. HINCHLIFFE
O'Casey: *'Juno and the Paycock', 'The Plough and the Stars' & 'The Shadow of a Gunman'* RONALD AYLING
Pinter: *'The Caretaker' & Other Plays* MICHAEL SCOTT
Sheridan: *Comedies* PETER DAVISON

Elizabethan Lyric & Narrative Poetry GERALD HAMMOND
Medieval English Drama PETER HAPPÉ
Poetry Criticism: Developments since the Symbolists A. E. DYSON
Post-Fifties Poets: Gunn, Hughes, Larkin & R. S. Thomas A. E. DYSON
Shakespeare: Approaches in Criticism JOHN RUSSELL BROWN
The Gothick Novel VICTOR SAGE

Yeats

Poems, 1919–1935

A CASEBOOK

EDITED BY

ELIZABETH CULLINGFORD

MACMILLAN

First published 1984 by
Higher and Further Education Division
MACMILLAN PUBLISHERS LTD
London and Basingstoke
Companies and representatives
throughout the world

Typeset by
Wessex Typesetters Ltd
Frome, Somerset

Printed in Hong Kong

British Library Cataloguing in Publication Data
Yeats poems, 1919–1935.—(Casebook series)
1. Yeats, W. B.—Criticism and interpretation
I. Cullingford, Elizabeth II. Series
821'.8 PR5907
ISBN 0-333-27422-9
ISBN 0-333-27423-7 Pbk

W.R.TUSON

CONTENTS

2 Studies on Specific Poems

GENERAL EDITOR'S PREFACE

The Casebook series, launched in 1968, has become a well-regarded library of critical studies. The central concern of the series remains the 'single-author' volume, but suggestions from the academic community have led to an extension of the original plan, to include occasional volumes on such general themes as literary 'schools' and genres.

Each volume in the central category deals either with one well-known and influential work by an individual author, or with closely related works by one writer. The main section consists of critical readings, mostly modern, collected from books and journals. A selection of reviews and comments by the author's contemporaries is also included, and sometimes comment from the author himself. The Editor's Introduction charts the reputation of the work or works from the first appearance to the present time.

Volumes in the 'general themes' category are variable in structure but follow the basic purpose of the series in presenting an integrated selection of readings, with an Introduction which explores the theme and discusses the literary and critical issues involved.

A single volume can represent no more than a small selection of critical opinions. Some critics are excluded for reasons of space, and it is hoped that readers will pursue the suggestions for further reading in the Select Bibliography. Other contributions are severed from their original context, to which some readers may wish to turn. Indeed, if they take a hint from the critics represented here, they certainly will.

A. E. Dyson

INTRODUCTION

The purpose of this Casebook is to illuminate the main issues that Yeats's work has raised in the minds of his critics, and to provide specific detailed commentary on some of his major poems. Here the beginning student will find tools which will enable him to extend his knowledge and appreciation: Tom Henn* on the Anglo-Irish background, or Richard Ellmann's* elucidation of *A Vision*, for example. The more advanced student will be able to sample the work of some of the best Yeats scholars, consider widely contrasting views and critical methods, and decide for himself which avenues of inquiry to follow. Such a student is urged to restore to their original context essays which have been extracted from longer books and articles.

This book is, above all, designed to save its readers time. There is an enormous amount of work about Yeats, and some of it is very bad. A glance at the monumental bibliography of Yeats criticism compiled by K. P. S. Jochum (Urbana, 1978), which lists over seven thousand items, is enough to depress the spirits of the hardiest aspiring researcher. The essays here offered, the suggestions in this Introduction, and the Select Bibliography, will provide a preliminary map of the wilderness. Time thus saved can be spent where it will do most good: in close consideration of the poems themselves.

The scope of the present selection is limited: we are looking at responses to poetry in collections published between 1919 and 1935 – *The Wild Swans at Coole* (1919), *Michael Robartes and the Dancer* (1921), *The Tower* (1928), *The Winding Stair and Other Poems* (1933), and *A Full Moon in March* (1935). Excluded are the early poems of the so-called 'Celtic Twilight', the 'transitional' verse of *Responsibilities* (1914), and the 'lust and rage' of the posthumously published *Last Poems*. (Criticism of the *Last Poems* appears in a Casebook edited by Jon Stallworthy.) The general essays included in Part Three, section 1 may range a little more widely, but all the specific commentary in section 2 following is restricted to poems of the 1919–35 period. As an obvious consequence of this focus, there is little discussion of one of the major issues which has preoccupied Yeats's critics: the question of

---

* All critics marked with an asterisk are represented by the relevant work in this volume – [Ed.]

his development. One exception, however, is T. S. Eliot,* whose classic memorial lecture on Yeats (1940) celebrates his self-transformation from the impersonal craftsman of a 'vague enchanted beauty' into a vigorous 'poet of middle age' who, 'out of intense and personal experience, is able to express a general truth'. Another is Richard Ellmann,* who stresses the continuity between the early and the later work, arguing in *The Identity of Yeats* (1954), that 'his themes and symbols are fixed in youth, and then renewed with increasing vigour and directness to the end of his life'.

If the topic of Yeats's development is discussed only briefly, much more space is given here to another major issue: the question of his beliefs. Early critics were less interested in aesthetic matters than in the poet's adherence to magical doctrines and creation of the philosophical system expounded in *A Vision* (1925, 1937). His alleged fascism disturbed readers like George Orwell* and W. H. Auden,* whose political consciousness was moulded in a different time and a different place. Those who objected to his *Vision* or to his politics had two avenues open to them: either to suggest, as did Yvor Winters,* that his 'cranky' beliefs vitiate the greatness of his verse, or that the verse somehow 'transcends' the beliefs, which may safely be ignored. Neither strategy appears satisfactory to a reader who thinks both that poetry and belief are inseparable, and that Yeats was a great poet. In a remarkably prophetic passage written in 1942, Allen Tate* examined this problem and concluded that it would determine the direction of Yeats studies. While wrestling with the sources and the implications of Yeats's esoteric symbolism, Tate said, critics would produce 'special studies of great ingenuity, but the more direct and more difficult problem of the poetry itself will probably be delayed'. He was, unfortunately, correct.

The first of the poems with which this Casebook is concerned was written when Yeats was forty-nine; the last in his seventieth year. The context in which this poetry was written includes not only private events like Yeats's marriage, but also the political drama of Ireland. To a significant extent the history of Yeats's mature poetry is the history of his country. English readers share with Yeats a common language, but they are divided from him by politics, culture and tradition. Though his work is taught in schools and universities as 'English Literature', he is no more an English poet than his erstwhile secretary Ezra Pound – which may explain why so many English critics (F. R. Leavis,* L. C. Knights, D. S. Savage and Frank

Kermode* among them) have found themselves somewhat uneasy in the face of his achievement. Leavis, for example, argues that the 'anaemic' Victorian poetic tradition in which Yeats began to write, continued, through its persistence in his use of 'symbol drawn from his cult of magic', to defeat his later attempts at full self-expression. Leavis's conclusion – that Yeats is ultimately a failure and that his poetry is 'little more than a marginal comment on the main activities of his life' – results more from his determination to expose the pernicious influence of English nineteenth-century poetry than from an informed understanding of his Irish subject. American critics, on the other hand, have found it easier to acknowledge Yeats's unique identity. Politics may play a part here, for Americans, many of them Irish by ancestry, have always been more eager than the English to foster Ireland's political and cultural aspirations. Closest in sympathy to the poet is the Anglo-Irish critic Tom Henn,* whose depiction of the Irish background provides an indispensable introduction to a world which he himself also knew: the world of the decaying Anglo-Irish gentry. For a detailed treatment of modern Irish history it is recommended that the student consult F. S. L. Lyons's magnificent *Ireland Since the Famine* (1971). Lyons's extensive bibliography also points the way to more specialised studies of particular events.

Since the earliest poems considered here were written in 1914 (see Richard Ellmann's helpful chronology of Yeats's poetry in *The Identity of Yeats*, pp. 287–94), a survey of their historical context may begin with the Great War. To an English reader Yeats's refusal to write a war poem because 'I think it better that in times like these / A poet's mouth be silent' ('On Being Asked for a War Poem'), sounds callous. But from an Irish perspective Britain, not Germany, was the traditional national enemy. England had treated Ireland as a conquered territory since the invasion of Strongbow in the twelfth century. As a young man Yeats, who took his politics from the old Fenian John O'Leary, was deeply involved with Irish nationalism, and he became the leader of a movement to revive Irish culture, literature and drama.[1] By 1914 his first political enthusiasm had been cooled by the constant squabbling and bitterness among Dublin's literary-political cliques, but as a 'nationalist of the school of John O'Leary'[2] he saw the European holocaust as Britain's war, not Ireland's. In stark contrast was his reaction to the failed Easter Rising of 1916, when a handful of extreme nationalists tried unsuccessfully to prove that, as the old saying goes, England's difficulty is Ireland's opportunity. Yeats was personally acquainted with several of the leaders executed by the British, including Pearse, MacDonagh, Plunkett, Connolly and MacBride. In his magnificent elegy 'Easter 1916' he mourned their deaths and celebrated their heroism, while also expressing a realistic scepticism about the political efficacy of their action. C. K. Stead* reads the poem as a dramatic construct, which turns from the comic to the tragic in order to transform its subjects into 'symbols that take life in the mind'.

One of the executed leaders, John MacBride, was the estranged husband of Yeats's great love Maud Gonne. Yeats seized this chance for what was, as it turned out, a last proposal. Refused not only by Maud, but also by her daughter Iseult, he married Georgie Hyde-Lees in 1917. This union, which was a success despite a somewhat difficult beginning, proved crucially important both for his poetry and for his philosophical development. Years earlier, congratulating his friend George Russell on the birth of a son, Yeats had said that the poet ought to participate in the 'great primary emotions'.[3] His late marriage gave him access to these emotions and thereby strengthened his work, as a poem like 'A Prayer for My Daughter' demonstrates. His wife, however, also brought him more esoteric gifts. She displayed a previously unsuspected talent for automatic writing, and at the dictation of so-called spirit 'instructors' helped to produce the manuscripts upon which Yeats's system, *A Vision*, was based. Work on the first (1925) and second (1937) editions of *A Vision* occupied Yeats's attention while he was writing most of the poems with which we are concerned. Verses in *The Wild Swans at Coole* collection (1919)† – 'Ego Dominus Tuus' and 'The Phases of the Moon', for example – reflect the substance of *A Vision* in highly undigested form, but by the time he came to write *The Tower* (1928) the 'hard symbolic skeleton', as he called it, was hidden beneath the flesh of a poetry which was deeply rooted in the actualities of time and place.

After the Rising, Yeats felt that he had become too alienated from his own land, and decided to renew his patriotic commitment by a symbolic purchase. In 1917 he bought an old Norman tower, Thoor Ballylee, which was situated near Lady Gregory's estate, Coole Park, in the West of Ireland. Daniel Harris* has devoted a whole book,

† Here and in the ensuing selection, Yeats's volume-titles, including those which use the title of an individual poem to denote the whole collection, are italicised; the individual poems are set in roman type between single quote marks – [Ed.]

Yeats: Coole Park and Ballylee (1974), to a study of the poems generated by these two places, which for Yeats were both real and imaginary dwellings: both homes and symbols. His celebration of the ordered aristocratic magnificence of Coole Park in such poems as 'Coole Park, 1929' and 'Coole Park and Ballylee, 1931' suggests Yeats's debt to the verse epistles of Ben Jonson. In the extract I have chosen, Harris discusses 'The Tower', which he sees as 'Yeats's most self-demanding revaluation of the imagination'. Written in 1925, when Yeats was sixty years old, 'The Tower' treats magnificently one of his perennial themes: the process of aging and the paradoxical vitality of spirit which accompanies corporeal decay.

As an elderly man Yeats felt himself shut out from the life of physical political action. In 1917 he added these lines to his early poem, 'The Lamentation of the Old Pensioner':

> Though lads are making pikes again
> For some conspiracy,
> . . .
> My contemplations are of Time
> That has transfigured me.

The outbreak of the Anglo-Irish War in 1919 confirmed his status as onlooker, but he was vehement in his support for the Irish cause, denouncing the British forces – in particular, the anti-terrorist terrorisers, the Black and Tans – in a strongly worded speech at the Oxford Union. Brutal killings by the Tans prompted his bitter accusation:

> . . . a drunken soldiery
> Can leave the mother, murdered at her door,
> To crawl in her own blood, and go scot-free;
> . . .
> ('Nineteen Hundred and Nineteen')

The Treaty which ended the Anglo-Irish War in 1922 gave Ireland Dominion status, but not the Republic for which the patriots had fought. Although the Irish Parliament – the Dáil – accepted the Treaty by 64 to 57 votes, Eamon De Valera and his followers repudiated the majority decision, and the Irish Civil War began.

Two long sequences, 'Nineteen Hundred and Nineteen' and 'Meditations in Time of Civil War', record Yeats's responses to the Anglo-Irish War and to the Civil War of 1922–23. Although both conflicts were destructive, the Civil War added the pain of divided loyalties to the agony of violence. Yeats had supported the Irish against the British, but after the split between Irishmen he found it less easy to choose sides. At first he tried to remain neutral, but eventually threw in his lot with the new government of the Irish Free State. To explicate the difficult poetry Yeats raised on these historical foundations I have chosen the work of Thomas Whitaker.* His important book *Swan and Shadow* (1964), from which two extracts are reproduced, explores the relationship of Yeats's work to history in the light of his philosophical system. Whitaker concludes that Yeats's historical vision alternates between impersonal panorama and personal drama. In his studies of 'Meditations' and 'Nineteen Hundred and Nineteen' he demonstrates how Yeats came to understand the Troubles through an imaginative apprehension of the forces of evil within himself. The poems present what Whitaker calls 'History as Dramatic Experience'.

Although Yeats portrays himself as an 'old scarecrow' in 'Sailing to Byzantium' and 'Among School Children' (both written in 1926), the years from 1922 to 1928 saw his emergence as a confident and fairly successful elder statesman. In 1923 he was appointed to a six-year term in the Senate of the newly founded Irish Free State. In the same year he was awarded the Nobel Prize for Literature. His work in the Senate, which he performed conscientiously, involved him in some apparently unlikely tasks. At the opening of 'Among School Children' he immortalised himself in the unexpected role of School Inspector: 'A sixty-year-old smiling public man'. No one could keep smiling for long in the contentious Irish political arena, however, and after various clashes with the illiberal Catholic nationalist majority on such issues as divorce, censorship, and even the designing of Ireland's new coinage (which was attacked as 'pagan' because it lacked Catholic symbols), Yeats was glad to retire in 1928 and attempt to restore his failing health at Rapallo in the company of his old friend Ezra Pound. He wanted to get away from Irish politics. 'I'd like to spend my old age as a bee and not as a wasp',[4] he said.

His return to Irish politics in the thirties, however, brought new waspishness in the form of a brief but intense interest in the Irish neo-Fascist organisation, the Blueshirts. This group, led by General Eoin O'Duffy, was formed in the early thirties as a counterweight to the growing threat to national stability supposedly posed by republican extremists of the IRA. Yeats, nurturing visions of a perfect civil order in which only the most educated men would govern, briefly saw the Blueshirts as a means to this end. By 1934, however, their brutality and the obvious megalomania of O'Duffy had demonstrated to a repentant Yeats that parties of violence can never establish public order. The marching songs originally written for the Blueshirts were published in a radically revised form in the volume *A Full Moon in March* (1935), as were 'Parnell's Funeral' and 'Church and State', the two poems which convey his rejection of O'Duffy and of the idea of an order imposed from above. The Blueshirt episode was important because it gave to critics who disliked Yeats's proclaimed allegiance to aristocratic ideals the chance to classify him under an even more unpleasant label. George Orwell's * denunciation of Yeats's tendencies as 'fascist' is only one of a number of such attacks, of which the most influential has certainly been Conor Cruise O'Brien's 'Passion and Cunning: An Essay on the Politics of W. B. Yeats' in *In Excited Reverie* (edited by A. N. Jeffares and K. G. W. Cross, 1965). A student interested in the topic of Yeats's politics should read this essay in conjunction with Elizabeth Cullingford's *Yeats, Ireland and Fascism* (1981), which presents an opposing view.

Surveying the history of Yeats criticism A. N. Jeffares, in his introduction to *W. B. Yeats: The Critical Heritage* (1977), has noted that reviews of Yeats's work published during his lifetime were generally descriptive rather than particularly insightful. Even John Middleton Murry's famous assessment of *The Wild Swans at Coole* as the end of the road for Yeats, his 'swansong . . . eloquent of final defeat', is interesting now only as a warning of the dangers of premature judgement. How embarrassing to have written of Yeats in 1919: 'He is empty now. He has the apparatus of enchantment, but no potency in his soul.' This review, together with many others, is to be found in the historically interesting *Critical Heritage* volume.

More rigorously selective is the collection entitled *The Permanence of Yeats* (edited by James Hall and Martin Steinmann, 1950). The extracts I have chosen from Edmund Wilson, F. R. Leavis, Cleanth Brooks, R. P. Blackmur, and Allen Tate are also to be found in this book, which marks a watershed in Yeats studies. Eleven years after Yeats's death, Hall and Steinmann gathered many of the most stimulating and provocative surveys of his achievement, and discussed early trends in Yeats criticism. Looking at this volume thirty and more years and many specialised studies later is like returning to first principles. The writers speak of Yeats without that mixture of awe and pedantry which deadens so much later scholarship. The issues stand out in raw, almost crude, distinctness. Although Yeats's greatness is conceded by most of these scholars, the challenges and detractions contained in the volume are stingingly direct. Despite the vast amounts of knowledge amassed by their successors, these pioneers raised questions which every new reader of Yeats must still answer for himself. Was he an intellectual genius or a misguided crank? Is his work richly dramatic or simply theatrical? Is he a great artist or a grandiose artificer? A poet or a poseur? Is he our foremost chronicler of love and friendship, or chillingly inhumane? As these queries suggest, much of the difficulty which Yeats presented to critics of the thirties and forties centred upon his personality, both as it was embodied in his verse and as it was revealed in his own prose and in the reminiscences of his contemporaries. W. H. Auden's* piece, 'The Public *v.* the Late Mr W. B. Yeats' (1939), wittily satirises this tendency to make poetical judgements on personal grounds, and offers a defence of Yeats which is similar to the one expressed in his famous elegy, 'In Memory of W. B. Yeats'. Time, according to Auden's poem, will pardon Yeats 'for writing well'; or, as he says in his essay, 'The diction of *The Winding Stair* is the diction of a just man'. In an extract from *Axel's Castle* (1931), Edmund Wilson* discusses the special nature of the 'personality truly and naturally poetic', and suggests that the pressures of modern society forced Yeats to invent a poetic Mask, an Anti-self which enabled him to create a symbolic art despite a largely antagonistic environment. Given the starkness of the challenge which Yeats – Irishman, nationalist, occultist, aristocratic liberal, enemy of materialism and mass society, and prophet of impending political apocalypse – offered to the cultural, democratic and scientific orthodoxies of his time, the attention paid to his personality and attitudes is not in itself surprising. More startling is the fact that many of the contributors to *The Permanence of Yeats* were leading exponents of the 'impersonal' doctrine of the 'New Criticism'. As the editors pointed out, 'an age of formalist criticism has chosen . . . to deal with Yeats as a problem in cultural values'. In other words, the collection suggests that, although Yeats's work demands the close linguistic and textual analysis advocated by the New Critics, he cannot be properly understood without some appreciation of his biography, his philosophy and his cultural context. As he said himself, he was 'a man of my time, through my poetical faculty living its history'.[5] In the face of his massively complex involvement with, say, the world of Irish politics, a purist New Criticism is manifestly inadequate. His philosophy presents a similar obstacle. Cleanth Brooks's* essay (1939) on the relation of Yeats's system to the Byzantium poems jettisons the concept of the work as self-sufficient icon and relies on external information and quotation drawn from Yeats's prose writings. In my view Brooks overdoes it, but his essay is a brave and early attempt to come to terms with what critics like George Orwell are all too ready to dismiss as 'hocus-pocus'.

Brooks's approach takes its cue from an earlier essay (1936) by R. P. Blackmur,* who argues that Yeats has an 'extraordinary grasp of the reality of emotion, character and aspiration; and that his chief resort and weapon for the grasping of that reality is magic'. While Blackmur feels that magic is a less than satisfactory basis for poetry, because its tradition is secret rather than public, he does his best to explain and justify Yeats's absorption in magical doctrines. He is right, I think, to argue that the discipline which magic provided for Yeats 'had an extraordinary structural, seminal and substantial importance to the degree that without it he could hardly have written at all'. Blackmur suggests that Yeats's readers, though they may not be adepts themselves, should accept his magic as a 'machinery of meaning' and should 'search out the prose parallels and reconstruct the symbols he uses on their own terms in order to come on the emotional reality, if it is there, actually in the poems – when the machinery may be dispensed with'.[6] This task he undertakes, in the extract I have chosen, for the poem 'The Second Coming'.

Blackmur and Brooks, though their emphases differ, employ basically similar approaches to Yeats's poetry. Their technique – which involves absorbing as much as possible of Yeats's thought, however esoteric or foreign to normal methods of apprehension it may be, and placing it in illuminating relation to the verse – cannot be faulted as a basic strategy. There is no doubt that Yeats is a difficult writer, and that in order to achieve the fullest pleasure from his poems we have to be prepared to put in some hard work. Unfortunately, however, much subsequent criticism has never reached the pleasure: the point where, as Blackmur advises, the 'machinery may be dispensed with'. Passages from Yeats's prose, sources for his visual imagery, facts about his magical, political or aesthetic theories, analysis of his debts to Blake, Shelley and Ben Jonson, or Plato, Berkeley and Gentile, are an important preliminary to, but cannot substitute for, what Tate demanded in 1942: a study of 'the poetry itself'.

The selections I have made for section 1 of Part Three of this Casebook, therefore, are from writers who wear their erudition lightly and who use it as a means to an end, not as an end in itself. Although Yeats is indeed a difficult and complex thinker, we are not helped by critics who take a perverse pleasure in being more obscure than the poet himself. For example I have chosen Richard Ellmann's* lucid discussion (1954) of *A Vision* over the more celebrated essay by Northrop Frye[7] because Ellmann's account will be more directly useful to a student who is unfamiliar with Yeats's myth, and because we are concerned here to illuminate facets of the poetry rather than to discuss Yeats's philosophy on its own merits. More advanced students who are interested in the 'archetypal' method of critical analysis should, of course, go on to explore Frye for themselves.

Several of my selections come from the golden decade of Yeats criticism, the sixties, during which Giorgio Melchiori, Edward Engelberg, Thomas Whitaker, Donald Torchiana and Thomas Parkinson all produced important books. These critics, however, were heavily indebted to the groundwork laid by previous scholars. The forties saw the publication of three major biographical studies: Joseph Hone's *W. B. Yeats* (1943), A. N. Jeffares's *W. B. Yeats: Man and Poet* (1949), and Richard Ellmann's *Yeats: The Man and the Masks* (1949). With the publication in 1954 of Allan Wade's edition of the letters, scholars had many of the tools with which to begin work which has not yet been superseded, despite the subsequent unearthing of numerous hitherto unknown manuscripts, drafts and prose writings. Until the *Collected Letters*, which are being edited by John Kelly, appear in print, Wade remains the authoritative source; and until the new authorised biography is completed, scholars will still have to read Ellmann, Jeffares and Hone. Hone's book, while full of useful facts, is a rather dull and pious work which smooths the rough edges off its subject. Jeffares's is extremely detailed, but it often reads like a paraphrase of Yeats's then unpublished prose. Only Ellmann's book takes up the definite attitude towards Yeats's life and poetry which gives it the right to be called a 'critical' biography. Ellmann is deeply interested in the influence of John Butler Yeats upon his son the poet, and for a complementary account students are encouraged to read William M. Murphy's *Prodigal Father: The Life of J. B. Yeats* (1978). (This detailed study makes it easier to appreciate why W. B. Yeats was so ready to fall into the arms of the dominating Lady Gregory. His mother's brooding withdrawal from life, combined with his father's chronic fecklessness and total inability to support the family, left him without a satisfactory parental role model. Looking, like Stephen Daedelus, for a 'true' father, he discovered Lady Gregory.) Ellmann's *The Man and the Masks*, as its title suggests, also explores Yeats's theory of the deliberately constructed personality, and stresses the crucial importance of his occult interests: interests adopted at least in part as a rebellion against the scepticism of his father.

Published in the same year as *The Man and the Masks* was Donald Stauffer's* *The Golden Nightingale* (1949). This brief but illuminating study is remarkable chiefly for its insistence upon an approach to Yeats's verse which helps in some measure to circumvent the problems caused by *A Vision* and by Yeats's use of 'learned' and often obscure source material. Taking his cue from Yeats's own remark that his poems would 'light up' each other, Stauffer examines 'The Wild Swans at Coole' in juxtaposition with other poems which make use of swans as central symbols. This method (which has much to commend it for the beginning student, since it requires only a copy of Yeats's works, an observant eye, and a certain amount of time) is refined and clarified by Hugh Kenner* in his famous essay, 'The Sacred Book of the Arts' (1956). Kenner's thesis, that Yeats 'was an architect, not a decorator; he didn't accumulate poems, he wrote books', has become an important guideline for later work. For example, the editors of the excellent centenary collection *An Honoured Guest* (1965), paid homage to Kenner by commissioning essays which treated each of Yeats's books as a coherent unit.

A very different method has been employed by two interesting critics, Jon Stallworthy and Thomas Parkinson.* Stallworthy approaches Yeats's work through its early drafts, many of which were preserved by Mrs Yeats. This insight into Yeats's methods of composition throws light on the development of themes from conception to execution, on his endless experimentation with vocabulary and syntax, and on his handling of rhyme and metre. Students are urged to consult Stallworthy's *Between the Lines: Yeats's Poetry in the Making* (1963) for the genesis of individual poems. Parkinson, who also makes extensive use of draft materials, develops slightly more sophisticated conclusions from his researches. The extract which I have chosen from his *W. B. Yeats: The Later Poetry* (1964) reveals the deliberateness of Yeats's persistent off-rhyme, and discusses his use of traditional stanza forms.

Source-hunting has always been a popular approach to Yeats's work. Henn started a promising line of inquiry in his chapter from *The Lonely Tower* (1949), 'Painter and Poet', where he explored Yeatsian images drawn directly from the world of painting. His successor, Giorgio Melchiori, provides in *The Whole Mystery of Art* (1960) such an elaborate account of pictorial sources that no one extract could do justice to the complexity of his work. This is a difficult but rewarding book, for in examining the probable originals of images such as the unicorn and the rape of Leda, Melchiori also throws light on Yeats's philosophy and characteristic habits of mind.

The emphasis by Henn and Melchiori upon the picture as source makes them participants in one of the great debates of Yeats criticism: what is the fundamental basis of Yeats's aesthetic? Donald Stauffer sees the essential Yeats in verses of what he calls 'lyric stasis'. He describes the poems as 'monuments' or sculptured objects. Implicitly, Henn and Melchiori are on his side of the argument: Melchiori argues directly for the importance of visual, even geometric, patterning as the foundation of Yeats's art. On the opposite side stand Parkinson, Whitaker, Stead and Harris, who read Yeats's poems as expressions of dramatic conflict. Frank Kermode's* *Romantic Image* (1957), while it examines the Dancer as an icon combining lyric stasis and dramatic movement, stresses the iconic rather than the dramatic function of the poem as a whole. Edward Engelberg, another critic whose work cannot be satisfactorily represented by selections, argues in *The Vast Design* (1964) that Yeats's aesthetic is actually based upon pairs of opposites, one of which is the lyric versus the dramatic principle. Readers will doubtless form their own opinions on the issue, but this sketch of the controversy suggests how dangerous it is to adopt a single point of view about so complex a poet as Yeats. The antinomies which dominate his philosophy are everywhere in his verse, and, as he once said, they cannot be resolved. Final solutions lead to death, or to God, which, as Ellmann wittily points out, are often interchangeable terms in Yeats. The best Yeats criticism acknowledges that the poet may, in his father's phrase, feel free to believe in marriage in the morning and not believe in it in the afternoon. What counts, according to J. B. Yeats, is not consistency of mind, but integrity of soul.

Debate on such a topic as 'Yeats: Last Romantic or Apologist for

Neo-Classicism', is therefore fruitful only if it is recognised that Yeats, while having a decided preference for romanticism, shares both the romantic and the classic impulses. (The fact that Yeats was given to balancing opposites must not obscure the equally important fact that his balance was seldom perfectly held.) Two of the critics whom I have chosen to include, Yvor Winters and Harold Bloom, consider Yeats to be a romantic, and both of them use this fact to launch attacks upon him. Winters* dislikes all romanticism, and his famous hatchet-job on Yeats (1960) consists mostly of an exposé of what he considers to be excessively romantic (in his definition, silly) social attitudes. It is included not because of its virtues as scholarship but because I find it both bracing and amusing. Harold Bloom,* on the other hand, a devotee of the romantic tradition, considers Yeats not only the last but also the least of its twentieth-century heirs. When Bloom's argument (1970) is carefully analysed (which is hard to do, for he is a master of the unsupported generalisation and the vague assertion), it appears that the problem with Yeats is that he is not Shelley: hardly a hanging crime, one would have thought. Despite his querulous tone and careless scholarship, however, Bloom can be provocative and stimulating: his reading of 'A Dialogue of Self and Soul', a poem he actually likes, juxtaposes Yeats and Shelley in a most illuminating fashion.

There can be no greater contrast to Bloom's work than that of Donald Torchiana, whose *W. B. Yeats and Georgian Ireland* (1966) is a massive study that makes extensive use of newspaper reports and unpublished manuscripts in order to prove the importance of Yeats's interest in the Anglo-Irish eighteenth century. Bloom dismisses Yeats's classicising tendency in a few lines: he concludes that there was something forced about it. Torchiana gives it his all. If Bloom is often flamboyantly wrong, Torchiana is often worthily dull: and both books are marred by their dismissal of the other side of the question. But Torchiana is at least factually reliable, and his work is recommended as a starting point for anyone interested in pursuing the subject of Yeats and the Protestant Ascendancy.

Bloom's book, which was published in 1970, stands at the end of a decade of important work on Yeats. Since then, valuable critical studies of the mature poetry have been few. *Yeats: Coole Park and Ballylee* (1974) by Daniel A. Harris* is the exception which proves the rule. In a review of Yeats criticism published in 1979, Thomas Parkinson observed gloomily that the history of the study of Yeats 'has a discouraging design'. This discouragement arises from the fact that, as Tate prophesied, peripheral studies have outnumbered direct discussions of the poetry: scholarship has swamped criticism. Parkinson suspects that 'the classical modern authors have been so over-documented as to paralyse the will'.[8] Yet Parkinson also points to an exciting opportunity not only for scholars but for every reader of Yeats. If most of the initial research has been done, we are free to engage in the far more stimulating process of evaluation. The great questions remain open. And what the seventies have brought is some new light on a major question, the question with which we began: what are we to think of Yeats's occult beliefs?

The serious work on Yeats's occultism takes us a long way from Orwell's 'hocus-pocus' and Auden's 'mumbo-jumbo'. Not all of it is very readable: Virginia Moore's *The Unicorn* (1954), for example, which contains much fascinating detail, is unsatisfactorily structured, and the argument is destroyed by its author's doomed attempt to prove that Yeats was a Christian. F. A. C. Wilson's extremely dogmatic *W. B. Yeats and Tradition* (1958), asserts that Yeats's poems and plays 'clearly require a definitive statement of meaning, proved up to the hilt', and goes on to provide one based upon Yeats's sources in 'heterodox mysticism'. Anyone who thinks that the meaning of a poem can be 'proved up to the hilt' is clearly not the most flexible of critics, but Wilson's book is a valuable reminder that the occult tradition is, in fact, quite close to the centre of Western symbolic thought. Yeats may, indeed, be seen as ahead of, rather than behind, his times. His interest in magic, myth and ritual was shared by 'respectable' anthropologists like Frazer, though his conclusions were different. His belief in archetypal symbols and in the Anima Mundi, though it derived from the Cambridge platonists, parallels the thought of C. G. Jung. James Olney's study, *The Rhizome and the Flower* (1980), shows that the correspondences between the ideas of the poet and the psychologist were remarkably exact, despite the lack of mutual influence. Olney's book is hard going; interested students may prefer to read his brief essay in a collection edited by G. M. Harper, *Yeats and the Occult* (1976). This collection – and a more specialised study by Harper, *Yeats's Golden Dawn* (1974), recommended for hard-core enthusiasts only – bears witness to a resurgence of enlightened interest in this difficult subject. In it Kathleen Raine, herself a disciple of Blake, argues that Yeats's anti-materialist philosophy and his adoption of the Blakean maxim

'All religions are one' put him in the forefront of those who will usher in the New Age. Raine's claims may sound a little far-fetched until we study Yeats's delighted reactions to modern Einsteinian physics and realise that he was not opposed to science itself, but only to the materialism and mechanism which had ruled the scientific establishment since the seventeenth century. With the new physics he found himself instinctively at home.

Let me conclude by reiterating that the purpose of this book is to stimulate questions, not to provide answers. None of the critics here represented can claim to understand Yeats fully, and even so detailed and sensitive a piece of work as the analysis of 'Byzantium' by G. S. Fraser* leaves plenty of room for expansion or dissent. My prime aim in compiling this collection has been to provoke informed and independent inquiry.

NOTES

1. The history of Yeats's involvement is too complex to summarise here, but it is charted, along with the rest of his political career, in Elizabeth Cullingford, *Yeats, Ireland and Fascism* (London, 1981).
2. *The Letters of W. B. Yeats*, ed. Allan Wade (London, 1954), pp. 920–1.
3. *Ibid*, p. 315.
4. Yeats, 'As a Bee – Not as a Wasp', *Irish Independent* (22 Oct. 1928), p. 6.
5. Yeats, Introduction, *Oxford Book of Modern Verse* (Oxford, 1936), p. *xxxiii*.
6. This quotation from Blackmur comes from a part of the essay I have not included.
7. For the Frye essay, see Select Biobliography.
8. Thomas Parkinson, 'Some Recent Work on Yeats: From Great Modern Poet to Canonical Classic', *Southern Review*, xv (1979).

PART ONE

Yeats on His Art and Its Inspiration

EXTRACTS FROM *ESSAYS AND INTRODUCTIONS*, *AUTOBIOGRAPHIES*, *EXPLORATIONS* AND CORRESPONDENCE

1. *Essays and Introductions* *

On Magic, Symbols and the Imagination

I believe in the practice and philosophy of what we have agreed to call magic, in what I must call the evocation of spirits, though I do not know what they are, in the power of creating magical illusions, in the visions of truth in the depths of the mind when the eyes are closed; and I believe in three doctrines, which have, as I think, been handed down from early times, and been the foundations of nearly all magical practices. These doctrines are: –

(1) That the borders of our mind are ever shifting, and that many minds can flow into one another, as it were, and create or reveal a single mind, a single energy.

(2) That the borders of our memories are as shifting, and that our memories are a part of one great memory, the memory of Nature herself.

(3) That this great mind and great memory can be evoked by symbols.

I often think I would put this belief in magic from me if I could, for I have come to see or to imagine, in men and women, in houses, in handicrafts, in nearly all sights and sounds, a certain evil, a certain ugliness, that comes from the slow perishing through the centuries of a quality of mind that made this belief and its evidences common over the world. . . .

---

* The collected edition cited here is *Essays and Introductions* (London, 1961), to which the page references in the text relate. The individual works from which the extracts are taken are indicated in the Source notes appended to them. [Ed.]

. . . I cannot now think symbols less than the greatest of all powers whether they are used consciously by the masters of magic, or half unconsciously by their successors, the poet, the musician and the artist. At first I tried to distinguish between symbols and symbols, between what I called inherent symbols and arbitrary symbols, but the distinction has come to mean little or nothing. Whether their power has arisen out of themselves, or whether it has an arbitrary origin, matters little, for they act, as I believe, because the Great Memory associates them with certain events and moods and persons. Whatever the passions of man have gathered about, becomes a symbol in the Great Memory, and in the hands of him who has the secret it is a worker of wonders, a caller-up of angels or of devils. The symbols are of all kinds, for everything in heaven or earth has its association, momentous or trivial, in the Great Memory and one never knows what forgotten events may have plunged it, like the toadstool and the ragweed, into the great passions. . . .

. . . [William Blake] had learned from Jacob Boehme and from old alchemist writers that imagination was the first emanation of divinity, 'the body of God', 'the Divine members', and he drew the deduction, which they did not draw, that the imaginative arts were therefore the greatest of Divine revelations, and that the sympathy with all living things, sinful and righteous alike, which the imaginative arts awaken, is that forgiveness of sins commanded by Christ. The reason, and by the reason he meant deductions from the observations of the senses, binds us to mortality because it binds us to the senses, and divides us from each other by showing us our clashing interests; but imagination divides us from mortality by the immortality of beauty, and binds us to each other by opening the secret doors of all hearts. He cried again and again that everything that lives is holy, and that nothing is unholy except things that do not live – lethargies, and cruelties, and timidities, and that denial of imagination which is the root they grew from in old times. Passions, because most living, are most holy – and this was a scandalous paradox in his time – and man shall enter eternity borne upon their wings. . . .

SOURCE: extracts from *Ideas of Good and Evil* (1903): *E. & I.*, pp. 28, 49–50, 112–13.

On Music and Oratory, the Poet and the Saint

. . . Walter Pater says music is the type of all the arts, but somebody else, I forget now who, that oratory is their type. You will side with the one or the other according to the nature of your energy, and I in my present mood am all for the man who, with an average audience before him, uses all means of persuasion – stories, laughter, tears, and but so much music as he can discover on the wings of words. . . .

. . . If it be true that God is a circle whose centre is everywhere, the saint goes to the centre, the poet and artist to the ring where everything comes round again. The poet must not seek for what is still and fixed, for that has no life for him; and if he did, his style would become cold and monotonous, and his sense of beauty faint and sickly, as are both style and beauty to my imagination in the prose and poetry of Newman, but be content to find his pleasure in all that is for ever passing away that it may come again, in the beauty of woman, in the fragile flowers of spring, in momentary heroic passion, in whatever is most fleeting, most impassioned, as it were, for its own perfection, most eager to return in its glory. Yet perhaps he must endure the impermanent a little, for these things return, but not wholly, for no two faces are alike, and, it may be, had we more learned eyes, no two flowers. Is it that all things are made by the struggle of the individual and the world, of the unchanging and the returning, and that the saint and the poet are over all, and that the poet has made his home in the serpent's mouth? . . .

SOURCE: extracts from *Discoveries* (1907), included in *The Cutting of an Agate* (1912; rev. edn, 1919): *E. & I.*, pp. 267–8, 287–8.

On Language and Tradition

. . . Literature decays when it no longer makes more beautiful, or more vivid, the language which unites it to all life, and when one finds the criticism of the student, and the purpose of the reformer, and the logic of the man of science, where there should have been the reveries of the common heart, ennobled into some raving Lear or unabashed Don Quixote. One must not forget that the death of language, the substitution of phrases as nearly impersonal as algebra for words and rhythms varying from man to man, is but a part of the tyranny of impersonal things. . . .

. . . works of art are always begotten by previous works of art, and every masterpiece becomes the Abraham of a chosen people. When we delight in a spring day there mixes, perhaps, with our personal emotion an emotion Chaucer found in Guillaume de Lorris, who had it from the poetry of Provence; we celebrate our draughty May with an enthusiasm made ripe by more meridian suns; and all our art has its image in the Mass that would lack authority were it not descended from savage ceremonies taught amid what perils and by what spirits to naked savages. The old images, the old emotions, awakened again to overwhelming life, like the gods Heine tells of, by the belief and passion of some new soul, are the only master-pieces. The resolution to stand alone, to owe nothing to the past, when it is not mere sense of property, the greed and pride of the counting-house, is the result of that individualism of the Renaissance which had done its work when it gave us personal freedom. . . .

SOURCE: extracts from *The Cutting of an Agate* (1912; rev. edn, 1919): *E. & I.*, pp. 301, 352–3.

On the Poet's First Principle

A poet writes always of his personal life, in his finest work out of its tragedy, whatever it be, remorse, lost love, or mere loneliness; he never speaks directly as to someone at the breakfast table, there is always a phantasmagoria. Dante and Milton had mythologies, Shakespeare the characters of English history or of traditional romance; even when the poet seems most himself, when he is Raleigh and gives potentates the lie, or Shelley 'a nerve o'er which do creep the else unfelt oppressions of this earth,' or Byron when 'the soul wears out the breast' as 'the sword outwears its sheath,' he is never the bundle of accident and incoherence that sits down to breakfast; he has been reborn as an idea, something intended, complete. A novelist might describe his accidence, his incoherence, he must not; he is more type than man, more passion than type. He is Lear, Romeo, Oedipus, Tiresias; he has stepped out of a play, and even the woman he loves is Rosalind, Cleopatra, never The Dark Lady. He is part of his own phantasmagoria and we adore him because nature has grown intelligible, and by so doing a part of our creative power. . . .

SOURCE: extract from 'A General Introduction for my Work'; written for a complete edition of Yeats's works which was not achieved by his death in 1939: *E. & I.*, p. 509.

On His Irish Subject-Matter

. . . It was through the old Fenian leader John O'Leary I found my theme. His long imprisonment, his longer banishment, his magnificent head, his scholarship, his pride, his integrity, all that aristocratic dream nourished amid little shops and little farms, had drawn around him a group of young men; I was but eighteen or nineteen and had already, under the influence of *The Faerie Queene* and *The Sad Shepherd*, written a pastoral play, and under that of Shelley's *Prometheus Unbound* two plays, one staged somewhere in the Caucasus, the other in a crater of the moon; and I knew myself to be vague and incoherent. He gave me the poems of Thomas Davis, said they were not good poetry but had changed his life when a young man, spoke of other poets associated with Davis and *The Nation* newspaper, probably lent me their books. I saw even more clearly than O'Leary that they were not good poetry. I read nothing but romantic literature; hated that dry eighteenth-century rhetoric; but they had one quality I admired and admire: they were not separated individual men; they spoke or tried to speak out of a people to a people; behind them stretched the generations. I knew, though but now and then as young men know things, that I must turn from that modern literature Jonathan Swift compared to the web a spider draws out of its bowels; I hated and still hate with an ever growing hatred the literature of the point of view. I wanted, if my ignorance permitted, to get back to Homer, to those that fed at his table. I wanted to cry as all men cried, to laugh as all men laughed, and the Young Ireland poets when not writing mere politics had the same want, but they did not know that the common and its befitting language is the research of a lifetime and when found may lack popular recognition.

. . . I had heard in Sligo cottages or from pilots at Rosses Point endless stories of apparitions, whether of the recent dead or of the people of history and legend, of that Queen Maeve whose reputed cairn stands on the mountain over the bay. Then at the British Museum I read stories Irish writers of the 'forties and 'fifties had written of such apparitions, but they enraged me more than pleased because they turned the country visions into a joke. But when I went from cottage to cottage with Lady Gregory and watched her hand recording that great collection she has called *Visions and Beliefs* I escaped disfiguring humour.

Behind all Irish history hangs a great tapestry, even Christianity had to accept it and be itself pictured there. Nobody looking at its dim folds can say where Christianity begins and Druidism ends; . . .

. . . That tapestry filled the scene at the birth of modern Irish literature, it is there in the Synge of *The Well of the Saints*, in James Stephens, and in Lady Gregory throughout, in all of George Russell that did not come from the Upanishads, and in all but my later poetry.

Sometimes I am told in commendation, if the newspaper is Irish, in condemnation if English, that my movement perished under the firing squads of 1916; sometimes that those firing squads made our realistic movement possible. If that statement is true, and it is only so in part, for romance was everywhere receding, it is because in the imagination of Pearse and his fellow soldiers the Sacrifice of the Mass had found the Red Branch in the tapestry; they went out to die calling upon Cuchulain: . . .

. . . Our mythology, our legends, differ from those of other European countries because down to the end of the seventeenth century they had the attention, perhaps the unquestioned belief, of peasant and noble alike; Homer belongs to sedentary men, even to-day our ancient queens, our mediaeval soldiers and lovers, can make a pedlar shudder. I can put my own thought, despair perhaps from the study of present circumstance in the light of ancient philosophy, into the mouth of rambling poets of the seventeenth century, or even of some imagined ballad singer of to-day, and the deeper my thought the more credible, the more peasant-like, are ballad singer and rambling poet. Some modern poets contend that jazz and music-hall songs are the folk art of our time, that we should mould our art upon them; we Irish poets, modern men also, reject every folk art that does not go back to

Olympus. Give me time and a little youth and I will prove that even 'Johnny, I hardly knew ye' goes back. . . .

If Irish literature goes on as my generation planned it, it may do something to keep the 'Irishry' living, nor will the work of the realists hinder, nor the figures they imagine, nor those described in memoirs of the revolution. These last especially, like certain great political predecessors, Parnell, Swift, Lord Edward, have stepped back into the tapestry. It may be indeed that certain characteristics of the 'Irishry' must grow in importance. When Lady Gregory asked me to annotate her *Visions and Beliefs* I began, that I might understand what she had taken down in Galway, an investigation of contemporary spiritualism. For several years I frequented those mediums who in various poor parts of London instruct artisans or their wives for a few pence upon their relations to their dead, to their employers, and to their children; then I compared what she had heard in Galway, or I in London, with the visions of Swedenborg, and, after my inadequate notes had been published, with Indian belief. If Lady Gregory had not said when we passed an old man in the woods, 'That man may know the secret of the ages', I might never have talked with Shri Purohit Swāmi nor made him translate his Master's travels in Tibet, nor helped him translate the Upanishads. . . .

. . . I am convinced that in two or three generations it will become generally known that the mechanical theory has no reality, that the natural and supernatural are knit together, that to escape a dangerous fanaticism we must study a new science; at that moment Europeans may find something attractive in a Christ posed against a background not of Judaism but of Druidism, not shut off in dead history, but flowing, concrete, phenomenal.

I was born into this faith, have lived in it, and shall die in it; my Christ, a legitimate deduction from the Creed of St Patrick as I think, is that Unity of Being Dante compared to a perfectly proportioned human body, Blake's 'Imagination', what the Upanishads have named 'Self': nor is this unity distant and therefore intellectually understandable, but imminent, differing from man to man and age to age, taking upon itself pain and ugliness, 'eye of newt, and toe of frog'.

Subconscious preoccupation with this theme brought me *A Vision*, its harsh geometry an incomplete interpretation. The 'Irishry' have preserved their ancient 'deposit' through wars which, during the sixteenth and seventeenth centuries, became wars of extermination; no people, Lecky said at the opening of his *Ireland in the Eighteenth Century*, have undergone greater persecution, nor did that persecution altogether cease up to our own day. No people hate as we do in whom that past is always alive, there are moments when hatred poisons my life and I accuse myself of effeminacy because I have not given it adequate expression. It is not enough to have put it into the mouth of a rambling peasant poet. Then I remind myself that though mine is the first English marriage I know of in the direct line, all my family names are English, and that I owe my soul to Shakespeare, to Spenser and to Blake, perhaps to William Morris, and to the English language in which I think, speak, and write, that everything I love has come to me through English; my hatred tortures me with love, my love with hate. I am like the Tibetan monk who dreams at his initiation that he is eaten by a wild beast and learns on waking that he himself is eater and eaten. This is Irish hatred and solitude, the hatred of human life that made Swift write *Gulliver* and the epitaph upon his tomb, that can still make us wag between extremes and doubt our sanity. . . .

SOURCE: extracts from 'A General Introduction . . .': *E. & I.*, pp. 510–11, 513–14, 515, 516, 517–18, 518–19.

On Style

. . . Style is almost unconscious. I know what I have tried to do, little what I have done. Contemporary lyric poems, even those that moved me – *The Stream's Secret*, *Dolores* – seemed too long, but an Irish preference for a swift current might be mere indolence, yet Burns may have felt the same when he read Thomson and Cowper. The English mind is meditative, rich, deliberate; it may remember the Thames valley. I planned to write short lyrics or poetic drama where every speech would be short and concentrated, knit by dramatic tension, and I did so with more confidence because young English poets were at that time writing out of emotion at the moment of crisis, though their old slow-moving meditation returned almost at once. Then, and in this English poetry has followed my lead, I tried to make the language of poetry coincide with that of passionate, normal speech. I wanted to write in whatever language comes most naturally when we soliloquise, as I do all day long, upon the events of our own lives or of any life where we can see ourselves for the moment. I sometimes compare myself with the mad old slum women I hear denouncing and remembering; 'How dare you', I heard one say of some imaginary suitor, 'and you without health or a home!' If I spoke my thoughts aloud they might be as angry and as wild. It was a long time before I had made a language to my liking; I began to make it when I discovered some twenty years ago that I must seek, not as Wordsworth thought, words in common use, but a powerful and passionate syntax, and a complete coincidence between period and stanza. Because I need a passionate syntax for passionate subject-matter I compel myself to accept those traditional metres that have developed with the language. Ezra Pound, Turner, Lawrence wrote admirable free verse, I could not. I would lose myself, become joyless like those mad old women. The translators of the Bible, Sir Thomas Browne, certain translators from the Greek when translators still bothered about rhythm, created a form midway between prose and verse that seems natural to impersonal meditation; but all that is personal soon rots; it must be packed in ice or salt. Once when I was in delirium from pneumonia I dictated a letter to George Moore telling him to eat salt because it was a symbol of eternity; the delirium passed, I had no memory of that letter, but I must have meant what I now mean. If I wrote of personal love or sorrow in free verse, or in any rhythm that left it unchanged, amid all its accidence, I would be full of self-contempt because of my egotism and indiscretion, and foresee the boredom of my reader. I must choose a traditional stanza, even what I alter must seem traditional. I commit my emotion to shepherds, herdsmen, cameldrivers, learned men, Milton's or Shelley's Platonist, that tower Palmer drew. Talk to me of originality and I will turn on you with rage. I am a crowd, I am a lonely man, I am nothing. Ancient salt is best packing. The heroes of Shakespeare convey to us through their looks, or through the metaphorical patterns of their speech, the sudden enlargement of their vision, their ecstasy at the approach of death: 'She should have died hereafter', 'Of many thousand kisses, the poor last', 'Absent thee from felicity awhile'. They have become God or Mother Goddess, the pelican, 'My baby at my breast', but all must be cold; no actress has ever sobbed when she played Cleopatra, even the shallow brain of a producer has never thought of such a thing. The supernatural is present, cold winds blow across our hands, upon our faces, the thermometer falls, and because of that cold we are hated by journalists and groundlings. There may be in this or that detail painful tragedy, but in the whole work none. I have heard Lady Gregory say, rejecting some play in the modern manner sent to the Abbey Theatre, 'Tragedy must be a joy to the man who dies.' Nor is it any different with lyrics, songs, narrative poems; neither scholars nor the populace have sung or read anything generation after generation because of its pain. The maid of honour whose tragedy they sing must be lifted out of history with timeless pattern, she is one of the four Maries, the rhythm is old and familiar, imagination must dance, must be carried beyond feeling into the aboriginal ice. Is ice the correct word? I once boasted, copying the phrase from a letter of my father's, that I would write a poem 'cold and passionate as the dawn'. . . .

SOURCE: extract from 'A General Introduction . . .': *E. & I.*, pp. 521–3.

2. *Autobiographies**

On Mask and Image

. . . As life goes on we discover that certain thoughts sustain us in defeat, or give us victory, whether over ourselves or others, and it is these thoughts, tested by passion, that we call convictions. Among subjective men (in all those, that is, who must spin a web out of their own bowels) the victory is an intellectual daily re-creation of all that exterior fate snatches away, and so that fate's antithesis; while what I have called 'the Mask' is an emotional antithesis to all that comes out of their internal nature. We begin to live when we have conceived life as tragedy. . . . [p. 189]

. . . as I look backward upon my own writing, I take pleasure alone in those verses where it seems to me I have found something hard and

* The version cited here is *Autobiographies* (London, 1955): a revised edition of *The Autobiography* (1938), and distinct from the work entitled *Autobiographies* published in 1926 as vol. 6 in the Collected Works of that period. The page reference for each extract relates to the 1955 edition. [Ed.]

cold, some articulation of the Image which is the opposite of all that I am in my daily life, and all that my country is; . . . [p. 274]

On Drama and Style

. . . Because [George Moore's] mind was argumentative, abstract, diagrammatic, mine sensuous, concrete, rhythmical, we argued about words. In later years, through much knowledge of the stage, through the exfoliation of my own style, I learnt that occasional prosaic words gave the impression of an active man speaking. In dream poetry, in *Kubla Khan*, in *The Stream's Secret*, every line, every word, can carry its unanalysable, rich associations; but if we dramatize some possible singer or speaker we remember that he is moved by one thing at a time, certain words must be dull and numb. Here and there in correcting my early poems I have introduced such numbness and dullness, turned, for instance, 'the curd-pale moon' into the 'brilliant moon', that all might seem, as it were, remembered with indifference, except some one vivid image. When I began to rehearse a play I had the defects of my early poetry; I insisted upon obvious all-pervading rhythm. Later on I found myself saying that only in those lines or words where the beauty of the passage came to its climax, must rhythm be obvious. . . . [pp. 434–5]

. . . There is a relation between discipline and the theatrical sense. If we cannot imagine ourselves as different from what we are and assume that second self, we cannot impose a discipline upon ourselves, though we may accept one from others. Active virtue as distinguished from the passive acceptance of a current code is therefore theatrical, consciously dramatic, the wearing of a mask. . . . [p. 469]

. . . I now see that the literary element in painting, the moral element in poetry, are the means whereby the two arts are accepted into the social order and become a part of life and not things of the study and the exhibition. Supreme art is a traditional statement of certain heroic and religious truths, passed on from age to age, modified by individual genius, but never abandoned. . . . A great work of art, the *Ode to a Nightingale* not less than the *Ode to Duty*, is as rooted in the early ages as the Mass which goes back to savage folk-lore. In what temple garden did the nightingale first sing? . . . [p. 490]

. . . Every now and then, when something has stirred my imagination, I begin talking to myself. I speak in my own person and dramatize myself, very much as I have seen a mad old woman do upon the Dublin quays, and sometimes detect myself speaking and moving as if I were still young, or walking perhaps like an old man with fumbling steps. Occasionally, I write out what I have said in verse, and generally for no better reason than because I remember that I have written no verse for a long time. I do not think of my soliloquies as having different literary qualities. They stir my interest, by their appropriateness to the men I imagine myself to be, or by their accurate description of some emotional circumstance, more than by any aesthetic value. When I begin to write I have no object but to find for them some natural speech, rhythm and syntax, and to set it out in some pattern, so seeming old that it may seem all men's speech, and though the labour is very great, I seem to have used no faculty peculiar to myself, certainly no special gift. I print the poem and never hear about it again, until I find the book years after with a page dog-eared by some young man, or marked by some young girl with a violet, and when I have seen that, I am a little ashamed, as though somebody were to attribute to me a delicacy of feeling I should but do not possess. What came so easily at first, and amidst so much drama, and was written so laboriously at the last, cannot be counted among my possessions. . . . [pp. 532–3]

3. *Explorations**

On Conflict and Unity

. . . I am trying to understand why certain metaphysicians whom I have spent years trying to master repel me, why those invisible beings

* The collected edition cited here is *Explorations* (London, 1962), to which the page references in the text relate. The individual works from which the extracts are taken are indicated in the Source notes appended to them. [Ed.]

I have learned to trust would turn me from all that is not conflict, that is not from sword in hand. Is it not like this? I cannot discover truth by logic unless that logic serve passion, and only then if the logic be ready to cut its own throat, tear out its own eyes – the cry of Hafiz, 'I made a bargain with that hair before the beginning of time', the cry of every lover. Those spiritual beings seem always as if they would turn me from every abstraction. I must not talk to myself about 'the truth' nor call myself 'teacher' nor another 'pupil' – these things are abstract – but see myself set in a drama where I struggle to exalt and overcome concrete realities perceived not with mind only but as with the roots of my hair. The passionless reasoners are pariah dogs and devour the dead symbols. . . .

SOURCE: extract from *Pages from a Diary Written in 1930* (1940): *Expl.*, pp. 301–2.

One day when I was twenty-three or twenty-four this sentence seemed to form in my head, without my willing it, much as sentences form when we are half-asleep: 'Hammer your thoughts into unity'. For days I could think of nothing else, and for years I tested all I did by that sentence. I had three interests: interest in a form of literature, in a form of philosophy, and a belief in nationality. None of these seemed to have anything to do with the other, but gradually my love of literature and my belief in nationality came together. Then for years I said to myself that these two had nothing to do with my form of philosophy, but that I had only to be sincere and to keep from constraining one by the other and they would become one interest. Now all three are, I think, one, or rather all three are a discrete expression of a single conviction. . . .

SOURCE: extract from *If I Were Four-and-Twenty* (1940) – written in 1919: *Expl.*, p. 263.

4. *Correspondence*

I

[Yeats here discusses with Lady Dorothy Wellesley trends in contemporary poetry. – Ed.]

. . . This difficult work, which is being written everywhere now (a professor from Barcelona tells me they have it there) has the substance of philosophy & is a delight to the poet with his professional pattern; but it is not your road or mine, & ours is the main road, the road of naturalness & swiftness and we have thirty centuries upon our side. We alone can 'think like a wise man, yet express our selves like the common people'. These new men are goldsmiths working with a glass screwed into one eye, whereas we stride ahead of the crowd, its swordsmen, its jugglers, looking to right & left. 'To right and left' by which I mean that we need like Milton, Shakespeare, Shelley, vast sentiments, generalizations supported by tradition.

[*Postmarked 20 April 1936.*]

. . . I wrote to-day to Laura Riding, with whom I carry on a slight correspondence, that her school was too thoughtful, reasonable & truthful, that poets were good liars who never forget that the Muses were women who liked the embrace of gay warty lads. I wonder if she knows that warts are considered by the Irish peasantry a sign of sexual power? Those little poems of yours are nonchalant, & nonchalance is declared by Castigleone[1] essential to all true courtiers – so it is to warty lads & poets. . . . [*Dated 22 May 1936.*]

. . . We have all something within ourselves to batter down and get our power from this fighting. I have never 'produced' a play in verse without showing the actors that the passion of the verse comes from the fact that the speakers are holding down violence or madness – 'down Hysterica passio'. All depends on the completeness of the holding down, on the stirring of the beast underneath. Even my poem 'To D.W.' should give this impression. The moon, the moonless night, the dark velvet, the sensual silence, the silent room and the violent bright Furies. Without this conflict we have no passion, only sentiment and thought. . . . [*Dated 5 August 1936.*]

SOURCE: extracts from *Letters on Poetry from W. B. Yeats to Dorothy Wellesley* (London, 1940; 2nd edn, 1964), pp. 58, 63, 86.

NOTE

1. [Ed.] Castigleone: a slip of the pen for Castiglione, author of *Il Cortegiano* (1528).

II

[This section presents miscellaneous comments from Yeats's general correspondence – Ed.]

. . . I understand my own race and in all my work, lyric or dramatic, I have thought of it. If the theatre fails I may or may not write plays – but I shall write for my own people – whether in love or hate of them matters little – probably I shall not know which it is. . . .
[*To Miss A. E. F. Horniman – dated (?) early 1908.*]

. . . All our art is but the putting our faith and the evidence of our faith into words or forms and our faith is in ecstasy. Of recent years instead of 'vision', meaning by vision the intense realization of a state of ecstatic emotion symbolized in a definite imagined region, I have tried for more self portraiture. I have tried to make my work convincing with a speech so natural and dramatic that the hearer would feel the presence of a man thinking and feeling. . . .
[*To his father, J. B. Yeats – dated 5 August 1913.*]

. . . I was delighted with your letter insisting on 'intimacy' as the mark of fine literature. The contrary thing to this intimacy, which is another name for experience, life, is I believe 'generalization'. And generalization creates rhetoric, wins immediate popularity, organizes the mass, gives political success, Kipling's poetry, Macaulay's essays and so on. Life is never the same twice and so cannot be generalized. When you go from an Irish country district, where there are good manners, old songs, old stories and good talk, the folk mind, to an Irish country town, generalization meets one in music-hall songs with their mechanical rhythm, or in thoughts taken from the newspapers. . . .

[*To his father, J. B. Yeats – dated 7 August 1909.*]

. . . In the last letter but one, you spoke of all art as imitation, meaning, I conclude, imitation of something in the outer world. To me it seems that it often uses the outer world as a symbolism to express subjective moods. The greater the subjectivity, the less the imitation. Though perhaps there is always some imitation. You say that music suggests now the roar of the sea, now the song of the bird, and yet it seems to me that the song of the bird itself is perhaps subjective, an expression of feeling alone. The element of pattern in every art is, I think, the part that is not imitative, for in the last analysis there will always be somewhere an intensity of pattern that we have never seen with our eyes. In fact, imitation seems to me to create a language in which we say things which are not imitation. . . .

[*To his father, J. B. Yeats – dated 5 March 1916.*]

. . . My own verse has more and more adopted – seemingly without any will of mine – the syntax and vocabulary of common personal speech. . . . The over childish or over pretty or feminine element in some good Wordsworth and in much poetry up to our date comes from the lack of natural momentum in the syntax. This momentum underlies almost every Elizabethan and Jacobean lyric and is far more important than simplicity of vocabulary. If Wordsworth had found it he could have carried any amount of elaborate English. . . .

[*To H. C. Grierson – dated 21 February 1926.*]

. . . When I try to put all into a phrase I say, 'Man can embody truth but he cannot know it'. I must embody it in the completion of my life. The abstract is not life and everywhere draws out its contradictions. You can refute Hegel but not the Saint or the Song of Sixpence. . . .

[*To Lady Elizabeth Pelham, 4 January 1939: written some three weeks before the poet's death.*]

SOURCE: extracts from Allan Wade (ed.), *The Letters of W. B. Yeats* (London, 1954), pp. 500, 583, 534, 607, 710, 922.

PART TWO

Early Critics

Edmund Wilson (1931)

'Symbolism versus Naturalism'

. . . In spite of the immense amount of poetry published and read today, the personality truly and naturally poetic seems to be becoming rarer and rarer. It may be true that the kind of dignity and distinction which have been characteristic of the poet in the past are becoming more and more impossible in our modern democratic society and during a period when the ascendancy of scientific ideas has made man conscious of his kinship with the other animals and of his subjection to biological and physical laws rather than of his relation to the gods. It was easy for the lyric poet, from Wyatt's age to Waller's, to express himself both directly and elegantly, because he was a courtier, or, in any case, a member of a comparatively small educated class, whose speech combined the candor and naturalness of conversation among equals with the grace of a courtly society. It was possible for him honestly to take up a residence in an intellectual world where poetic images stood for actualities because the scientific language and technique for dealing with these actualities had not yet come to permeate thought. But the modern poet who would follow this tradition, and who would yet deal with life in any large way, must create for himself a special personality, must maintain a state of mind, which shall shut out or remain indifferent to many aspects of the contemporary world. This necessity accounts partly, I suppose, for Yeats's preoccupation in his prose writings with what he calls the Mask or Anti-Self, a sort of imaginary personality, quite antagonistic to other elements of one's nature, which the poet must impose upon himself. It is hard to imagine a seventeenth-century poet being driven to such a theory – a theory which makes one's poetic self figure as one of the halves of a split personality; and it seems true that Yeats himself has not been able to keep up his poetic rôle without a certain effort. We find, at any rate, in his criticism and his autobiographical writings a remarkably honest and illuminating account of the difficulties of remaining a poet during the age in which we live.

Yeats seems to be conscious from the first of an antagonism between the actual world of industry, politics and science, on the one hand, and the imaginative poetic life, on the other. He tells us, in his autobiography, that a vital issue seemed to be raised for him, in his boyhood, by the then popular and novel realism of Bastien-Lepage and Carolus Durand as against the mysticism of the Pre-Raphaelite painters. Bastien-Lepage's 'clownish peasant staring with vacant eyes at her great boots' represented already to the young Yeats that Naturalistic, scientific vision which contradicted and warred with his own. And he takes up from the beginning, in his criticism, a definite and explicit position in regard to Naturalism: he will stand apart from the democratic, the scientific, modern world – his poetic life shall be independent of it; his art shall owe nothing to its methods. His principles in literature are those of the Symbolists, but he formulates them more clearly and defends them with more vigor than any-one else has yet done in English.

'There is', he asserts in his early essay on the symbolism of Shelley, 'for every man some one scene, some one adventure, some one picture that is the image of his secret life, for wisdom first speaks in images, and . . . this one image, if he would but brood over it his life long, would lead his soul, disentangled from unmeaning circumstance and the ebb and flow of the world, into that far household where the undying gods await all whose souls have become simple as flame, whose bodies have become quiet as an agate lamp.' All great literature, says Yeats, is created out of symbols: observations and statistics mean nothing; works of art which depend upon them can have no enduring value. 'There is something', he says, 'of an old wives' tale in fine literature. The makers of it are like an old peasant telling stories of the great famine or the hangings of '98 or from his own memories. He has felt something in the depth of his mind and he wants to make it as visible and powerful to our senses as possible. He will use the most extravagant words or illustrations if they will suit his purpose. Or he will invent a wild parable, and the more his mind is on fire or the more creative it is, the less will he look at the outer world or value it for its own sake. It gives him metaphors and examples, and that is all. He is even a little scornful of it, for it seems to him while the fit is on that the fire has gone out of it and left it but white ashes. I cannot explain it, but I am certain that every high thing was invented in this way, between sleeping and waking, as it were, and that peering and peeping persons are but hawkers of stolen goods. How else could their noses have grown so ravenous or their eyes so sharp?' . . .

SOURCE: extract from *Axel's Castle* (New York, 1931; paperback edn., London, 1961), pp. 38–41.

F. R. Leavis (1932)

'Yeats and the Nineteenth-Century Tradition'

. . . The poetry of this later phase [*The Green Helmet* (1910; revised edition 1912) and after – Ed.] is a remarkable positive achievement: Mr Yeats was strong enough to force a triumph out of defeat. He speaks of a beauty

> . . . won
> From bitterest hours,

and it is this he served instead of the cloudy glamour of the *Celtic Twiiight*[1]; a

> . . . beauty like a tightened bow, a kind
> That is not natural in an age like this.

The verse, in its rhythm and diction, recognises the actual world, but holds against it an ideal of aristocratic fineness. It is idiomatic, and has the run of free speech, being at the same time proud, bare and subtle. To pass from the earlier verse to this is something like passing from Campion to Donne. The parallel, indeed, is not so random as it might seem. At any rate, Donne's name in connection with a poet capable of passionate intellectual interests, who from such a start achieved such a manner, leads us to reflect that if the poetic tradition of the nineteenth century had been less completely unlike the Metaphysical tradition, Mr Yeats might have spent less of his power outside poetry. The speculation is perhaps idle, but it calls attention to the way in which his verse developed into something that has the equivalent of certain seventeenth-century qualities. His use of the idiom and rhythm of speech is not all:

> Plato thought nature but a spume that plays
> Upon a ghostly paradigm of things;
> Solider Aristotle played the taws
> Upon the bottom of a king of kings;
> World-famous golden-thighed Pythagoras
> Fingered upon a fiddle-stick or strings
> What a star sang and careless Muses heard:
> Old clothes upon old sticks to scare a bird.
>
> ['Among School Children', VI]

This (and the context more than bears out the promise of flexibility and variety of tone) is surely rather like seventeenth-century 'wit'; more like it than anything we expect to find in modern verse outside the work of certain post-war poets – poets who exhibit no completer escape from the Victorian poetical. The volume it comes from, indeed, appeared after the war. But *The Tower* (1928) merely develops the manner of *The Green Helmet*, *Responsibilities* (1914) and *The Wild Swans at Coole* (1919).

In *The Tower* Mr Yeats achieves a kind of ripeness in disillusion. The scorn so pervasive before is gone: his tragic horror at the plight of Ireland (as, for instance, in 'Meditations in Time of Civil War') is something different and more generous. There is indeed bitterness, but it is not the sterile kind. His raging against

> Decrepit age that has been tied to me
> As to a dog's tail

goes with a sense of ardent vitality:

> Never had I more
> Excited, passionate, fantastical
> Imagination, nor an ear and eye
> That more expected the impossible – ['The Tower', I]

and the excitement is as apparent as the bitterness in this poetry of the last phase. Each gives value to the other. He is capable of excitement, for instance, about the 'abstract things' that he describes as a *pis aller*. He turns with a pang from the varied 'sensual music' of the world, but he is drawn positively towards the 'monuments of unaging intellect':

> An aged man is but a paltry thing,
> A tattered coat upon a stick, unless
> Soul clap its hands and sing, and louder sing,
> For every tatter in its mortal dress.
> ['Sailing to Byzantium', II]

This (though there is always an ironical overtone) is the voice of one who knows intellectual passion. He does not deceive himself about what he has lost, but the regret itself becomes in the poetry something positive. His implications, in short, are very complex; he has achieved a difficult and delicate sincerity, an extraordinarily subtle poise.

What, then, it might be asked after this account of Mr Yeats's achievement, is there to complain of? Does it really show that the tradition in the nineteenth century might with advantage have been other than it was? If he had to struggle with uncongenial circumstances, has not every great artist had to do so; and did he not, by admission, make triumphs of them? Mr Yeats himself gives the answer in the bitter sense of waste he expresses characteristically, in the latest work as elsewhere. His poetry is little more than a marginal comment on the main activities of his life. No one can read his *Autobiographies* and his *Essays*[2] without being struck by the magnificent qualities of intelligence and character he exhibits. His insight shows itself in his analysis of his own case, an analysis that suggests at the same time the complete achievement he was fated to miss: 'In literature', he wrote in 1906, 'partly from the lack of that spoken word which knits us to normal man, we have lost in personality, in our delight in the whole man – blood, imagination, intellect, running together – but have found a new delight, in essences, in states of mind, in pure imagination, in all that comes to us most easily in elaborate music.'[3] And we find him remarking in *Autobiographies* 'how small a fragment of our nature can be brought to perfect expression, nor that even but with great toil, in a much divided civilisation'.[4] Again, by quoting his own verse, he explicitly relates the general reflection to his own case: 'Nor did I understand as yet how little that Unity [of Being], however wisely sought, is possible without a Unity of Culture in class or people that is no longer possible at all.

> The fascination of what's difficult
> Has dried the sap out of my veins, and rent
> Spontaneous joy and natural content
> Out of my heart.'[5]

At this point it might be commented that Mr Yeats turns out an unfortunate witness to have called. What he testifies against is not the poetic tradition, but the general state of civilisation and culture: a state which, he contends, makes waste inevitable for the sensitive. But he implies nothing against holding that if the poetic tradition had been different, he might have brought more of himself to expression. Writing of the early Synge he says significantly: '. . . the only language that interested him was the conventional language of modern poetry which has begun to make us all weary. I was very weary of it, for I had finished *The Secret Rose*,[6] and felt how it had separated my imagination from life, sending my Red Hanrahan, who should have trodden the same roads with myself, into some undiscoverable country.'[7] It is true that he successfully dropped this 'conventional language of modern poetry'; but early habits of mind and sensibility are not so easily dropped. The incidental confession he makes in a later poem ['Upon a Dying Lady'] –

> I have no speech but symbol, the pagan speech I made
> Amid the dreams of youth

– has much significance. For 'symbol' in his technical sense – symbol drawn from his cult of magic and the Hermetic sciences – is commonly felt to be an unsatisfactory element in his later verse, and to come from an unfortunate habit of mind. And his magic and occultism, of course, are the persistent and intense expression of the bent that expressed itself first of all in the 'conventional language of modern poetry':

> . . . The abstract joy,
> The half read wisdom of daemonic images,
> Suffice the aging man as once the growing boy.
> ['Meditations in Time of Civil War']

Disillusion and waste were indeed inevitable; but not in the form in which Mr Yeats suffered them. They might have been more significant. For Victorian romanticism was not the only possible answer to those modern conditions that Mr Yeats deplores. If it were, poetry would cease to matter. Adult minds could no longer take it seriously. Losing all touch with the finer consciousness of the age it would be, not only irresponsible, but anaemic – as, indeed, Victorian poetry so commonly is. Mr Yeats's career, then, magnificent as the triumph was that he compelled out of defeat, is a warning. It illustrates the special disability of the poet in the last century, and impressively bears out my argument about the poetic tradition. No Englishman in any case could have profited by the sources of strength open to Mr Yeats as an Irishman, and no such source is open to any one now. No serious poet could propose to begin again where Mr Yeats began. . . .

SOURCE: extract from *New Bearings in English Poetry* (London, 1932; new edn, 1950; paperback edn, Ann Arbor, 1960), pp. 43–50.

NOTES

[Revised and reorganised from the original – Ed.]

1. [Ed.] Yeats's first volume of essays (1893; revised edn, 1902).

2. [Ed.] Leavis refers to earlier versions of these works (1926 and 1924 respectively). In subsequent annotation his references are related to later publications.

3. *Essays and Introductions* (London, 1961), p. 266. Cf. *Autobiographies* (London, 1955), p. 326: 'Donne could be as metaphysical as he pleased . . . because he could be as physical as he pleased.'

4. *Autobiographies*, pp. 295–6.

5. Ibid., p. 355.

6. [Ed.] Yeats's collection of stories, published in 1897.

7. *Essays and Introductions*, pp. 298–9.

R. P. Blackmur (1936)

'The Later Poetry'

. . . The major facts I hope to illustrate are these: that Yeats has, if you accept his mode, a consistent extraordinary grasp of the reality of emotion, character and aspiration; and that his chief resort and weapon for the grasping of that reality is magic; and that if we would make use of that reality for ourselves we must also make some use of the magic that inspirits it. What is important is that the nexus of reality and magic is not by paradox or sleight of hand, but is logical and represents, for Yeats in his poetry, a full use of intelligence. Magic performs for Yeats the same fructifying function that Christianity does for Eliot, or that ironic fatalism did for Thomas Hardy; it makes a connection between the poem and its subject matter and provides an adequate mechanics of meaning and value. If it happens that we discard more of Hardy than we do of Yeats and more of Yeats than we do of Eliot, it is not because Christianity provides better machinery for the movement of poetry than fatalism or magic, but simply because Eliot is a more cautious craftsman. Besides, Eliot's poetry has not even comparatively worn long enough to show what parts are permanent and what merely temporary. The point here is that fatalism, Christianity and magic are none of them disciplines to which many minds can consciously appeal today, as Hardy, Eliot, and Yeats do, for emotional strength and moral authority. The supernatural is simply not part of our mental furniture, and when we meet it in our reading we say: Here is débris to be swept away. But if we sweep it away without first making sure what it is, we are likely to lose the poetry as well as the débris. It is the very purpose of a supernaturally derived discipline, as used in poetry, to set the substance of natural life apart, to give it a form, a meaning, and a value which cannot be evaded. What is excessive and unwarranted in the discipline we indeed ought to dismiss; but that can be determined only when what is integrating and illuminating is known first. The discipline will in the end turn out to have had only a secondary importance for the reader; but its effect will remain active even when he no longer considers it. That is because for the poet the discipline, far from seeming secondary, had an extraordinary structural seminal and substantial importance to the degree that without it he could hardly have written at all.

Poetry does not flow from thin air but requires always either a literal faith, an imaginative faith, or, as in Shakespeare, a mind full of many provisional faiths. The life we all live is not alone enough of a subject for the serious artist; it must be life with a leaning, life with a tendency to shape itself only in certain forms, to afford its most lucid revelations only in certain lights. If our final interest, either as poets or as readers, is in the reality declared when the forms have been removed and the lights taken away, yet we can never come to the reality at all without the first advantage of the form and lights. Without them we should *see* nothing but only glimpse something unstable. We glimpse the fleeting but do not see what it is that fleets.

So it was with Yeats; his early poems are fleeting, some of them beautiful and some that sicken, as you read them, to their own extinction. But as he acquired for himself a discipline, however unacceptable to the bulk of his readers, his poetry obtained an access to reality. So it is with most of our serious poets. It is almost the mark of the poet of genuine merit in our time – the poet who writes serious works with an intellectual aspect which are nonetheless poetry – that he performs his work in the light of an insight, a group of ideas and a faith, with the discipline that flows from them, which taken together form a view of life most readers cannot share, and which, furthermore, most readers feel as repugnant, or sterile, or simply inconsequential.

All this is to say generally – and we shall say it particularly for Yeats later – that our culture is incomplete with regard to poetry; and the poet has to provide for himself in that quarter where authority and value are derived. It may be that no poet ever found a culture complete for his purpose; it was a welcome and arduous part of his business to make it so. Dante, we may say, completed for poetry the Christian culture of his time, which was itself the completion of centuries. But there was at hand for Dante, and as a rule in the great ages of poetry, a fundamental agreement or convention between the poet and his audience about the validity of the view of life of which the poet deepened the reality and spread the scope. There is no such agreement today. We find poets either using the small conventions of the individual life as if they were great conventions, or attempting to resurrect some great convention of the past, or, finally, attempting to discover the great convention that must lie, willy-nilly, hidden in the life about them. This is a labor, whichever form it takes, which leads as often to subterfuge, substitution, confusion and failure, as to success; and it puts the abnormal burden upon the reader of determining what the beliefs of the poet are and how much to credit them before he can satisfy himself of the reality which those beliefs envisage. The alternative is to put poetry at a discount – which is what has happened.

This the poet cannot do who is aware of the possibilities of his trade: the possibilities of arresting, enacting and committing to the language through his poems the expressed value of the life otherwise only lived or evaded. The poet so aware knows, in the phrasing of that prose-addict Henry James, both the sacred rage of writing and the muffled majesty of authorship; and knows, as Eliot knows, that once to have been visited by the muses is ever afterwards to be haunted. These are qualities that once apprehended may not be discounted without complete surrender, when the poet is no more than a haunt haunted. Yeats has never put his poetry at a discount. But he has made it easy for his readers to do so – as Eliot has in his way – because the price he has paid for it, the expense he has himself been to in getting it on paper, have been a price most readers simply do not know how to pay and an expense, in time and labor and willingness to understand, beyond any initial notion of adequate reward.

The price is the price of a fundamental and deliberate surrender to magic as the ultimate mode for the apprehension of reality. The expense is the double expense of, on the one hand, implementing magic with a consistent symbolism, and on the other hand, the greatly multiplied expense of restoring, through the *craft* of poetry, both the reality and its symbols to that plane where alone their experience becomes actual – the plane of the quickened senses and the concrete emotions. That is to say, the poet (and, as always, the reader) has to combine, to fuse inextricably into something like an organic unity the constructed or derived symbolism of his special insight with the symbolism animating the language itself. It is, on the poet's plane, the labor of bringing the representative forms of knowledge home to the experience which stirred them: the labor of keeping in mind *what* our knowledge is of: the labor of craft. With the poetry of Yeats this labor is, as I say, doubly hard, because the forms of knowledge, being magical, do not fit naturally with the forms of knowledge that ordinarily preoccupy us. But it is possible, and I hope to show it, that the difficulty is, in a sense, superficial and may be overcome with familiarity, and that the mode of magic itself, once familiar, will even seem rational for the purposes of poetry – although it will not thereby seem inevitable. Judged by its works in the representation of emotional reality – and that is all that can be asked in our context – magic and its burden of symbols may be a major tool of the imagination. A tool has often a double function; it performs feats for which it was designed, and it is heuristic, it discovers and performs new feats which could not have been anticipated without it, which it indeed seems to instigate for itself and in the most unlikely quarters. It is with magic as a tool in its heuristic aspect – as an agent for discovery – that I wish here directly to be concerned.

One of the finest, because one of the most appropriate to our time and place, of all Yeats's poems, is his 'The Second Coming'.

> Turning and turning in the widening gyre
> The falcon cannot hear the falconer;
> Things fall apart; the centre cannot hold;
> Mere anarchy is loosed upon the world,
> The blood-dimmed tide is loosed, and everywhere
> The ceremony of innocence is drowned;
> The best lack all conviction, while the worst
> Are full of passionate intensity.
>
> Surely some revelation is at hand;
> Surely the Second Coming is at hand.
> The Second Coming! Hardly are those words out
> When a vast image out of *Spiritus Mundi*
> Troubles my sight: somewhere in sands of the desert
> A shape with lion body and the head of a man,
> A gaze blank and pitiless as the sun,
> Is moving its slow thighs, while all about it

Reel shadows of the indignant desert birds.
The darkness drops again; but now I know
That twenty centuries of stony sleep
Were vexed to nightmare by a rocking cradle,
And what rough beast, its hour come round at last,
Slouches towards Bethlehem to be born?

There is about it, to any slowed reading, the immediate conviction of pertinent emotion; the lines are stirring, separately and in their smaller groups, and there is a sensible life in them that makes them seem to combine in the form of an emotion. We may say at once then, for what it is worth, that in writing his poem Yeats was able to choose words which to an appreciable extent were the right ones to reveal or represent the emotion which was its purpose. The words deliver the meaning which was put into them by the craft with which they were arranged, and that meaning is their own, not to be segregated or given another arrangement without diminution. Ultimately, something of this sort is all that can be said of this or any poem, and when it is said, the poem is known to be good in its own terms or bad because not in its own terms. But the reader seldom reaches an ultimate position about a poem; most poems fail, through craft or conception, to reach an ultimate or absolute position: parts of the craft remain machinery and parts of the conception remain in limbo. Or, as in this poem, close inspection will show something questionable about it. It is true that it can be read as it is, isolated from the rest of Yeats's work and isolated from the intellectual material which it expresses, and a good deal gotten out of it, too, merely by submitting to it. That is because the words are mainly common, both in their emotional and intellectual senses; and if we do not know precisely what the familiar words drag after them into the poem, still we know vaguely what the weight of it feels like; and that seems enough to make a poem at one level of response. Yet if an attempt is made at a more complete response, if we wish to discover the precise emotion which the words mount up to, we come into trouble and uncertainty at once. There is an air of explicitness to each of the separate fragments of the poem. Is it, in this line or that, serious? Has it a reference? – or is it a rhetorical effect, a result only of the persuasive overtones of words? – or is it a combination, a mixture of reference and rhetoric?

Possibly the troubled attention will fasten first upon the italicised phrase in the twelfth line: *Spiritus Mundi*; and the question is whether the general, the readily available senses of the words are adequate to supply the specific sense wanted by the poem. Put another way, can the poet's own arbitrary meaning be made, merely by discovering it, to participate in and enrich what the 'normal' meanings of the words in their limiting context provide? The critic can only supply the facts; the poem will in the end provide its own answer. Here there are certain facts that may be extracted from Yeats's prose writings which suggest something of what the words symbolise for him. In one of the notes to the limited edition of *Michael Robartes and the Dancer*, Yeats observes that his mind, like another's, has been from time to time obsessed by images which had no discoverable origin in his waking experience. Speculating as to their origin, he came to deny both the conscious and the unconscious memory as their probable seat, and finally invented a doctrine which traced the images to sources of supernatural character. I quote only that sentence which is relevant to the phrase in question 'Those [images] that come in sleep are (1) from the state immediately preceding our birth; (2) from the *Spiritus Mundi* – that is to say, from a general storehouse of images which have ceased to be a property of any personality or spirit.' It apparently follows, for Yeats, that images so derived have both an absolute meaning of their own and an operative force in determining meaning and predicting events in this world. In another place (the Introduction to 'The Resurrection', in *Wheels and Butterflies* [1934]) he describes the image used in this poem, which he had seen many times, 'always at my left side just out of the range of the sight, a brazen winged beast that I associated with laughing, ecstatic destruction'. Ecstasy, it should be added, comes for Yeats just before death, and at death comes the moment of revelation, when the soul is shown its kindred dead and it is possible to see the future.

Here we come directly upon that central part of Yeats's magical beliefs which it is one purpose of this poem emotionally to represent: the belief in what is called variously *Magnus Annus*, The Great Year, The Platonic Year, and sometimes in a slightly different symbolism, The Great Wheel. This belief, with respect to the history of epochs, is associated with the procession of the equinoxes, which bring, roughly every two thousand years, a Great Year of death and rebirth, and this belief, with respect to individuals, seems to be associated with the phases of the moon; although individuals may be influenced by the equinoxes and there may be a lunar interpretation of history. These beliefs have a scaffold of geometrical figures, gyres, cones, circles, etc., by the application of which exact interpretation is secured. Thus it is possible to predict, both in biography and history, and in time, both forwards and backwards the character, climax, collapse and rebirth in antithetical form of human types and cultures. There is a subordinate but helpful belief that signs, warnings, even direct messages, are always given, from *Spiritus Mundi* or elsewhere, which the poet and the philosopher have only to see and hear. As it happens, the Christian era, being nearly two thousand years old, is due for extinction and replacement, in short for the Second Coming, which this poem heralds. In his note to its first publication (in *Michael Robartes and the Dancer*) Yeats expresses his belief as follows:

> At the present moment the life gyre is sweeping outward, unlike that before the birth of Christ which was narrowing, and has almost reached its greatest expansion. The revelation which approaches will however take its character from the contrary movement of the interior gyre. All our scientific, democratic, fact-accumulating, heterogeneous civilization belongs to the outward gyre and prepares not the continuance of itself but the revelation as in a lightning flash, though in a flash that will not strike only in one place, and will for a time be constantly repeated, of the civilization that must slowly take its place.

So much for a major gloss upon the poem. Yeats combined, in the best verse he could manage, the beliefs which obsessed him with the image which he took to be a specific illustration of the beliefs. Minor and buttressing glosses are possible for many of the single words and phrases in the poem, some flowing from private doctrine and some from Yeats's direct sense of the world about him, and some from both at once. For example: The 'ceremony of innocence' represents for Yeats one of the qualities that made life valuable under the dying aristocratic social tradition; and the meaning of the phrase in the poem requires no magic for completion but only a reading of other poems. The 'falcon and the falconer' in the second line has, besides its obvious symbolism, a doctrinal reference. A falcon is a hawk, and a hawk is symbolic of the active or intellectual mind; the falconer is perhaps the soul itself or its uniting principle. There is also the apposition which Yeats has made several times that 'Wisdom is a butterfly / And not a gloomy bird of prey'. Whether the special symbolism has actually been incorporated in the poem, and in which form, or whether it is private débris merely, will take a generation of readers to decide. In the meantime it must be taken provisionally for whatever its ambiguity may seem to be worth. Literature is full of falcons, some that fly and some that lack immediacy and sit, archaic, on the poet's wrist; and it is not always illuminating to determine which is which. But when we come on such lines as

> The best lack all conviction, while the worst
> Are full of passionate intensity,

we stop short, first to realise the aptness of the statement to every plane of life in the world about us, and then to connect them with the remote body of the poem they illuminate. There is a dilemma of which the branches grow from one trunk but which cannot be solved; for these lines have, not two meanings, but two sources for the same meaning. There is the meaning that comes from the summary observation that this is how men are – and especially men of power – in the world we live in; it is knowledge that comes from knowledge of the 'fury and the mire of human veins'; a meaning the contemplation of which has lately (April 1934) led Yeats to offer himself to any government or party that, using force and marching men, will 'promise not this or that measure but a discipline, a way of life'. And there is in effect the same meaning, at least at the time the poem was written, which comes from a different source and should have, one would think, very different consequences in prospective party loyalties. Here the meaning has its source in the doctrines of the Great Year and the Phases of the Moon; whereby, to cut exegesis short, it is predicted as necessary that, at the time we have reached, the best minds, being subjective, should have lost all faith though desiring it, and the worst minds, being so nearly objective, have no need of faith and may be full of 'passionate intensity' without the control of any faith or wisdom. Thus we have on the one side the mirror of observation and on the other side an imperative, magically derived, which come to the conclusion of form in identical words. . . .

SOURCE: extract from 'The Later Poetry of W. B. Yeats', *Southern Review*, II, 2 (1936); reproduced in Blackmur's *The Expense of Greatness* (New York, 1940), pp. 74–85; and also in his *Language as Gesture* (London, 1952) and its shortened version, *Form and Value in Modern Poetry* (Garden City, N.Y., 1957).

W. H. Auden (1939)

'Prosecution and Defence'

The Public Prosecutor:

Gentlemen of the jury. Let us be quite clear in our minds as to the nature of this case. We are here to judge, not a man, but his work. Upon the character of the deceased, therefore, his affectations of dress and manner, his inordinate personal vanity, traits which caused a fellow countryman and former friend to refer to him as the greatest literary fop in history, I do not intend to dwell. I must only remind you that there is usually a close connection between the personal character of a poet and his work, and that the deceased was no exception.

Again I must draw your attention to the exact nature of the charge. That the deceased had talent is not for a moment in dispute; so much is freely admitted by the prosecution. What the defence are asking you to believe, however, is that he was a great poet, the greatest of this century writing in English. That is their case, and it is that which the prosecution feels bound most emphatically to deny.

A great poet. To deserve such an epithet, a poet is commonly required to convince us of these things: firstly a gift of a very high order for memorable language, secondly a profound understanding of the age in which he lived, and thirdly a working knowledge of and sympathetic attitude toward the most progressive thought of his time.

Did the deceased possess these? I am afraid, gentlemen, that the answer is, no.

On the first point I shall be brief. My learned friend, the counsel for the defence, will, I have no doubt, do his best to convince you that I am wrong. And he has a case, gentlemen. O yes, a very fine case. I shall only ask you to apply to the work of the deceased a very simple test. How many of his lines can you remember?

Further, it is not unreasonable to suppose that a poet who has a gift for language will recognise that gift in others. I have here a copy of an anthology edited by the deceased entitled *The Oxford Book of Modern Verse*. I challenge anyone in this court to deny that it is the most deplorable volume ever issued under the imprint of that highly respected firm which has done so much for the cause of poetry in this country, the Clarendon Press.

But in any case you and I are educated modern men. Our fathers imagined that poetry existed in some private garden of its own, totally unrelated to the workaday world, and to be judged by pure aesthetic standards alone. We know that now to be an illusion. Let me pass, then, to my second point. Did the deceased understand his age?

What did he admire? What did he condemn? Well, he extolled the virtues of the peasant. Excellent. But should that peasant learn to read and write, should he save enough money to buy a shop, attempt by honest trading to raise himself above the level of the beasts, and O, what a sorry change is there. Now he is the enemy, the hateful huxter whose blood, according to the unseemly boast of the deceased, never flowed through *his* loins. Had the poet chosen to live in a mud cabin in Galway among swine and superstition, we might think him mistaken, but we should admire his integrity. But did he do this? O dear no. For there was another world which seemed to him not only equally admirable, but a deal more agreeable to live in, the world of noble houses, of large drawing rooms inhabited by the rich and the decorative, most of them of the female sex. We do not have to think very hard or very long, before we shall see a connection between these facts. The deceased had the feudal mentality. He was prepared to admire the poor just as long as they remained poor and deferential, accepting without protest the burden of maintaining a little Athenian band of literary landowners, who without their toil could not have existed for five minutes.

For the great struggle of our time to create a juster social order, he felt nothing but the hatred which is born of fear. It is true that he played a certain part in the movement for Irish Independence, but I hardly think my learned friend will draw your attention to that. Of all the modes of self-evasion open to the well-to-do, nationalism is the easiest and most dishonest. It allows to the unjust all the luxury of righteous indignation against injustice. Still, it has often inspired men and women to acts of heroism and self-sacrifice. For the sake of a free Ireland the poet Pearse and the Countess Markiewicz gave their all. But if the deceased did give himself to this movement, he did so with singular moderation. After the rebellion of Easter Sunday 1916, he wrote a poem on the subject which has been called a masterpiece. It is. To succeed at such a time in writing a poem which could offend neither the Irish Republicans nor the British army was indeed a masterly achievement.

And so we come to our third and last point. The most superficial glance at the last fifty years is enough to tell us that the social struggle toward a greater equality has been accompanied by a growing intellectual acceptance of the scientific method and the steady conquest of irrational superstititon. What was the attitude of the deceased toward this? Gentlemen, words fail me. What are we to say of a man whose earliest writings attempted to revive a belief in fairies and whose favourite themes were legends of barbaric heroes with unpronounceable names, work which has been aptly and wittily described as Chaff about Bran!

But you may say, he was young: youth is always romantic; its silliness is part of its charm. Perhaps it is. Let us forgive the youth, then, and consider the mature man, from whom we have a right to expect wisdom and common sense. Gentlemen, it is hard to be charitable when we find that the deceased, far from outgrowing his folly, has plunged even deeper. In 1900 he believed in fairies; that was bad enough; but in 1930 we are confronted with the pitiful, the deplorable spectacle of a grown man occupied with the mumbo-jumbo of magic and the nonsense of India. Whether he seriously believed such stuff to be true, or merely thought it pretty, or imagined it would impress the public, is immaterial. The plain fact remains that he made it the centre of his work. Gentlemen, I need say no more. In the last poem he wrote, the deceased rejected social justice and reason, and prayed for war. Am I mistaken in imagining that somewhat similar sentiments are expressed by a certain foreign political movement which every lover of literature and liberty acknowledges to be the enemy of mankind?

The Counsel for the Defence:

Gentlemen of the jury. I am sure you have listened with as much enjoyment as I to the eloquence of the prosecution. I say enjoyment because the spectacle of anything well done, whether it be a feat of engineering, a poem, or even an outburst of impassioned oratory, must always give pleasure.

We have been treated to an analysis of the character of the deceased which for all I know, may be as true as it is destructive. Whether it proves anything about the value of his poetry is another matter. If I may be allowed to quote my learned friend, 'We are here to judge, not a man but his work.' We have been told that the deceased was conceited, that he was a snob, that he was a physical coward, that his taste in contemporary poetry was uncertain, that he could not understand physics and chemistry. If this is not an invitation to judge the man I do not know what is. Does it not bear an extraordinary resemblance to the belief of an earlier age that a great artist must be chaste? Take away the frills, and the argument of the prosecution is reduced to this: 'A great poet must give the right answers to the problems which perplex his generation. The deceased gave the wrong answers. Therefore the deceased was not a great poet.' Poetry in such a view is the filling up of a social quiz; to pass with honours the poet must score not less than 75 per cent. With all due respect to my learned friend, this is nonsense. We are tempted so to judge contemporary poets because we really do have problems which we really do want solved, so that we are inclined to expect everyone, politicians, scientists, poets, clergymen, to give us the answer, and to blame them indiscriminately when they do not. But who reads the poetry of the past in this way? In an age of rising nationalism, Dante looked back with envy to the Roman Empire. Was this socially progressive? Will only a Catholic admit that Dryden's *The Hind and the Panther* is a good poem? Do we condemn Blake because he rejected Newton's theory of light, or rank Wordsworth lower than Baker, because the latter had a deeper appreciation of the steam engine?

Can such a view explain why

> Mock Emmet, mock Parnell;
> All the renown that fell

is good; and bad, such a line as

> Somehow I think that you are rather like a tree.

In pointing out that this is absurd, I am not trying to suggest that art exists independently of society. The relation between the two is just as intimate and important as the prosecution asserts.

Every individual is from time to time excited emotionally and intellectually by his social and material environment. In certain individuals this excitement produces verbal structures which we call poems; if such a verbal structure creates an excitement in the reader, we call it a good poem. Poetic talent, in fact, is the power to make personal excitement socially available. Poets, i.e. persons with poetic talent, stop writing good poetry when they stop reacting to the world they live in. The nature of that reaction, whether it be positive or negative, morally admirable or morally disgraceful, matters very little, what is essential is that the reaction should genuinely exist. The later Wordsworth is not inferior to the earlier because the poet had altered his political opinions, but because he had ceased to feel and think so strongly, a change which happens, alas, to most of us as we grow older. Now, when we turn to the deceased, we are confronted by the amazing spectacle of a man of great poetic talent, whose capacity for excitement not only remained with him to the end, but actually increased. In two hundred years when our children have made a different and, I hope, better social order, and when our science has developed out of all recognition, who but a historian will care a button whether the deceased was right about the Irish Question or wrong about the transmigration of souls? But because the excitement out of which his poems arose was genuine, they will still, unless I am very much mistaken, be capable of exciting others, different though their circumstances and beliefs may be from his.

However since we are not living two hundred years hence, let us play the schoolteacher a moment, and examine the poetry of the deceased with reference to the history of our time.

The most obvious social fact of the last forty years is the failure of liberal capitalist democracy, based on the premises that every individual is born free and equal, each an absolute entity independent of all others. And that a formal political equality, the right to vote, the right to a fair trial, the right of free speech, is enough to guarantee his freedom of action in his relations with his fellow men. The results are only too familiar to us all. By denying the social nature of personality, and by ignoring the social power of money, it has created the most impersonal, the most mechanical, and the most unequal civilisation the world has ever seen, a civilisation in which the only emotion common to all classes is a feeling of individual isolation from everyone else, a civilisation torn apart by the opposing emotions born of economic injustice, the just envy of the poor and the selfish terror of the rich.

If these latter emotions meant little to the deceased, it was partly because Ireland compared with the rest of western Europe was economically backward, and the class struggle was less conscious there. My learned friend has sneered at Irish nationalism, but he knows as well as I that nationalism is a necessary stage towards socialism. He has sneered at the deceased for not taking arms, as if shooting were the only honourable and useful form of social action. Has the Abbey Theatre done nothing for Ireland?

But to return to the poems. From first to last they express a sustained protest against the social atomisation caused by industrialism, and both in their ideas and their language a constant struggle to overcome it. The fairies and heroes of the early work were an attempt to find through folk tradition a binding force of society; and the doctrine of Anima Mundi found in the later poems is the same thing, in a more developed form, which has left purely local peculiarities behind, in favour of something that the deceased hoped was universal; in other words, he was working for a world religion. A purely religious solution may be unworkable, but the search for it is, at least, the result of a true perception of a social evil. Again, the virtues that the deceased praised in the peasantry and aristocracy, and the vices he blamed in the commercial classes were real virtues and vices. To create a united and just society where the former are fostered and the latter cured is the task of the politician, not the poet.

For art is a product of history, not a cause. Unlike some other products, technical inventions for example, it does not re-enter history as an effective agent, so that the question whether art should or should not be propaganda is unreal. The case for the prosecution rests on the fallacious belief that art ever makes anything happen, whereas the honest truth, gentlemen, is that if not a poem had been written, not a picture painted, not a bar of music composed, the history of man would be materially unchanged.

But there is one field in which the poet is a man of action, the field of language, and it is precisely in this that the greatness of the deceased is most obviously shown. However false or undemocratic his ideas, his diction shows a continuous evolution toward what one might call the true democratic style. The social virtues of a real democracy are brotherhood and intelligence, and the parallel linguistic virtues are strength and clarity, virtues which appear even more clearly through successive volumes by the deceased.

The diction of *The Winding Stair* is the diction of a just man, and it is for this reason that just men will always recognise the author as a master.

SOURCE: 'The Public *v.* the Late Mr William Butler Yeats', article in *Partisan Review*, VI, 3 (Spring 1939), pp. 46–51.

Cleanth Brooks (1939)

'*A Vision* and the Byzantium Poems'

William Butler Yeats has produced in his *Vision* one of the most remarkable books of the last hundred years. It is the most ambitious attempt made by any poet of our time to set up a 'myth'. The framework is elaborate and complex; the concrete detail constitutes some of the finest prose and poetry of our time. But the very act of boldly setting up a myth will be regarded by most critics as an impertinence, or, at the least, as a fantastic vagary. And the latter view will be reinforced by Yeats's account of how he received the system from the spirits through the mediumship of his wife.

The privately printed edition of *A Vision* appeared so long ago as 1925, but it has been almost completely ignored by the critics even though there has been, since the publication of *The Tower* in 1928, a remarkable resurgence of interest in Yeats's poetry. Indeed, Edmund Wilson has been the only critic thus far to deal with *A Vision* in any detail. His treating it in any detail is all the more admirable in view of his general interpretation of the significance of Yeats's system. For Wilson, as we have already seen, considers the symbolist movement as a retreat from science and reality; and Yeats's system, with its unscientific paraphernalia, its gyres and cones, its strange psychology described in terms of Masks and Bodies of Fate, and most of all its frank acceptance of the supernatural, is enough to try the patience of any scientific modernist. A very real regard for the fineness of Yeats's later poetry has kept him from carrying too far the view of Yeats as an escapist. But to regard the magical system as merely a piece of romantic furniture is to miss completely the function which it has performed for Yeats.

The central matter is science, truly enough, and Edmund Wilson is right in interpreting the symbolist movement as an antiscientific tendency. But the really important matter to determine is the grounds for Yeats's hostility to science. The refusal to accept the scientific account in matters where the scientific method is valid and relevant is unrealistic, but there is nothing 'escapist' about a hostility to science which orders science off the premises as a trespasser when science has taken up a position where it has no business to be. For example, Victorian poetry will illustrate the illegitimate intrusion of science, and Yeats in his frequent reprehension of the 'impurities' in such poetry – far from being a romantic escapist – is taking a thoroughly realistic position. The formulas which Edmund Wilson tends to take up – scientific, hard-headed, realistic; antiscientific-romantic, escapist – are far too simple.

We have argued in earlier chapters that all poetry since the middle of the seventeenth century has been characterised by the impingement of science upon the poet's world. Yeats, after a brief enthusiasm for natural science as a boy, came, he tells us, to hate science 'with a monkish hate'. 'I am', Yeats tells us, 'very religious, and deprived by Huxley and Tyndall . . . of the simple-minded religion of my childhood, I had made a new religion, almost an infallible church of poetic tradition, of a fardel of stories, and of personages, and of emotions, inseparable from their first expression, passed on from generation to generation by poets and painters with some help from philosophers and theologians.' Here is the beginning of Yeats's system.

It is easy, when one considers the system as expressed in *A Vision* to argue that Yeats's quarrel with science was largely that the system of science allowed no place for the supernatural – visions, trances and incredible happenings – which began to manifest itself to Yeats at a very early period in his life. Undoubtedly Yeats wished for an account of experience which would make room for such happenings. But if we insist on this aspect of the matter, as most critics have done, we neglect elements which are far more important. Granting that Yeats had never had a single supernatural manifestation, many of his objections to science would have remained. The account given by science is still abstract, unconcerned with values, and affording no interpretations. Yeats wished for an account of experience which would surmount such defects: as he once put it, a philosophy which was at once 'logical and boundless'. The phrase is an important one. Had Yeats merely been content to indulge himself in fairy tales and random superstitions, he would never, presumably, have bothered with a system of beliefs at all. A philosophy which was merely 'boundless' would allow a person to live in a pleasant enough anarchy. The 'logical' quality demands a systematisation, though in Yeats's case one which would not violate and oversimplify experience.

The whole point is highly important. If Yeats had merely been anxious to indulge his fancy, not caring whether the superstition accepted for the moment had any relation to the world about him – had he been merely an escapist, no system would have been required at all. For the system is an attempt to make a coherent formulation of the natural and the supernatural. The very existence of the system set forth in *A Vision* therefore indicates that Yeats refused to run away from life.

But if he refused to run away from life he also refused to play the game with the counters of science. For the abstract, meaningless, valueless system of science, he proposed to substitute a concrete, meaningful system, substituting symbol for concept. As he states in the introduction to *A Vision*, 'I wished for a system of thought that would leave my imagination free to create as it chose and yet make all it created, or could create, part of the one history, and that the soul's.'[1] Or if we prefer Mr Eliot's terms, Yeats set out to build a system of references which would allow for a unification of sensibility. Yeats wanted to give the authority of the intellect to attitudes and the intensity of emotion to judgements. The counsel of I. A. Richards is to break science and the emotions cleanly apart – to recognise the separate validity and relevance of 'statements' (scientific propositions) on the one hand and of 'pseudo-statements' (unscientific but emotionally valid statements) on the other.

Yeats, on the contrary, instead of breaking science and poetry completely apart, has preferred to reunite these elements in something of the manner in which they are fused in a religion. His system has for him, consequently, the authority and meaning of a religion, combining intellect and emotion as they were combined before the great analytic and abstracting process of modern science broke them apart. In short, Yeats has created for himself a myth. He says so frankly in the closing paragraphs of *A Vision* (1925 edition): 'A book of modern philosophy may prove to our logical capacity that there is a transcendental portion of our being that is timeless and spaceless . . . and yet our imagination remain subjected to nature as before. . . . It was not so with ancient philosophy because the ancient philosopher had something to reinforce his thought, – the Gods, the Sacred Dead, Egyptian Theurgy, the Priestess Diotime. . . . I would restore to the philosopher his mythology.'

It is because most of us misunderstand and distrust the myth and because we too often trust science even when it has been extended into contexts where it is no longer science that most of us misunderstand the function of Yeats's mythology. A further caution is in order. Yeats has called his system 'magical', and the term may mislead us. Yeats even claims for the system a capacity for prediction. In 1917, in his 'Anima Hominis', he wrote: 'I do not doubt those heaving circles, those winding arcs, whether in one man's life or in that of an age, are mathematical, and that some in the world, or beyond the world, have foreknown the event and pricked upon the calendar the life-span of a Christ, a Buddha, a Napoleon'; and in the earlier edition of *A Vision*, there actually occurs a prophecy of the next two hundred years. But the system does not serve the ends of 'vulgar magic'. Yeats obviously does not propose to use his system to forecast the movements of the stock market, or to pick the winner of the Grand National. The relation of the system to science and the precise nature of Yeats's belief in it will be discussed later. For the present, the positive qualities of the myth may be best discussed by pointing out its relation to Yeats's poetry. . . .

The relation of the artist to the souls of the dead is apparently a highly important one for Yeats, and two of Yeats's finest poems, the 'Byzantium' poems, depend heavily upon a knowledge of this relationship.

Byzantium, as Mr R. P. Blackmur has pointed out, is the heaven of man's mind. But more especially it is a symbol of the heaven of man's imagination, and pre-eminently of a particular kind of imagination, the nature of which Yeats suggests for us in the following passage from *A Vision*. 'I think if I could be given a month of Antiquity and leave to spend it where I chose, I would spend it in Byzantium a little before Justinian opened St Sophia and closed the Academy of Plato. I think I could find in some little wineshop some philosophical worker in mosaic who could answer all my questions, the supernatural descending nearer to him than to Plotinus even. . . .'

I think that in early Byzantium, maybe never before or since in recorded history, religious, aesthetic and practical life were one, that architect and artificers – though not, it may be, poets, for language had been the instrument of controversy and must have grown abstract – spoke to the multitude and the few alike. . . . .

[In Byzantium of this period] . . . all about . . . is an incredible splendour like that which we see pass under our closed eyelids as we lie between sleep and waking, no representation of a living world but the dream of a somnambulist. Even the drilled pupil of the eye, when the drill is in the hand of some Byzantine worker in ivory, undergoes a somnambulistic change, for its deep shadow among the faint lines of the tablet, its mechanical circle, where all else is rhythmical and flowing, give to Saint or Angel a look of some great bird staring at miracle.

So much for the symbol of Byzantium itself. The poem 'Sailing to Byzantium', as the less difficult of the two, may properly be considered first. . . . [Brooks quotes the first two stanzas – Ed.]

The poet appeals to the

> . . . sages standing in God's holy fire
> As in the gold mosaic of a wall

asking them to

> Come from the holy fire, perne in a gyre,
> And be the singing-masters of my soul.

A quotation from 'Anima Mundi' is illuminating at this point: 'There are two realities, the terrestrial and the condition of fire. All power is from the terrestrial condition, for there all opposites meet and there only is the extreme of choice possible, full freedom. And there the heterogeneous is, and evil, for evil is the strain one upon another of opposites; but in the condition of fire is all music and all rest . . . .' The dead whose souls have gone through all the sequences, and whose sequences have come to an end are in the condition of fire: '. . . the soul puts on the rhythmic or spiritual body or luminous body and contemplates all the events of its memory and every possible impulse in an eternal possession of itself in one single moment'.

There is a close connection between the dead living in their passionate memories, and Yeats's theory of *Anima Mundi* or the Great Memory. In the same essay he tells us: 'Before the mind's eye whether in sleep or waking, came images that one was to discover presently in some book one had never read, and after looking in vain for explanation to the current theory of forgotten personal memory, I came to believe in a great memory passing on from generation to generation.' From this great memory come two influences: First, 'that inflowing coming alike to men and to animals is called natural'. It is this, for example, that teaches a bird to build her nest or which shapes the child in the womb. But the second inflowing 'which is not natural but intellectual . . . is from the fire . . . .' It is this inflow which the poet wishes to come to him and to transform him, shaping him to a 'bodily form' which is not taken

> . . . from any natural thing,
> But such a form as Grecian goldsmiths make
> Of hammered gold and gold enamelling
> . . .

And if we inquire why the symbol of this 'unnatural' form is denoted by that of a bird, though a bird of metal, we may find the reason in reading further in 'Anima Mundi': 'From tradition and perception, one thought of one's own life as symbolized by earth, the place of heterogeneous things [compare "the terrestrial condition" *supra*], the images as mirrored in water and the images themselves one could divine but as air; and beyond it all there was, I felt confident, certain aims and governing loves, the fire that makes all simple. Yet the images themselves were four-fold, and one judged their meaning in part from the predominance of one out of the four elements, or that of the fifth element, the veil hiding another four, a bird born out of the fire.'

The poem can be taken on a number of levels: as the transition from sensual art to intellectual art; as the poet's new and brilliant insight into the nature of the Byzantine imagination; as the poet's coming to terms with age and death. The foregoing account of the development of the symbols in the poet's personal experience will not in itself explain the fineness of the poem, or even indicate its aesthetic structure: it will not indicate, for example, the quality of self-irony in his characterisation of himself as a 'monument of unageing intellect' or as a 'tattered coat upon a stick' or the play of wit achieved in such a phrase as 'the artifice of eternity'. The account given will, for that matter, do no more than indicate the series of contrasts and paradoxes on which the poem is founded – it will not assess their function in giving the poem its power. But it may indicate the source of the authority which dictates the tone of the poem. The real importance of the symbolic system is that it allows the poet a tremendous richness and coherency.

'Sailing to Byzantium', as we have seen, derives its direction from the poet's own sense of loss and decay. The focus of the poem rests in the reader's sense that the poet is in Ireland, *not* Byzantium. The appeal to the sages of Byzantium is made in terms of the man whose soul is 'fastened to a dying animal'. 'Byzantium', on the other hand, a more difficult poem, concerns itself directly with the 'condition of fire' and the relation of the living to the living dead. It will furnish therefore perhaps the best illustration of the extent to which Yeats can successfully rely upon his system, for the poem is an undoubted success and yet its relation to the system is detailed and intricate. . . . [Brooks quotes the whole poem – Ed.]

. . . Consider the lines [in the first stanza]

> A starlit or a moonlit dome disdains
> All that man is,
> All mere complexities,
> The fury and the mire of human veins.

A starlit dome, in contradistinction to a moonlit dome, is one at the dark of the moon (phase 1), and the implication of 'moonlit dome' is one lighted by the full moon (phase 15).

Now . . . at phase 1, complete objectivity, and phase 15, complete subjectivity, human life cannot exist; for all human life represents a mixture of the subjective and the objective, 'complexities', 'mere complexities' as compared with the superhuman purity of phases 1 or 15. The dependence on the system may also seem excessive. And yet, even in this instance, one may show that the use is not merely arbitrary. The poem describes an appeal to the superhuman, to the deathless images of the imagination; and the starlit or moonlit dome, freed of the 'unpurged images of day', and silent with the 'Emperor's drunken soldiery' abed, may seem a place unhuman and supernatural, and a place in which one might fittingly invoke the superhuman. Yeats's symbols, though they are interwoven into complex organisations, never give way to a merely allegorical construct; the proof that they do not lies in the fact that on their literal level they tend to take the reader in the direction of the system, as in the present case.

The second stanza will be much clarified by a consideration of a number of passages in Yeats's prose. For example, consider with regard to the first four lines of the stanza –

> Before me floats an image, man or shade,
> Shade more than man, more image than a shade;
> For Hades' bobbin bound in mummy-cloth
> May unwind the winding path;

– the following passage from 'Hodos Chameliontos' (Yeats is pondering in this passage on the possibility of a great memory of the world): 'Is there nation-wide multiform reverie, every mind passing through a stream of suggestion, and all streams acting and reacting upon one another, no matter how distant the minds, how dumb the lips? A man walked, as it were, casting a shadow, and yet one could never say which was man and which was shadow, or how many the shadows that he cast.' The general idea we have already quoted above: 'Before the mind's eye whether in sleep or waking, came images that one was to discover presently in some book one had never read . . . .' The image here, 'man or shade', is such an image, and a part of the great memory. 'Hades' bobbin bound in mummy-cloth' occurs in the earlier poem, 'All Souls' Night', where Yeats again summons the dead:

> I need some mind that, if the cannon sound
> From every quarter of the world, can stay
> Wound in mind's pondering,
> As mummies in the mummy-cloth are wound.

All activity for Yeats, as we have seen, partakes of the whirling motion of the gyre, and the thread wound about the spool is continually used by Yeats as a symbol for experience wound up. Each age unwinds what the previous age has wound, and the life after death unwinds the thread wound on the spool by life. The 'winding path' which 'Hades' bobbin' may unwind is mentioned in 'Anima Mundi'. It is the 'path of the Serpent' or the 'winding movement of nature' as contrasted with the straight path open to the saint or sage. Once more, then, the natural and the human are contrasted with the supernatural and the superhuman. 'Death-in-life and life-in-death' are of course the dead themselves, who are for Yeats more alive than the living: 'It is even possible that being is only possessed completely by the dead . . . .'

The symbol of the bird, in the third stanza, we have already come upon in 'Sailing to Byzantium', and also in two passages quoted in this chapter from Yeats's prose – that in which he describes Byzantine art and that in which he uses the bird 'born out of the fire' to symbolise the fifth element – the supernatural – the veil hiding another four. The allusion to the 'cocks of Hades' is to be compared with the reference to the cockerel in the earlier poem, 'Solomon and the Witch':

> . . . A cockerel
> Crew from a blossoming apple bough
> Three hundred years before the Fall,
> And never crew again till now,
> And would not now but that he thought,
> Chance being at one with Choice at last,
> All that the brigand apple brought
> And this foul world were dead at last.

Chance is that which is Fated; Choice, that which is destined or chosen; and they coincide at phases 1 and 15, for at these phases Mask and Body of Fate are superimposed upon each other. 'At Phase 15 mind [is] completely absorbed by Being' – at phase 1 'body is completely absorbed in its supernatural environment'. The cockerel in the earlier poem 'crowed out eternity [and] / Thought to have crowed it in again'. The 'miracle, bird or golden handiwork' may thus fittingly crow in 'the artifice of eternity'.

But we shall not understand the third stanza nor the fourth fully unless we understand something of Yeats's theory of spirits. For example the phrase 'blood-begotten spirits' [in the fourth stanza] is explicable if we consider the following passage from 'Anima Mundi': 'All souls have a vehicle or body. . . . The vehicle of the human soul is what used to be called the animal spirits', and Yeats quotes from Hippocrates, 'The mind of man is . . . not nourished from meats and drinks from the belly, but by a clear luminous substance that redounds by separation from the blood.' These vehicles can be molded to any shape by an act of the imagination. Moreover, 'our animal spirits or vehicles are but as it were a condensation of the vehicle of *Anima Mundi*, and give substance to its images in the faint materialisation of our common thought, or more grossly when a ghost is our visitor'.

The description of the spirits as flames accords with the fact that they are in the condition of fire, but the additional phrase, 'flames begotten of flame', requires reference to Yeats's statement that 'the spirits do not get from it [the vehicle] the material from which their forms are made, but their forms take light from it as one candle takes light from another'. Indeed, Yeats tells us in the earlier version of *A Vision* that spirits can actually be born of spirits. Beings called 'arcons' are born from spirits which are at phases 15 and 1. Those born from spirits at phase 15 are antithetical arcons. The spirit at phase 15, desiring to rid itself of all traces of the primary, accomplishes this by 'imposing upon a man or woman's mind an *antithetical* image . . . .' This image may be expressed as an action or as a work of art. The expression of it 'is a harmonization which frees the Spirit from terror and the man from desire . . . .' So much from *A Vision.* In an essay published still earlier, Yeats says that Shelley 'must have expected to receive thoughts and images from beyond his own mind, just in so far as that mind transcended its preoccupation with particular time and place, for he believed *inspiration a kind of death* [italics mine]; and he could hardly have helped perceiving that an image that has transcended particular time and place becomes a symbol, passes beyond death, as it were, and becomes a living soul'. The passage from *A Vision* quoted above gives merely a schematisation of this earlier thought: an explanation of what the dead man gives and what the living man receives, and the reason for the giving. One notices, however, that whereas Yeats gives in the poem a most complex theory of the relation of the dead to the Great Memory and of their relations to the living, the symbols form more than an exposition of the esoteric: they dramatise the emotional relationships. The spirits must be originally blood-begotten but the blood gives place to flame; the mere complexities give way to purity; the fire 'makes all simple'. Yet power is of the blood and the flames which 'no faggot feeds' are powerless and cannot 'singe a sleeve'. The balance is maintained.

As for the dance of the spirits, another passage from 'Anima Mundi' is relevant: 'Then gradually they [the dead] perceive, although they are still but living in their memories, harmonies, symbols, and patterns, as though all were being refashioned by an artist, and they are moved by emotions, sweet for no imagined good but in themselves, like those of children dancing in a ring. . . . Hitherto shade has communicated with shade in moments of common memory that recur like the figures of a dance in terror or in joy, but now they run together like to like, and their Covens and Fleets have rhythm and pattern.'

The fifth stanza is a recapitulation, but a recapitulation with the addition of a new and important image for the Great Memory, an image which Yeats has earlier used for it in his prose: the image of the sea. In 'Anima Mundi', after speaking of the Great Memory, Yeats has written: 'The thought was again and again before me that this study had created a contact or mingling with minds who had followed a like study in some other age, and that these minds still saw and thought and chose. Our daily thought was certainly but the line of foam at the shallow edge of a vast luminous sea; Henry More's *Anima Mundi*, Wordsworth's "immortal sea which brought us hither". . . .'

Again, in an essay on 'The Tragic Theatre', Yeats has used the figure: 'Tragic art, passionate art, the drowner of dykes, the confounder of understanding, moves us by setting us to reverie, by alluring us almost to the intensity of trance. . . . We feel our minds expand convulsively or spread out slowly like some moon-brightened image-crowded sea.' The phrase 'gong-tormented' emphasises the connection of the images of the *Anima Mundi* with drama:

> All men are dancers and their tread
> Goes to the barbarous clangour of a gong.
> ('Nineteen Hundred and Nineteen')

The image of the Great Memory as a sea is introduced by the reference to Arion and the dolphin. The poet can travel in that sea, but only supported on the dolphin's mire and blood. The 'golden smithies of the Emperor' are of course those referred to in 'Sailing to Byzantium':

> Once out of nature I shall never take
> My bodily form from any natural thing,
> But such a form as Grecian goldsmiths make
> Of hammered gold and gold enamelling
> . . .

These artists – the Byzantine 'painter, the worker in mosaic, the worker in gold and silver' – are those to whom, because of their craftsmanship, the 'supernatural descended nearer . . . than to Plotinus even'.

One can allow that much of the poem would be intelligible to a person entirely unacquainted with Yeats's system. But this rather detailed comparison of the poem with the passages from Yeats's prose given above is perhaps justified in showing how rich and intricate the poem becomes when a knowledge of the system is brought to bear on the poem. 'Byzantium' is admittedly a somewhat special case, but many of Yeats's other poems – especially those written around 1917 – are hardly less dependent on the system.

Most important of all, however, is to notice that from the poet's standpoint the richness and *precision* of such a poem as 'Byzantium' is only made possible by the poet's possession of such a system. The system, in these terms, is an instrument for, as well as a symbol of, the poet's reintegration of his personality. It is the instrument through which Yeats has accomplished the unification of his sensibility.

A brief summary of the general function of Yeats's system may be in order here. We have already spoken of the advantages which the poet gains by using concrete symbols rather than abstract ideas and of traditional symbols which make available to him the great symbolism out of the past. The system, to put it concisely, allows Yeats to see the world as a great drama, predictable in its larger aspects (so that the poet is not lost in a welter of confusion), but in a pattern which allows for the complexity of experience and the apparent contradictions of experience (so that the poet is not tempted to oversimplify). The last point is highly important and bears directly on the dramatic aspect of the system, for the system demands, as it were, a continually repeated victory over the contradictory whereby the contradictory is recognised, and through the recognition, resolved into agreement. Yeats's finest poems not only state this thesis but embody such a structure, and his increasing boldness in the use of the contradictory and the discordant in his own poetry springs directly from his preoccupation with antithesis. . . .

SOURCE: extracts from the chapter, 'Yeats: The Poet as Mythmaker', in *Modern Poetry and the Tradition* (Chapel Hill, N.C., 1939; 2nd edn, 1965), pp. 173–87, 189–200.

NOTE

1. This statement occurs in the privately printed edition of *A Vision* which appeared in 1925. The new edition does not differ from the earlier fundamentally in the system that it sets forth, though it has many omissions and revisions of statement, and some extensions. [For fuller discussion of *A Vision*, see Richard Ellmann's second excerpt in Part Three, section 1, below – Ed.]

T. S. Eliot (1940)

'The Development of Yeats'

. . . This, I am sure, was part of the secret of his ability, after becoming unquestionably the master, to remain always a contemporary. Another is the continual development of which I have spoken. This has become almost a commonplace of criticism of his work. But while it is often mentioned, its causes and its nature have not been often analysed. One reason, of course, was simply concentration and hard work. And behind that is character: I mean the special character of the artist as artist – that is, the force of character by which Dickens, having exhausted his first inspiration, was able in middle age to proceed to such a masterpiece, so different from his early work, as *Bleak House*. It is difficult and unwise to generalise about ways of composition – so many men, so many ways – but it is my experience that towards middle age a man has three choices: to stop writing altogether, to repeat himself with perhaps an increasing skill of virtuosity, or by taking thought to adapt himself to middle age and find a different way of working. Why are the later long poems of Browning and Swinburne mostly unread? It is, I think, because one gets the essential Browning or Swinburne entire in earlier poems; and in the later, one is reminded of the early freshness which they lack, without being made aware of any compensating new qualities. When a man is engaged in work of abstract thought – if there is such a thing as wholly abstract thought outside of the mathematical and the physical sciences – his mind can mature, while his emotions either remain the same or only atrophy, and it will not matter. But maturing as a poet means maturing as the whole man, experiencing new emotions appropriate to one's age, and with the same intensity as the emotions of youth.

One form, a perfect form, of development is that of Shakespeare, one of the few poets whose work of maturity is just as exciting as that of their early manhood. There is, I think, a difference between the development of Shakespeare and Yeats, which makes the latter case still more curious. With Shakespeare, one sees a slow, continuous development of mastery of his craft of verse, and the poetry of middle age seems implicit in that of early maturity. After the first few verbal exercises you say of each piece of work: 'This is the perfect expression of the sensibility of that stage of his development.' That a poet should develop at all, that he should find something new to say, and say it equally well, in middle age, has always something miraculous about it. But in the case of Yeats the kind of development seems to me different. I do not want to give the impression that I regard his earlier and his later work almost as if they had been written by two different men. Returning to his earlier poems after making a close acquaintance with the later, one sees, to begin with, that in technique there was a slow and continuous development of what is always the same medium and idiom. And when I say development, I do not mean that many of the early poems, for what they are, are not as beautifully written as they could be. There are some, such as 'Who Goes with Fergus', which are as perfect of their kind as anything in the language. But the best, and the best known of them, have this limitation: that they are as satisfactory in isolation, as 'anthology pieces', as they are in the context of his other poems of the same period.

I am obviously using the term 'anthology piece' in a rather special sense. In any anthology, you find some poems which give you complete satisfaction and delight in themselves, such that you are hardly curious who wrote them, hardly want to look further into the work of that poet. There are others, not necessarily so perfect or complete, which make you irresistibly curious to know more of that poet through his other work. Naturally, this distinction applies only to short poems, those in which a man has been able to put only a part of his mind, if it is a mind of any size. With some such you feel at once that the man who wrote them must have had a great deal more to say, in different contexts, of equal interest. Now among all the poems in Yeats's earlier volumes I find only in a line here or there, that sense of a unique personality which makes one sit up in excitement and eagerness to learn more about the author's mind and feelings. The intensity of Yeats's own emotional experience hardly appears. We have sufficient evidence of the intensity of experience of his youth, but it is from the retrospections in some of his later work that we have our evidence.

I have, in early essays, extolled what I called impersonality in art, and it may seem that, in giving as a reason for the superiority of Yeats's later work the greater expression of personality in it, I am contradicting myself. It may be that I expressed myself badly, or that I had only an adolescent grasp of that idea – as I can never bear to re-read my own prose writings, I am willing to leave the point unsettled – but I think now, at least, that the truth of the matter is as follows. There are two forms of impersonality: that which is natural to the mere skilful craftsman, and that which is more and more achieved by the maturing artist. The first is that of what I have called the 'anthology piece', of a lyric by Lovelace or Suckling, or of Campion, a finer poet than either. The second impersonality is that of the poet who, out of intense and personal experience, is able to express a general truth; retaining all the particularity of his experience, to make of it a general symbol. And the strange thing is that Yeats, having been a great craftsman in the first kind, became a great poet in the second. It is not that he became a different man, for, as I have hinted, one feels sure that the intense experience of youth had been lived through – and indeed, without this early experience he could never have attained anything of the wisdom which appears in his later writing. But he had to wait for a later maturity to find expression of early experience; and this makes him, I think, a unique and especially interesting poet.

Consider the early poem which is in every anthology, 'When You Are Old', or 'A Dream of Death' in the same volume of 1893. They are beautiful poems, but only craftsman's work, because one does not feel present in them the particularity which must provide the material for the general truth. By the time of the volume of 1904 there is a development visible in a very lovely poem, 'The Folly of Being Comforted', and in 'Adam's Curse', something is coming through, and in beginning to speak as a particular man he is beginning to speak for man. This is clearer still in the poem 'Peace', in the 1910 volume. But it is not fully evinced until the volume of 1914, in the violent and terrible epistle dedicatory of *Responsibilities*, with the great lines

> Pardon that for a barren passion's sake,
> Although I have come close on forty-nine,
> . . .

And the naming of his age in the poem is significant. More than half a lifetime to arrive at this freedom of speech. It is a triumph.

There was much also for Yeats to work out of himself, even in technique. To be a younger member of a group of poets, none of them certainly of anything like his stature, but further developed in their limited path, may arrest for a time a man's development of idiom. Then again, the weight of the pre-Raphaelite prestige must have been tremendous. The Yeats of the Celtic twilight – who seems to me to have been more the Yeats of the pre-Raphaelite twilight – uses Celtic folklore almost as William Morris uses Scandinavian folklore. His longer narrative poems bear the mark of Morris. Indeed, in the pre-Raphaelite phase, Yeats is by no means the least of the pre-Raphaelites. I may be mistaken, but the play, *The Shadowy Waters*, seems to me one of the most perfect expressions of the vague enchanted beauty of that school: yet it strikes me – this may be an impertinence on my part – as the western seas descried through the back window of a house in Kensington, an Irish myth for the Kelmscott Press; and when I try to visualise the speakers in the play, they have the great dim, dreamy eyes of the knights and ladies of

Burne-Jones. I think that the phase in which he treated Irish legend in the manner of Rossetti or Morris is a phase of confusion. He did not master this legend until he made it a vehicle for his own creation of character – not, really, until he began to write the *Plays for Dancers*. The point is, that in becoming more Irish, not in subject-matter but in expression, he became at the same time universal.

The points that I particularly wish to make about Yeats's development are two. The first, on which I have already touched, is that to have accomplished what Yeats did in the middle and later years is a great and permanent example – which poets-to-come should study with reverence – of what I have called Character of the Artist: a kind of moral, as well as intellectual, excellence. The second point, which follows naturally after what I have said in criticism of the lack of complete emotional expression in his early work, is that Yeats is pre-eminently the poet of middle age. By this I am far from meaning that he is a poet only for middle-aged readers: the attitude towards him of younger poets who write in English, the world over, is enough evidence to the contrary. Now, in theory, there is no reason why a poet's inspiration or material should fail, in middle age or at any time before senility. For a man who is capable of experience finds himself in a different world in every decade of his life; as he sees it with different eyes, the material of his art is continually renewed. But in fact, very few poets have shown this capacity of adaptation to the years. It requires, indeed, an exceptional honesty and courage to face the change. Most men either cling to the experiences of youth, so that their writing becomes an insincere mimicry of their earlier work, or they leave their passion behind, and write only from the head, with a hollow and wasted virtuosity. There is another and even worse temptation: that of becoming dignified, of becoming public figures with only a public existence – coat-racks hung with decorations and distinctions, doing, saying, and even thinking and feeling only what they believe the public expects of them. Yeats was not that kind of poet: and it is, perhaps, a reason why young men should find his later poetry more acceptable than older men easily can. For the young can see him as a poet who in his work remained in the best sense always young, who even in one sense became young as he aged. But the old, unless they are stirred to something of the honesty with oneself expressed in the poetry, will be shocked by such a revelation of what a man really is and remains. They will refuse to believe that *they* are like that.

> You think it horrible that lust and rage
> Should dance attendance upon my old age;
> They were not such a plague when I was young;
> What else have I to spur me into song? ['The Spur']

These lines are very impressive and not very pleasant, and the sentiment has recently been criticised by an English critic whom I generally respect. But I think he misread them. I do not read them as a personal confession of a man who differed from other men, but of a man who was essentially the same as most other men; the only difference is in the greater clarity, honesty and vigour. To what honest man, old enough, can these sentiments be entirely alien? They can be subdued and disciplined by religion, but who can say that they are dead? Only those to whom the maxim of La Rochefoucauld applies: 'Quand les vices nous quittent, nous nous flattons de la créance que c'est nous qui les quittons.' The tragedy of Yeats's epigram is all in the last line.

Similarly, the play *Purgatory* is not very pleasant, either. There are aspects of it which I do not like myself. I wish he had not given it this title, because I cannot accept a purgatory in which there is no hint of, or at least no emphasis upon, Purgation. But, apart from the extraordinary theatrical skill with which he has put so much action within the compass of a very short scene of but little movement, the play gives a masterly exposition of the emotions of an old man. I think that the epigram I have just quoted seems to me just as much to be taken in a dramatic sense as the play *Purgatory*. The lyric poet – and Yeats was always lyric, even when dramatic – can speak for every man, or for men very different from himself; but to do this he must for the moment be able to identify himself with every man or other men; and it is only his imaginative power of becoming this that deceives some readers into thinking that he is speaking for and of himself alone – especially when they prefer not to be implicated.

I do not wish to emphasise this aspect only of Yeats's poetry of age. I would call attention to the beautiful poem in *The Winding Stair*, in memory of Eva Gore-Booth and Con Markiewicz, in which the picture at the beginning, of:

> Two girls in silk kimonos, both
> Beautiful, one a gazelle,

gets great intensity from the shock of the later line:

> When withered old and skeleton gaunt,

and also to 'Coole Park, 1929', beginning

> I meditate upon a swallow's flight,
> Upon an aged woman and her house.

In such poems one feels that the most lively and desirable emotions of youth have been preserved to receive their full and due expression in retrospect. For the interesting feelings of age are not just different feelings; they are feelings into which the feelings of youth are integrated. . . .

To be able to praise, it is not necessary to feel complete agreement; and I do not dissimulate the fact that there are aspects of Yeats's thought and feeling which to myself are unsympathetic. I say this only to indicate the limits which I have set to my criticism. The questions of difference, objection and protest arise in the field of doctrine, and these are vital questions. I have been concerned only with the poet and dramatist, so far as these can be isolated. In the long run they cannot be wholly isolated. A full and elaborate examination of the total work of Yeats must some day be undertaken; perhaps it will need a longer perspective. There are some poets whose poetry can be considered more or less in isolation, for experience and delight. There are others whose poetry, though giving equally experience and delight, has a larger historical importance. Yeats was one of the latter: he was one of those few whose history is the history of their own time, who are a part of the consciousness of an age which cannot be understood without them. This is a very high position to assign to him: but I believe that it is one which is secure.

SOURCE: extracts from the first annual Yeats lecture, delivered to the Friends of the Irish Academy at the Abbey Theatre, Dublin, in 1940; reproduced in *On Poetry and Poets* (London, 1957), pp. 253–9, 262.

George Orwell (1943)

'Yeats's Politics'

One thing that Marxist criticism has not succeeded in doing is to trace the connection between 'tendency' and literary style. The subject-matter and imagery of a book can be explained in sociological terms, but its texture seemingly cannot. Yet some such connection there must be. One knows, for instance, that a Socialist would not write like Chesterton or a Tory imperialist like Bernard Shaw, though *how* one knows it is not easy to say. In the case of Yeats, there must be some kind of connection between his wayward, even tortured, style of writing and his rather sinister vision of life. Mr Menon[1] is chiefly concerned with the esoteric philosophy underlying Yeats's work, but the quotations which are scattered all through his interesting book serve to remind one how artificial Yeats's manner of writing was. As a rule, this artificiality is accepted as Irishism, or Yeats is even credited with simplicity because he uses short words, but in fact one seldom comes on six consecutive lines of his verse in which there is not an archaism or an affected turn of speech. To take the nearest example:

> Grant me an old man's frenzy,
> Myself must I remake
> Till I am Timon and Lear
> Or that William Blake
> Who beat upon the wall
> Till Truth obeyed his call.

The unnecessary 'that' imports a feeling of affectation, and the same tendency is present in all but Yeats's best passages. One is seldom long away from a suspicion of 'quaintness', something that links up not only with the nineties, the Ivory Tower and the 'calf covers of pissed-on green', but also with Rackham's drawings, Liberty art-fabrics and the *Peter Pan* never-never land, of which, after all, 'The Happy Townland' is merely a more appetising example. This does not matter because, on the whole, Yeats gets away with it, and if his straining after effect is often irritating, it can also produce phrases ('the chill, footless years', 'the mackerel-crowded seas') which suddenly overwhelm one like a girl's face seen across a room. He is an exception to the rule that poets do not use poetical language:

How many centuries spent
The sedentary soul
In toil of measurement
Beyond eagle or mole,
Beyond hearing or seeing,
Or Archimedes' guess,
To raise into being
That loveliness?

Here he does not flinch from a squashy vulgar word like 'loveliness', and after all it does not seriously spoil this wonderful passage. But the same tendencies, together with a sort of raggedness which is no doubt intentional, weaken his epigrams and polemical poems. For instance (I am quoting from memory)[2] the epigram against the critics who damned *The Playboy of the Western World*:

Once, when midnight smote the air,
Eunuchs ran through Hell and met
On every crowded street to stare
Upon great Juan riding by:
Even like these to rail and sweat
Staring upon his sinewy thigh.

The power which Yeats has within himself gives him the analogy ready made and produces the tremendous scorn of the last line, but even in this short poem there are six or seven unnecessary words. It would probably have been deadlier if it had been neater.

Mr Menon's book is incidentally a short biography of Yeats, but he is above all interested in Yeats's philosophical 'system', which in his opinion supplies the subject-matter of more of Yeats's poems than is generally recognised. This system is set forth fragmentarily in various places, and at full length in *A Vision*, a privately printed book which I have never read but which Mr Menon quotes from extensively. Yeats gave conflicting accounts of its origin, and Mr Menon hints pretty broadly that the 'documents' on which it was ostensibly founded were imaginary. Yeats's philosophical system, says Mr Menon, 'was at the back of his intellectual life almost from the beginning. His poetry is full of it. Without it his later poetry becomes almost completely unintelligible.' As soon as we begin to read about the so-called system we are in the middle of a hocus-pocus of Great Wheels, gyres, cycles of the moon, reincarnation, disembodied spirits, astrology and what not. Yeats hedges as to the literalness with which he believed in all this, but he certainly dabbled in spiritualism and astrology, and in earlier life had made experiments in alchemy. Although almost buried under explanations, very difficult to understand, about the phases of the moon, the central idea of his philosophical system seems to be our old friend, the cyclical universe, in which everything happens over and over again. One has not, perhaps, the right to laugh at Yeats for his mystical beliefs – for I believe it could be shown that *some* degree of belief in magic is almost universal – but neither ought one to write such things off as mere unimportant eccentricities. It is Mr Menon's perception of this that gives his book its deepest interest. 'In the first flush of admiration and enthusiasm', he says, 'most people dismissed the fantastical philosophy as the price we have to pay for a great and curious intellect. One did not quite realise where he was heading. And those who did, like Pound and perhaps Eliot, approved the stand that he finally took. The first reaction to this did not come, as one might have expected, from the politically-minded young English poets. They were puzzled because a less rigid or artificial system than that of *A Vision* might not have produced the great poetry of Yeats's last days.' It might not, and yet Yeats's philosophy has some very sinister implications, as Mr Menon points out.

Translated into political terms, Yeats's tendency is Fascist. Throughout most of his life, and long before Fascism was ever heard of, he had the outlook of those who reach Fascism by the aristocratic route. He is a great hater of democracy, of the modern world, science, machinery, the concept of progress – above all, of the idea of human equality. Much of the imagery of his work is feudal, and it is clear that he was not altogether free from ordinary snobbishness. Later these tendencies took clearer shape and led him to 'the exultant acceptance of authoritarianism as the only solution. Even violence and tyranny are not necessarily evil because the people, knowing not evil and good, would become perfectly acquiescent to tyranny. . . . Everything must come from the top. Nothing can ever come from the masses.' Not much interested in politics, and no doubt disgusted by his brief incursions into public life, Yeats nevertheless makes political pronouncements. He is too big a man to share the illusions of Liberalism, and as early as 1920 he foretells in a justly famous passage ('The Second Coming') the kind of world that we have actually moved into. But he appears to welcome the coming age, which is to be 'hierarchical, masculine, harsh, surgical', and is influenced both by

Ezra Pound and by various Italian Fascist writers. He describes the new civilisation which he hopes and believes will arrive: 'an . . . aristocratic civilisation in its completed form, every detail of life hierarchical, great wealth everywhere in few men's hands, all dependent upon a few, up to the Emperor himself who is a God dependent upon a greater God, and everywhere in Court, in the family, an inequality made law'. The innocence of this statement is as interesting as its snobbishness. To begin with, in a single phrase, 'great wealth in few men's hands', Yeats lay bare the central reality of Fascism, which the whole of its propaganda is designed to cover up. The merely political Fascist claims always to be fighting for justice: Yeats, the poet, sees at a glance that Fascism means injustice, and acclaims it for that very reason. But at the same time he fails to see that the new authoritarian civilisation, if it arrives, will not be aristocratic, or what he means by aristocratic. It will not be ruled by noblemen with Van Dyck faces, but by anonymous millionaires, shiny-bottomed bureaucrats and murdering gangsters. Others who have made the same mistake have afterwards changed their views, and one ought not to assume that Yeats, if he had lived longer, would necessarily have followed his friend Pound, even in sympathy. But the tendency of the passage I have quoted above is obvious, and its complete throwing overboard of whatever good the past two thousand years have achieved is a disquieting symptom.

How do Yeats's political ideas link up with his leaning towards occultism? It is not clear at first glance why hatred of democracy and a tendency to believe in crystal-gazing should go together. Mr Menon only discusses this rather shortly, but it is possible to make two guesses. To begin with, the theory that civilisation moves in recurring cycles is one way out for people who hate the concept of human equality. If it is true that 'all this', or something like it, 'has happened before', then science and the modern world are debunked at one stroke and progress becomes for ever impossible. It does not matter much if the lower orders are getting above themselves, for, after all, we shall soon be returning to an age of tyranny. Yeats is by no means alone in this outlook. If the universe is moving round on a wheel, the future must be foreseeable, perhaps even in some detail. It is merely a question of discovering the laws of its motion, as the early astronomers discovered the solar year. Believe that, and it becomes difficult not to believe in astrology or some similar system. A year before the war, examining a copy of *Gringoire*, the French Fascist weekly, much read by army officers, I found in it no less than thirty-eight advertisements of clairvoyants. Secondly, the very concept of occultism carries with it the idea that knowledge must be a secret thing, limited to a small circle of initiates. But the same idea is integral to Fascism. Those who dread the prospect of universal suffrage, popular education, freedom of thought, emancipation of women, will start off with a predilection towards secret cults. There is another link between Fascism and magic in the profound hostility of both to the Christian ethical code.

No doubt Yeats wavered in his beliefs and held at different times many different opinions, some enlightened, some not. Mr Menon repeats for him Eliot's claim that he had the longest period of development of any poet who has ever lived. But there is one thing that seems constant, at least in all of his work that I can remember, and that is his hatred of modern western civilisation and desire to return to the Bronze Age, or perhaps to the Middle Ages. Like all such thinkers, he tends to write in praise of ignorance. The Fool in his remarkable play, *The Hour-Glass*, is a Chestertonian figure, 'God's Fool', the 'natural born innocent', who is always wiser than the wise man. The philosopher in the play dies in the knowledge that all his lifetime of thought has been wasted (I am quoting from memory again):

> The stream of the world has changed its course,
> And with the stream my thoughts have run
> Into some cloudy thunderous spring
> That is its mountain source –
> Ay, to some frenzy of the mind,
> For all that we have done's undone,
> Our speculation but as the wind.

Beautiful words, but by implication profoundly obscurantist and reactionary; for if it is really true that a village idiot, as such, is wiser than a philosopher, then it would be better if the alphabet had never been invented. Of course, all praise of the past is partly sentimental, because we do not live in the past. The poor do not praise poverty. Before you can despise the machine, the machine must set you free from brute labour. But that is not to say that Yeats's yearning for a more primitive and more hierarchical age was not sincere. How much of all this is traceable to mere snobbishness, product of Yeats's own position as an impoverished offshoot of the aristocracy, is a different question. And the connection between his obscurantist opinions and his tendency towards 'quaintness' of language remains to be worked out; Mr Menon hardly touches upon it.

This is a very short book, and I would greatly like to see Mr Menon go ahead and write another book on Yeats, starting where this one leaves off. 'If the greatest poet of our times is exultantly ringing in an era of Fascism, it seems a somewhat disturbing symptom', he says on the last page, and leaves it at that. It is a disturbing symptom, because it is not an isolated one. By and large the best writers of our time have been reactionary in tendency, and though Fascism does not offer any real return to the past, those who yearn for the past will accept Fascism sooner than its probable alternatives. But there are other lines of approach, as we have seen during the past two or three years. The relationship between Fascism and the literary intelligentsia badly needs investigating, and Yeats might well be the starting-point. He is best studied by someone like Mr Menon, who can approach a poet primarily as a poet, but who also knows that a writer's political and religious beliefs are not excrescences to be laughed away, but something that will leave their mark even on the smallest detail of his work.

SOURCE: review article on V. K. Narayana Menon's *The Development of William Butler Yeats*, in *Horizon*, VII, 37 (1943); reproduced in Sonia Orwell and Ian Angus (eds), *The Collected Essays, Journalism and Letters of George Orwell* (London, 1968), vol. 2, pp. 271–5.

NOTES

1. *The Development of William Butler Yeats* by V. K. Narayana Menon.
2. [Ed.] Here and in other quotations from Yeats, Orwell's text has been silently revised to harmonise with the poet's definitive version.

Allen Tate (1942)

'How Yeats will be studied'

. . . Mr Eliot's view, that Yeats got off the central tradition into a 'minor mythology', and Mr Blackmur's view [see excerpt in Part Two, above – Ed.], that he took 'magic' (as opposed to religion) as far as any poet could, seem to me to be related versions of the same fallacy. Which is: that there must be a direct and effective correlation between the previously established truth of the poet's ideas and the value of the poetry. (I am oversimplifying Blackmur's view, but not Eliot's.) In this difficulty it is always useful to ask: *Where* are the poet's ideas? Good sense in this matter ought to tell us that while the ideas doubtless exist in some form outside the poetry, as they exist for Yeats in the letters, the essays and *A Vision*, we must nevertheless test them in the poems themselves, and not 'refute' a poem in which the gyres supply certain images by showing that gyres are amateur philosophy.

> Turning and turning in the widening gyre
> The falcon cannot hear the falconer;

– the opening lines of 'The Second Coming': and they make enough sense apart from our knowledge of the system; the gyre here can be visualised as the circling flight of the bird constantly widening until it has lost contact with the point, the center, to which it ought to be able to return. As a symbol of disunity it is no more esoteric than Eliot's 'Gull against the wind', at the end of 'Gerontion', which is a casual, not traditional or systematic symbol of disunity. Both Mr Blackmur and Mr Brooks – Mr Brooks [see excerpt in part Two, above – Ed.] more than Mr Blackmur – show us the systematic implications of the symbols of the poem 'Byzantium'. The presence of the system at its most formidable cannot be denied to this poem. I should like to see nevertheless an analysis of it in which no special knowledge is used; I should like to see it examined with the ordinary critical equipment of the educated critic; I should be surprised if the result were very different from Mr Brooks's reading of the poem. The symbols are 'made good' in the poem; they are drawn into a wider convention (Mr Blackmur calls it the 'heaven of man's mind') than they would imply if taken separately.

I conclude these notes with the remark: the study of Yeats in the coming generation is likely to overdo the scholarly procedure, and the result will be the occultation of a poetry which I believe is nearer the center of our main traditions of sensibility and thought than the poetry of Eliot or of Pound. Yeats's special qualities will instigate special studies of great ingenuity, but the more direct and more difficult problem of the poetry itself will probably be delayed. This is only to say that Yeats's romanticism will be created by his critics.

SOURCE: extract from 'Yeats's Romanticism', *Southern Review*, VII, 3 (1942); reproduced in Tate's *On the Limits of Poetry* (New York, 1948), pp. 223–4, and also in his *Essays of Four Decades* (Chicago, 1968).

PART THREE

Later Critics

1. General Studies
2. Studies on Specific Poems

1. GENERAL STUDIES

Richard Ellmann 'The Continuity of Yeats' (1954)

Explorers come to a new land full of dreams of their private Cathays, and their first reactions to it depend upon how well it can be accommodated to their hopes. Only gradually do they begin to separate what is there from what is not, and to chart the true country.

Having all Yeats's poems before us is itself a guide to reading them. The oldest, written in the eighties and nineties of the last century, and the newest, written up to two days before his death in 1939, take on a different complexion. The first seem less remote and spiritual, the last less exclusively sensual. There are seasonal changes, but no earthquakes or tidal waves. His themes and symbols are fixed in youth, and then renewed with increasing vigour and directness to the end of his life.

This continuity is the more surprising because it does not strike the reader at once, as does the continuity of other poets like Wallace Stevens, E. E. Cummings and T. S. Eliot. Changes in diction are likely to blind us to the constancy of themes. The substitution of one symbol for another is likely to conceal their equivalence. Yeats's powerful creative energy deceives us into thinking that its movement is spasmodic rather than regular.

The more one reads Yeats, the more his works appear to rotate in a few orbits. Again and again we are obliged to ask the same questions he asked. He was greatly concerned, for example, over the relations of his themes to his beliefs, especially because from the very beginning he adopted attitudes in different poems which seemingly conflicted with one another. This diversity, which he perhaps hit upon intuitively, he came to defend rationally in ways that most modern poets have left unexpressed. He displayed and interpreted the direction in which poetry was to go.

How the poet's statements and affirmations relate to his symbols was another issue that Yeats found crucial. Symbols, after all, may be simply traditional metaphors used with special emphasis, but they may also be conduits to a world of Platonic forms. The poet may use them as counters for his fancy to disport with, or imply through them a scale of values and a metaphysic. What, for example, does the cross mean to a man who is not a Christian? Yeats persistently returned to this subject until it no longer tormented him.

Themes and symbols in Yeats are questions of execution as well as of content; and style, with which he was so deeply concerned, was a question of content as well as of execution. Changes in rhythm, vocabulary and syntax were substantive. Style, he considered, was the self-conquest of the writer who was not a man of action. Altering a word like 'dream' to 'image' or 'curd-pale' to 'climbing' involved the whole man. Stages of stylistic development were stages of personal development.

Beyond theme, symbol and style is the general pattern or framework of Yeats's verse, in which each of these participates. Every poem embodies a schematisation, conscious as well as unconscious, of his way of living and seeing; and all his poems form a larger scheme which we can watch in the process of evolving. The stature of his work, which seems to tower over that of his contemporaries, comes largely from this ultimate adhesion of part to part to form a whole.

In weighing Yeats's work from these points of view, criticism finds its justification in the sentence of Spinoza, 'The intellectual love of a thing consists in the understanding of its perfections'. Spread out in full panoply, Yeats's poetry best reveals his originality and genius.

At the outset some first principles may be arrived at. Yeats's work, so strongly individualised, remains difficult to classify. It has been described as magical or occult poetry, but both terms must be rejected. The case for occultism is simple and tempting. He undoubtedly had a lifelong interest in the subject, beginning with Theosophy in the eighties, continuing with magical invocation in the nineties, and proceeding to spiritualism and automatic writing in later life. These activities have understandably made everyone uneasy. It would be more comfortable if the outstanding poet of our time had hobnobbed with, say, Thomas Henry Huxley, instead of Helena Petrovna Blavatksy, Samuel Liddell MacGregor Mathers, a medium in Soho, or Shri Purohit Swami. But he has not obliged us, and a number of critics have therefore attacked him for failing to attach himself to a more decent and gentlemanly creed.

Yeats lent some support to the charge when, as a young man, he wrote John O'Leary that occultism, to which he gave the wider name of 'the mystical life', was the centre of his work and bore to it the same relation that Godwin's philosophy held to the work of Shelley. But occultism is a big centre, a much bigger one, in fact, than is generally acknowledged. Along with spells and spooks from every culture, it has managed to assimilate many of the leading philosophical notions of eastern and western thought. To identify it with hocus-pocus alone is evidence of a socially acceptable common sense but not of acquaintance with the subject. Yeats found in occultism, and in mysticism generally, a point of view which had the virtue of warring with accepted beliefs, and of warring enthusiastically and authoritatively. He wanted to secure proof that experimental science was limited in its results, in an age when science made extravagant claims; he wanted evidence that an ideal world existed, in an age which was fairly complacent about the benefits of actuality; he wanted to show that the current faith in reason and in logic ignored a far more important human faculty, the imagination. And, in his endeavour to construct a symbolism, he went where symbols had always been the usual mode of expression.

Predilections of this sort made him not a mystic or an occultist but one of what he called 'the last romantics'. In so referring to himself, however, he was writing ironically, equating the word with all defenders of 'traditional sanctity and loveliness', and would no doubt have said that the first romantics were Homer and Sophocles. He might have called himself 'the last Quixote' or 'the last traditionalist' or even 'the last poet' with about the same significance. Following T. E. Hulme, we may take romanticism to be 'the view which regards man as a well, a reservoir full of possibilities', and classicism to be the view 'which regards him as a very finite and fixed creature'. Yeats is a romantic, but with compunctions. He admires imagination and individualism and excess and the golden future as much as Blake did, but he also at times evinces a strong strain of awareness that man's possibilities may not be limitless. He is unexpectedly interested in determinism; he insists on stateliness, courtliness, control and orderliness as criteria for judging past, present and future. His nature is not Wordsworthian, his heroes are not Byronic, his emotional expression is not Shelleyan. His outlook is, in fact, close at points to what Hulme describes as classicism: 'In the classical attitude you never seem to swing right along to the infinite nothing. If you say an extravagant thing which does exceed the limits inside which you know man to be fastened, yet there is always conveyed in some way at the end an impression of yourself standing outside it, and not quite believing it, or consciously putting it forward as a flourish. You never go blindly into an atmosphere more than the truth, an atmosphere too rarefied for man to breathe for long. You are always faithful to the conception of a limit.' Considered in the light of Hulme's statement, what seems at times in Yeats's poetry to be romantic extravagance needs always to be read twice for its possible backspin.

It was as an Irish poet that he aspired to become known, and now that he is dead the category seems more fully established and distinguished from the state of being an English poet. Yeats's Irishism is of a special kind. Like Joyce's prose, his poetry makes use of national and local borders only to transcend them. He is Irish; he is also anti-Irish in an Irish way; and his interest in Irishmen is always subordinated to an interest in men. His method of treating his Irish background and subject-matter is therefore exceedingly complex. Ireland is his symbol for the world, and he is caught between estrangement and love for both.

His work finds its real centre in the imagination, which is both sensual and spiritual, with no other aim than the creation of images as lusty as itself. At its most extreme he asserts that the imagination creates its own world. There is also the reverse of this medal, an acknowledgement that the world should be the creation of the imagination but is not. These two conceptions underlie Yeats's early work as well as his late, and bring the 'far-off, most secret, and inviolate Rose' and Crazy Jane's ideal of a love which shall be 'sole' and 'whole' into the same web.

To voice these conceptions Yeats created three principal dramatic roles. The first, that of the seer, presents the power of the imagination and the comparative frailty of experience most strikingly. The seer has little or no personality of his own; he is often at pains to declare that his images are not remembered from experience but imaginatively inspired. He reports on moments of crisis when the tension between the ideal and the actual is greatest, as when the swan descends to Leda or the dreadful beast of the second coming slouches towards Bethlehem. Not many of the poems present so momentous a view, but those that do lend a prophetic firmness to the whole.

More often the protagonist of the poems takes the parts of victim and assessor. As the frustrated, unsuccessful lover of the early verse, as the hounded public figure of the middle period, as the time-struck, age-worn old man of the later work, he has always something of the scapegoat about him. The scapegoat's sacrifice is not, however, an empty one. To abandon himself to a hopeless passion and all its attendant suffering has the fruitful result of glorifying the beloved and, by implication, the perfect concord which his imagination conceives but cannot proffer. The lover's failure becomes symbolic of the defect of all life. To give up easy comfort and calm for the dangerous losing battle with vulgarity and prudery, as the protagonist and his friends do in Yeats's middle period, has the virtue of perpetuating those qualities which are imaginatively sacred, such as courage, freedom from abstract restraints, and creative force. To struggle against 'dull decrepitude' and death enables the speaker to defend life to its bitter end.

So, although at each stage he is victimised, the victimisation is only half the story, the other half being the endowment of the situation with heroic consequence. If he takes 'all the blame out of all sense and reason', as in 'The Cold Heaven', or thirsts 'for accusation', as in 'Parnell's Funeral', it is because such sacrifices are parts of rituals through which they are transcended. The speaker is himself transcended; one forgets his plight to regard the qualities represented in it. That is why the poems, although in them he constantly talks about himself, rarely seem self-preoccupied.

The agent of transcendence is the assessor, standing at once inside and outside his own experience. He is perpetually evaluating, weighing in a scale ('A Friend's Illness'), balancing ('An Irish Airman Foresees His Death'), counting his good and bad ('Friends'), turning all he has said and done into a question until he stays awake night after night ('The Man and the Echo'). The assessment is conducted passionately, and disregards conventional morality to arrive at only those decisions which the imagination can accept because they are positive, imprudent and dignified, never mean or narrow. A poet has a miller's thumb, and his scales operate in an unusual way. A consideration of wrongs done him does not lead to heaping insult upon his enemies, but to a secret, proud exultation, as in 'To a Friend Whose Work Has Come to Nothing', that he can escape the limitations of petty enmity.

Because the assessment is made in particular and personal terms, arising directly from some incident or development of the poet's life, the poems rarely seem didactic. When they do, their message is almost invariably iconoclastic. The protagonist flaunts his heterodoxy as superior to the impartial conclusions of abstract logic and to the traditional formulations of Puritan morality. So he inculcates an arrant subjectivism in several poems in part because any other theory reduces man's stature as against a monopolistic God's, or life's stature as against an overwhelming heaven's or against the state of nothingness. Or he frightens the bourgeois by having Crazy Jane announce that

> '. . . Love has pitched his mansion in
> The place of excrement;
> . . .'

or makes Tom O'Roughley say, in defiance of sentimental mourning,

> . . .
> 'And if my dearest friend were dead
> I'd dance a measure on his grave.'

Many of his most direct statements of this sort go into the mouths of fools and madmen, who speak as if they desired no audience for their unconventional wisdom but themselves.

Frequently the assessment takes the form of establishing differences. There are the mob and the poet, trade and art, various stages of the soul ascending from confusion to unity of being. The table of differences serves much the same function as the conception of degree in the Elizabethan age; that is, it establishes differences only to bring all into a pattern. As Yeats noted in a manuscript book when he was twenty-one, 'Talent perceives differences, Genius unity'. If he contrasts the natural world with a more ideal or supernatural one, it is to conclude that 'Natural and supernatural with the self-same ring are wed'. His work can be read as a concerted effort to bring such contrasting elements as man and divinity, man and woman, man and external nature, man and his ideal, into a single circle. His sages, wrapt in their perfect sphere, must whirl down from eternity as he rises from time to meet them, and other spirits descend for 'desecration and the lover's night'; his heaven is never remote or ineffable. Against the spirit of anarchy Yeats offers his own conception of degree. When he declares that his 'medieval knees lack health until they bend', he longs for no idol but for a principle of organisation in which reverence and a sense of the fitness and orderliness of things will be possible.

But his organisation of the world is never placid. It is enlivened by a keen sense of tension. He upset the Indian Abinash Bose, who came to see him in 1937, when he replied to Bose's request for a message to India: 'Let 100,000 men of one side meet the other. That is my message to India.' He then, as Bose describes the scene, 'strode swiftly across the room, took up Sato's sword, and unsheathed it dramatically and shouted, "Conflict, more conflict".' The message sounds savage enough, but can serve more purpose if we put aside the histrionics which made Yeats for the moment oblivious to India and politics and everything but his momentary dramatic role. It had its origin in a view of the world as almost incessant strife between opposites, and in a similar view of the poem. He wrote Ethel Mannin late in life, 'I find my peace by pitting my sole nature against something and the greater the tension the greater my self-knowledge'. What came easy could not be trusted. In explaining to Dorothy Wellesley how he wrote a poem addressed to her, he said, 'We have all something within ourselves to batter down and get our power from this fighting. I have never "produced" a play in verse without showing the actors that the passion of the verse comes from the fact that the speakers are holding down violence or madness – "down Hysterica passio". All depends on the completeness of the holding down, on the stirring of the beast underneath.'

This determination and resistance are everywhere visible in Yeats's writings. 'Summer and Spring' is a useful illustration because in it the processes of composition and thought show through. The poem opens single-mindedly enough:

> We sat under an old thorn-tree
> And talked away the night,
> Told all that had been said or done
> Since first we saw the light,
> And when we talked of growing up
> Knew that we'd halved a soul
> And fell the one in t'other's arms
> That we might make it whole;
> . . .

But love cannot come to rest so easily in a Yeats poem; it has to be fortified by opposition, provided here by one Peter:

> . . .
> Then Peter had a murdering look,
> For it seemed that he and she

Had spoken of their childish days
Under that very tree.
. . .

Now Peter, having supplied the sourness to make love sweet, is dropped from sight, and we are left with the image of young love which grows out of his misery:

. . .
O what a bursting out there was,
And what a blossoming,
When we had all the summer-time
And she had all the spring!

The speaker brazenly takes for granted that his listeners will share in his satisfaction at the thwarting of Peter, but he does so in the name of love and, if he wins us, it is by reducing Peter's hatred to the status of a catalyst. The rivalry of the two young men cements the successful lover's happiness. If this conclusion seems cruel, Yeats will tell us that love is compounded of cruelty as well as sweetness.

So, in his greater poem, 'A Dialogue of Self and Soul', he sets earthly against heavenly glory; the soul at first appears to have all blessedness as its exclusive preserve, and offers it with the confidence that the self has nothing so good. But at the height of the rivalry the self realises it has a blessedness of its own, a secular blessedness; this discovery is called forth by the heat of battle, and enables the self to triumph:

I am content to follow to its source
Every event in action or in thought;
Measure the lot; forgive myself the lot!
When such as I cast out remorse
So great a sweetness flows into the breast
We must laugh and we must sing,
We are blest by everything,
Everything we look upon is blest.

Self and soul are not reconciled, but their opposition has generated in the victorious self a new knowledge and a new strength.

The opposition is often less overt; sometimes Yeats creates it by neglecting one side while he overstates the other. This is the method of 'All Things Can Tempt Me':

> All things can tempt me from this craft of verse:
> One time it was a woman's face, or worse –
> The seeming needs of my fool-driven land;
> Now nothing but comes readier to the hand
> Than this accustomed toil. When I was young,
> I had not given a penny for a song
> Did not the poet sing it with such airs
> That one believed he had a sword upstairs;
> Yet would be now, could I but have my wish,
> Colder and dumber and deafer than a fish.

The poet, as a young man, had believed that poetry should be written by a man of action; but now he would like nothing better than to isolate himself from action so as to devote himself wholeheartedly to his art. But in choosing a fish for his model he betrays the absurdity of his own wish; he is not renouncing action, but only impatient with it. For if he were really colder and dumber and deafer than a fish, he would not be a writer at all. So the fascination and necessity of action are implied in their seeming rejection. Yeats's desire to be turned into a beautiful but mechanical bird in 'Sailing to Byzantium' is also a wish which qualifies itself by its very excess; half of the poet's mind rejects the escape from life for which the other half longs.

Seeing life as made up of such stresses, Yeats naturally looks about for events and personages where the tension is greatest. He is addicted to analysing his friends as men torn between different aspects of character; Wilde, for example, seemed to him a frustrated man of action. All kinds of relations whether between man and woman, man and God, man and fate, or man and death, involve to Yeats's mind some admixture of enmity and love.

This perpetual conflict, with victories so Pyrrhic that the poet is compelled to return again and again to the field of battle, makes his world chequered and dense. His lifelong occupation with tragic drama is understandable as a consequence, for life is an endless competition between the imaginative hero and the raw material of his experience, the experience being necessary to bring out the heroic qualities to the full. The hero is one who sacrifices nothing of the ideal he has imagined for himself; death can do nothing but confirm his integrity.

Such are the lineaments that mark Yeats's work from first to last. They lend a strange excitement to it, as if it had all been written for an emergency, and to the search for what lie behind it, the choice among literary directions, the development of theme, symbol, style, and pattern.

SOURCE: Introductory chapter in *The Identity of Yeats* (London, 1954; 2nd edn, 1964), pp. 1–11.

T. R. Henn The Background (1949)

> ... 'You have come again.
> And surely after twenty years it was time to come.'
> I am thinking of a child's vow sworn in vain
> Never to leave that valley his fathers called their home.
>
> ['Under Saturn']

Sligo town lies in a cup of the hills, where a short but broad river takes the waters of Lough Gill into the Atlantic. As you stand facing the sea, there are two mountains: Knocknarea on the left hand, with a tumulus on the summit, said to be Queen Maeve's grave. On the right, far beyond the town and river, a great shoulder of mountain drops to the plain that stretches towards Lissadell and the sea; this is Ben Bulben, where Diarmuid and Grainne were pursued by Finn, and where Diarmuid, Adonis-like, was wounded by the enchanted boar. The river flows through a long twisting estuary, guarded towards the mouth by a beacon, The Metal Man,[1] which is to be seen in Jack Yeats's foreshortened drawing of Rosses Point; the little village that lies among the sand-dunes, with the sea to the west of it. The two mountains are full of legend. An old servant of Yeats's uncle, George Pollexfen, described Maeve and her women on Knocknarea: '... They are fine and dashing-looking, like the men one sees riding their horses in twos and threes on the slopes of the mountains with their swords swinging.'[2]

Both mountains and plains are ancient battlegrounds. After the Battle of Sligo in AD 537 Eoghan Bel 'was buried standing, his red javelin in his hand, as if bidding defiance to his enemies'.

> There in the tomb stand the dead upright ...

Beside Glencar there is a precipice where a troop of horsemen were led to their death; and at least one living person has heard on Ben Bulben the beat of miniature horse-hoofs on the plateau at the mountain top, and seen the grass beaten down and springing up again as if a troop of horse had passed that way.

> What marches through the mountain pass?
> No, no, my son, not yet;
> That is an airy spot,
> And no man knows what treads the grass.
> ['Three Marching Songs']

The whole neighbourhood is 'airy'[3]: perhaps because of the battle-fields that the conformation of the ground has determined through the centuries, perhaps because the fresh and the salt waters from the mountains and the estuary meet so violently and quickly there.[4]

At the head of the lake, which is studded with wooded islets (Innisfree among them), there is the village of Dromahair, where a man stood among a crowd and dreamed of faery-land. Near the coast, north-west of Sligo town, is the village of Drumcliff ('An ancestor was rector there'); the church among its rook-delighting trees beside the river that flows out of Glencar. It is full of ancient history; near it there is a monastery said to have been founded by St Columba, and this part of the Sligo plain was an ancient battlefield. On the wooded sides of the lake stood the great houses, Hazelwood of the Wynnes, Cleaveragh of the Wood-Martins, Markree of the Coopers, and many more up and down the countryside; Lissadell of the Gore-Booths was the most important in Yeats's development. In and about Sligo there were relatives of the Yeats family; and farther south, in Mayo and Galway, the 'half-legendary men,' the ancestors whom he drew into his own legend of great place.

The society and life of the early part of the century was in many ways peculiar. It is a very different world from that of Synge or of O'Casey. Everywhere the Big House, with its estates surrounding it, was a centre of hospitality, of county life and society, apt to breed a passionate attachment, so that the attempt to save it from burning or bankruptcy became an obsession (in the nineteen-twenties and onwards) when that civilisation was passing. The gradual sale of the outlying properties, as death duties and taxation rose higher, is recorded in Lady Gregory's struggle to save Coole Park, and was the fate of many estates.[5] The great families were familiar with each other and with each other's history; often, perhaps commonly, connected by blood or marriage. They had very definite and narrow traditions of life and service. The sons went to English Public Schools, and thence to Cambridge, or Oxford, or Trinity College, Dublin: the eldest would return to the estate and its management, the younger went to the Services, the Bar, the Church. There were

> . . .
> Great rooms where travelled men and children found
> Content or joy; a last inheritor
> Where none has reigned that lacked a name and fame
> Or out of folly into folly came.
>
> ['Coole Park and Ballylee, 1931']

The great age of that society had, I suppose, been the eighteenth and early nineteenth centuries; from the 1850s onwards it seems to have turned its eyes too much towards England, too conscious of its lost influence in its hereditary rôle of The Ascendancy. By 1912 it was growing a little tired, a little purposeless, but the world still seemed secure:

> We too had many pretty toys when young:
> A law indifferent to blame or praise,
> To bribe or threat; habits that made old wrong
> Melt down, as it were wax in the sun's rays;
> Public opinion ripening for so long
> We thought it would outlive all future days.
> . . .
>
> ['Nineteen Hundred and Nineteen']

The image of the house and its fall lingered with Yeats to the end, as in the play *Purgatory* of *Last Poems*:

> . . .
> Great people lived and died in this house;
> Magistrates, colonels, members of Parliament,
> Captains and Governors, and long ago
> Men that had fought at Aughrim and the Boyne.
> . . .
> . . . to kill a house
> Where great men grew up, married, died,
> I here declare a capital offence.

In the furnishings of a great house, or in its library, one became aware that most of the work had been done between, say 1750 and 1850, over the bones of a rebellion and two famines. The original building might date from Cromwell's time, or before; modernised, perhaps, by adding a frontage from a Loire chateau, or a portico from Italy. Some of these were of great beauty:

> Many ingenious lovely things are gone
> That seemed sheer miracle to the multitude,
> Protected from the circle of the moon
> That pitches common things about. . . .
>
> ['Nineteen Hundred and Nineteen']

It is against this background, I believe, we must see the Recognition and Reversal in Yeats's poetry that came out of the Rebellion and its aftermath. Before the First World War that aristocratic culture seemed to have given so much: pride of race, independence of thought, and a certain integrity of political values. It could be perceived (even then) in relation to the great eighteenth-century tradition, which, foreshortened and perhaps not wholly understood, held so much fascination for Yeats. It could be seen as representing the Anti-Self or Mask to which he was striving: whether in the image of the hero, or soldier, or horseman, or that symbolic Fisherman who occurs repeatedly:

> . . .
> I choose upstanding men
> That climb the streams until
> The fountain leap, and at dawn
> Drop their cast at the side
> Of dripping stone; I declare
> They shall inherit my pride,
> The pride of people that were
> Bound neither to Cause nor to State,
> Neither to slaves that were spat on,
> Nor to the tyrants that spat,
> The people of Burke and of Grattan
> That gave, though free to refuse –
> Pride, like that of the morn,
> . . .
>
> ['The Tower']

Lady Gregory and the Gore-Booths had shown him the security that came from the wealth of the great estates, and the life, leisured and cultured, that it seemed to make possible:

Surely among a rich man's flowering lawns,
Amid the rustle of his planted hills,
Life overflows without ambitious pains;
And rains down life until the basin spills,
And mounts more dizzy high the more it rains
As though to choose whatever shape it wills
And never stoop to a mechanical
Or servile shape, at others' beck and call.

['Meditations in Time of Civil War']

To this society, in the main Protestant, Unionist, and of the 'Ascendancy' in character, the peasantry was linked. The great demesnes had their tenantry, proud, idle, careless, kindly, with a richness of speech and folk-lore that Lady Gregory had been the first to record.[6] The days of *Castle Rackrent* and the absentee landlord were, in the main, over; the relationship between landlord and tenant varied, but was on the whole a kindly one, and carried a good deal of respect on either side. The bitterness of famine, the evictions and burnings described with such bitterness by Maud Gonne in *A Servant of the Queen*, belonged to an earlier period. The members of the family would be known either by the titles of their professions: the Counsellor, the Bishop, the Commander, and so on: or by the Christian names of their boyhood. They mixed with the peasantry more freely and with greater intimacy (especially in childhood) than would have been possible in England.[7] Yeats's memories of conversations with servants, and particularly with Mary Battle, gave him much material. Sport of every kind was a constant bond: the ability to shoot, or fish, or ride a horse was of central importance. At its best there was something not unlike a survival of the Renaissance qualities:

. . .
Soldier, scholar, horseman, he,
And all he did done perfectly
As though he had but that one trade alone.

['In Memory of Major Robert Gregory']

But even at its best the tradition had outlived its usefulness, as Yeats knew:

O what if gardens where the peacock strays
With delicate feet upon old terraces,
Or else all Juno from an urn displays
Before the indifferent garden deities;

O what if levelled lawns and gravelled ways
Where slippered Contemplation finds his ease
And Childhood a delight for every sense,
But take our greatness with our violence?
['Meditations in Time of Civil War']

There were various aspects of that life. Land or local troubles flared out from time to time. There were occasions when one did not sit in the evening between a lamp and the open; though Lady Gregory, in reply to threats on her life during the Civil War, replied proudly that she was to be found each evening, between six and seven, writing before an unshuttered window. . . .

. . . In every district there were many superstitions, with a curiously ambivalent attitude to them on the part of country-folk and gentry alike. The early Christian missionaries had taken over many of the features of the Elder Faiths of the locality. Holy wells are numerous and display the offerings of the pious. In my own youth pieces of gorse were placed on the lintels of the cottages on May Day to discourage the Good People from alighting there. A relic of the Baal Fire ritual was rehearsed in the lane below our house on St John's Eve when young men leaped through the flames of bonfires. The sacred pilgrimage to Croagh Patrick fired Yeats's mind with a vision of a new synthesis of paganism and Christianity. The 'cleft that's christened Alt' ['The Man and the Echo'] is near Sligo, and has magical associations; it was no violence of Yeats to think of it in terms of the chasm at Delphi, just as the Sphinx might be transplanted to the Rock of Cashel ['The Double Vision of Michael Robartes']. A good Catholic might well half-believe in the older magic and yet go to Mass with a clear conscience; a Protestant, while in theory superior to all superstitious practices, might yet catch something of half-belief from speech with servants, grooms and fishermen, and innate romanticism could readily build upon their stories.

I believe that it is important to realise something of this background of Yeats's work. It has many bearings. The world of the great houses offered security, a sense of peace, beautiful things to look on and handle:

. . .
Great works constructed there in nature's spite
For scholars and for poets after us,
Thoughts long knitted into a single thought,
A dance-like glory that those walls begot
['Coole Park, 1929'][8]

The truth about the great houses of the South and West lies, perhaps, somewhere between Yeats's pictures of Coole Park, the romantic descriptions of some recent novelists, and MacNeice's 'snob idyllicism'. For every family that produced 'travelled men and children' there was another that produced little but 'hard-riding country gentlemen', who had scarcely opened a book. An eighteenth-century house might be half-filled with Sheraton and Adam work, and half with Victorian rubbish. Families nursed the thought of past greatness, fed their vanity with old achievement or lineage or imagined descent from the ancient kings; and in the warm damp air, with its perpetual sense of melancholy, of unhappy things either far off or present, many of them decayed. Standish O'Grady could write bitterly of *The Great Enchantment*, that web of apathy in a country with an alien government and an alien religion, subject at every turn to patronage and the servility it brings, into which Ireland had fallen. That, too, is a narrow view of the whole. The aristocracy had, at its best, possessed many of the qualities that Yeats ascribed to it: the worlds of Somerville and Ross, the Dublin of Joyce or of Sean O'Casey differ merely in accordance with the position of the onlooker.

Of the paradox of Ireland, and its challenge, Yeats was aware almost from the beginning: 'But remember always that now you are face to face with Ireland, its tragedy and its poverty, and if we would express Ireland we must know her to the heart and in all her moods. You will be a far more powerful mystic and poet and teacher because of this knowledge. . . . You are face to face with the heterogeneous, and the test of one's harmony is our power to absorb it and make it harmonious. . . . Absorb Ireland and her tragedy and you will be the poet of a people, perhaps the poet of a new insurrection.'[9]

One effect of this society, organised into sharply divided classes, living a life that was perpetually seeking reassurance from the past, was to accentuate a certain rhetorical habit of thought and speech. The attitude to 'brave and glorious words' had something Elizabethan about it; just as the richness of idiom, of a certain happy valiancy of phrase that is so easily parodied or misunderstood, goes back to that tradition of speech. This instinct lies deep, but does lead to what is normally described as 'insincerity'. It is deliberate, cultivated, but still an essential part of the Irish character: remembering always that it is false to speak of any constant feature in that heterogeneous race. The reply of Nora in Synge's *In the Shadow of the Glen* to the Tramp's outburst of poetry is a fair comment: 'I'm thinking it's myself will be wheezing that time with lying down under the Heavens when the night is cold: but you've a fine bit of talk, stranger, and it's with yourself I'll go.'

Yeats found in these surroundings, security, companionship, encouragement, and some honour as a poet. The passing of that world, as it passed between 1916 and 1923, was a magnificent theme. There was a war within a war; Hugh Lane's drowning on the *Lusitania*, Robert Gregory's death in Italy in 1918, were symbols of the outer conflict that was imaged in the larger movement of the gyres, the cyclic movements of history. It was a kind of phoenix-ending of Ireland's great past; the burning of the eighteenth-century houses was half a terror, half the price of resurrection. The poet's ancestors were in the great tradition of political or literary achievement, men who had protested against tyranny or social decay:

> THE FIRST: My great-grandfather spoke to Edmund Burke
> In Grattan's house.
> THE SECOND: My great-grandfather shared
> A pot-house bench with Oliver Goldsmith once.
> ['The Seven Sages'][10]

In contrast with the great past, the fall was greater:

> Even from that delight memory treasures so,
> Death, despair, division of families, all entanglements of mankind grow,
> As that old wandering beggar and these God-hated children know.
> [*Oedipus at Colonus*]

In that setting he would be the last Romantic, or Lear, or Timon, or the prophetic Blake; the rôles were infinite. From the present he could go back through ancestral memories and see the folk-lore of the Sligo and Galway mountains behind those men and women who were fighting for the Irish Republic: so that the mythologies seem to meet and blend, the great eddies of history repeating themselves in a pattern. Cuchulain, bound by the belt to a pillar in his last fight, as in that great statue in the Post Office in Dublin, stood for the great paradox of heroic defeat:

> Some had no thought of victory
> But had gone out to die
> That Ireland's mind be greater,
> Her heart mount up on high;
> . . . ['Three Songs to the One Burden', III]

The irony was apparent, too; that life with which he identified himself was to be broken by the very forces which he believed he had launched. So, of the burning of the houses:

> But is there any comfort to be found?
> Man is in love and loves what vanishes,
> What more is there to say? That country round
> None dared admit, if such a thought were his,
> Incendiary or bigot could be found
> To burn that stump on the Acropolis,
> Or break in bits the famous ivories
> Or traffic in the grasshoppers or bees.
> ['Nineteen Hundred and Nineteen']

In all this there was, of course, a certain vanity. Yeats was a great actor; but his greatness was in part that his pose, while it was of the skin of his poetry, was never of its bone. (I shall suggest that this is true also of his psychical investigations.) For though he knew his ancestry far back, among the farmers and traders of the West, his world was, initially, outside that with which he tried to identify himself.[11] Nor did he attempt to falsify his pedigree, as many romantic writers have done. Dublin's gossip might tell malicious stories of his preoccupation with his ancestry, but it does not matter greatly. It was an easy and harmless game to magnify his lineage in verse, to claim entry into that pathetically pedigreed world that linked itself to Ormondes or Butlers or the High Kings. But, in point of fact, it is the other side of his genealogy, his descent from the smaller professional families, that he seeks to stress. Ancestral virtues came from seafaring men, from horsemen, from an integrity of the blood that had passed through no huxter's loin:

> He that in Sligo at Drumcliff
> Set up the old stone Cross,
> That red-headed rector in County Down,
> A good man on a horse,
> Sandymount Corbets, that notable man
> Old William Pollexfen,
> The smuggler Middleton, Butlers far back,
> Half legendary men. ['Are You Content?']

The West, like the Roman Campagna, is a country of ruins. There is a perpetual reminder, in ruined Norman castle and round tower, in the mysterious forts of Aran, of the heroic age, of past power that conjures up the emotions that Dryden, or Dyer in *The Ruins of Rome*, or Richard

Wilson, found in the Roman scene. There is endless melancholy, sprouting easily in the soft rain, in the contrast with a shiftless and idle countryside, beneath the drums and tramplings of four conquests. A ruined castle, with a couple of cottages beside, could be bought for thirty pounds and become a dominant symbol with memories of Spenser, Herbert,[12] Shelley:

> . . .
> There, on blood-saturated ground, have stood
> Soldier, assassin, executioner,
> Whether for daily pittance or in blind fear
> Or out of abstract hatred, and shed blood,
> . . .
>
> ['Blood and the Moon']

It is something that is easy to stigmatise as fantasy, escapism, self-dramatisation, snobbery, nostalgia, and so forth: but all such dismissals are too simple. Unless the duality of mood is realised and accepted for what it is, unless we cease to laugh at Yeats as not conforming to Arnold's 'criticism of life', or to deride the plays on the grounds that Aristotle would not have considered them as plays at all, we are condemned to a supercilious critical attitude which will vitiate all understanding.

The rebuilding of the Tower, Thoor Ballylee, near Lady Gregory's place at Coole, was a gesture, too: half-believed in, half-mocked at, but serving as a symbol, by turns cosmic and absurd; viewed with that peculiar irony that was necessary to preserve the sense of mystery.

> Blessed be this place,
> More blessed still this tower;
> A bloody, arrogant power
> Rose out of the race
> Uttering, mastering it,
> Rose like these walls from these
> Storm-beaten cottages –
> In mockery I have set
> A powerful emblem up,
> And sing it rhyme upon rhyme
> In mockery of a time
> Half dead at the top.   ['Blood and the Moon']

For the Tower was never finished; and a great empty room remained at the top. Yeats used to say that *A Vision* would be finished when the room was finally restored; neither was ever completed.[13] . . .

SOURCE: extracts from *The Lonely Tower* (London, 1949; rev. edn, 1965), pp. 1–6, 7–13.

NOTES

[Reorganised and renumbered from the original – Ed.]

1. MacNeice remarks acutely that Yeats's deliberate avoidance of it as a symbol is typical of his practice.
2. *Autobiographies* (London, 1955), p. 266.
3. Yeats's note: ' "airy" may be an old pronunciation of "eerie", often heard in Galway and Sligo.'
4. Jack B. Yeats spoke to me of this: but something of the kind was a belief in the seventeenth century.
5. See Lady Gregory, *Journals* (London, 1946): in particular the chapters called 'The Terror' and 'The Civil War'.
6. As in *Visions and Beliefs* (New York and London, 1920). She had popularised it, though Standish O'Grady and Douglas Hyde were the pioneers.
7. See *Autobiographies*, pp. 258, 260, 265, 267.
8. The idea of the dance and story are linked elsewhere: perhaps a memory of Nietzsche's remark as to the connection between the dance and tragedy. Compare the fourth stanza of 'Byzantium'.
9. *The Letters of W. B. Yeats*, ed. Allan Wade (London, 1954), pp. 294–5. Compare the quotation from Standish O'Grady's speech: 'We have now a literary movement, it is not very important; it will be followed by a political movement, that will not be very important; then must come a military movement, that will be important indeed' – *Autobiographies*, p. 424.
10. It is worth noting, as Peter Allt has pointed out, that the three men were sprung from the professional middle class, not from the great land-owning families.
11. Mr Day Lewis is, I think, wrong when he suggests that Yeats belonged as of right to this aristocracy, or was accepted by it until he was 'taken up' by Lady Gregory. There was a vast gap between the 'squirearchy' to which he refers and the great houses: cf. his 'Yeats and the Aristocratic Tradition', in Stephen Gwynn (ed.), *Scattering Branches* (London, 1940), pp. 162–3, 166.
12. 'Is all true doctrine in a winding stair?'
13. This information, from Mrs Yeats, differs from the account given by Hone – *W. B. Yeats*, 2nd edn (London, 1962), p. 331 – where the phrase 'half dead at the top' is related to the flat cement roof.

Richard Ellmann '*A Vision* Elucidated' (1954)

. . . Within the new Yeatsland the configuration of symbols and themes owes much to the strange phenomenon of Mrs Yeats's automatic writing which her husband and his critics have made famous.[1] A few days after their marriage, Mrs Yeats tried to distract her preoccupied husband by 'faking' automatic writing, and then discovered, to her astonishment, that she could write it without meaning to. The writing continued sporadically over several years, but had to be sorted, organised, and completely revised before it could be published.

The reader of *A Vision* may have difficulty in accepting this account, even though masses of automatic writing exist to authenticate it, because the ideas in the book are not novel in Yeats's work. He had said them all before, in one way or another. Aside from particular symbols, the thematic basis is much the same as the one he developed in his youth. There are the cycles, the reincarnating souls, the possible escape from the wheel of time to a timeless state, the millennial reversal of civilisations that corresponds to the rebirth of individuals, the heroic, unconventional ethic, the unknown and problematical god, the battle between the spiritual and material worlds. All these are taken up and reworked.

Alongside them are other conceptions familiar to Yeats, though expressed in combinations that make them look new. The running antithesis in the book between Christian and Renaissance values was an application of his psychology to history, with character apportioned to the first and personality to the second; it was also related to his early antithesis between Christianity and paganism, and to his contrast of the dried pips of Puritanism with the cornucopia of the Renaissance. What was new was the methodical tracing of the antithesis over more than 2000 years. The concern with the afterlife, and the proposition that during it the soul 'dreamed back' its lifetime experiences, stemmed naturally from folk-tales, spiritualism, Henry More and Swedenborg, a group of authorities he had convoked in 1914 in an essay for Lady Gregory's *Visions and Beliefs in the West of Ireland.* The classification of types of human personality was also an ingrained habit in Yeats, and its particular form in *A Vision* owed much, as will become apparent, to his earlier pursuits.

That Georgie Hyde-Lees Yeats's automatic writing should have assumed so Yeatsian a form is not surprising. She had belonged to the same or similar occult organisations as her husband and had read many of the same books. She knew his work thoroughly, especially the most recent, such as *Per Amica Silentia Lunae* (1917), a long essay which discusses the mask, the anti-self, and their supernatural counterpart, the daimon. And she spoke of these matters every day with a talkative husband. Consequently her mind, in a state which may be regarded naturalistically as partial self-hypnosis, could not escape focussing on the same subjects which beset it at conscious moments.

Mrs Yeats's role was nevertheless important. For the material of the automatic writing emerged in an unpredictable way, and the possibility of disclosure of some entirely new truth lent excitement to speculations which might otherwise have proved wearisome even to an inveterate investigator like Yeats, as in fact they did to his wife. Then, too, the revelations were diversified; some cosmological insight would be associated with an intimate personal reminiscence of Mrs Yeats, and with repercussions of their lives together, so that the notebooks were often extremely personal. This intimacy, and the unpremeditated character of the writing, were for Yeats a guarantee that he was not dealing with abstractions. It seemed likely that he had tapped what spiritualists call the subliminal mind, what Jung considers the racial unconscious, and what Henry More called *Anima Mundi*. While Yeats was uncertain of the precise depth of the revelations, as he sometimes confessed, he knew that Newton and Locke and the whole rationalist tradition had little or no part in the sporadic cacography of his sitting-room.

Although the themes were familiar to him, they never appeared without modifications which enlarged their import, and they rarely appeared except in the form of images. Here was a storehouse the like of which he had not been able to discover in a hundred trips to seances. *A Vision* is pictorial, at times even diagrammatic, but always unspeculative.

THE NEW SYMBOLS

The *Vision* is most accessible if regarded as a group of three symbols which mirror one another. The root symbol is a sphere inside of which whirl a pair of interpenetrating gyres or cones, or, as Yeats sometimes refers to them, vortexes. These are inextricably entwined yet perpetually at war with one another, now one and now the other triumphant in a series of regular, inconclusive battles. . . . [Ellmann here reproduces Yeats's 'Great Wheel' diagram from *A Vision*, rev. edn (London, 1962), p. 66 – Ed.]

With the sphere Yeats represents the unified reality beyond chaotic appearance or the experience of that reality. On consideration we realise that the sphere is the mature equivalent of the rose. It differs from the rose in that Yeats only occasionally mentions it in his verse; that is because it had come to seem a remoter ideal. The sphere is 'There' in the little poem of that name:

> There all the barrel-hoops are knit,
> There all the serpent-tails are bit,
> There all the gyres converge in one,
> There all the planets drop in the Sun.

The gyres, on the other hand, stand for the world of appearance, a world in which, as he says, 'Consciousness is conflict'. Wedded in antagonism, they symbolise any of the opposing elements that make up existence, such as sun and moon, day and night, life and death, love and hate, man and God, man and woman, man and beast, man and his spiritual counterpart or 'daimon'; on a more abstract level, they are permanence and change, the one and the many, objectivity and subjectivity, the natural and the supernatural worlds. With the gyres Yeats had a more excited and interesting picture of the universal conflict than, for example, two armies drawn up against one another would have afforded him; for the point of one gyre was in the other's base, as if a fifth column were operating in the very headquarters of the enemy. He concurred with Hegel that every thesis had implied in it an antithesis, and modified the notion that every movement holds the seeds of its own decay by identifying the seeds as those of a counter-movement. He was further confirmed in his symbol by the fact that it applied to his verse, which he realised with increasing clarity was guided by the principle of the containment of the utmost passion by the utmost control.

Like the sphere, the gyres are not often explicitly mentioned in his poems; they occupy a place equivalent to that of the cross in his early work, which appeared rarely also, because the opposition might be put less formally. But they furnish him with the title and subject of a late poem, 'The Gyres':

> The gyres! the gyres! Old Rocky Face, look forth;
> Things thought too long can be no longer thought,

For beauty dies of beauty, worth of worth,
And ancient lineaments are blotted out.
Irrational streams of blood are staining earth;
Empedocles has thrown all things about;
Hector is dead and there's a light in Troy;
We that look on but laugh in tragic joy.

What matter though numb nightmare ride on top,
And blood and mire the sensitive body stain?
What matter? Heave no sigh, let no tear drop,
A greater, a more gracious time has gone;
For painted forms or boxes of make-up
In ancient tombs I sighed, but not again;
What matter? Out of cavern comes a voice,
And all it knows is that one word 'Rejoice!'

Conduct and work grow coarse, and coarse the soul,
What matter? Those that Rocky Face holds dear,
Lovers of horses and of women, shall,
From marble of a broken sepulchre,
Or dark betwixt the polecat and the owl,
Or any rich, dark nothing disinter
The workman, noble and saint, and all things run
On that unfashionable gyre again.

Such a poem makes clear the limits as well as the uses of *A Vision*: 'The Gyres' is not the product of the automatic writing, except in its name for the symbols, but of all Yeats's experience. 'Old Rocky Face' is the Delphic Oracle, who spoke through a cleft in the rock, and is a proper muse for a prophetic poem. Yeats brings the oracle into his neighbourhood by addressing it directly with this familiar epithet, and then by ranging its supposed predilections, like those of his ghosts earlier, so that they will be identical with his own. Although he celebrates the eternal recurrence of things, he is not pleased by the recurrence of all things, but only of the things he likes, which are here traditional (therefore 'unfashionable' in this age) beauty and worth and a hierarchical dream of 'workman, noble and saint'. The saint, often treated by Yeats with less courtesy, is included as part of an orderly society in contrast to the growing anarchic confusion of the present. The description of the state of the world tallies, even in its imagery, with that of the poems 'The Second Coming' and 'Nineteen Hundred and Nineteen', but his exultation in the face of tragedy in 'The Gyres' is not paralleled in those comfortless poems. It cannot be too much emphasised that he modified the symbols to suit the states of mind, irrespective of their consistency with *A Vision*. The gyres are his servants, not his masters. In the same way he treats Empedocles and Troy with a fine casualness as symbols of the present scene rather than as allusions to the past. All ages are equally present to his prophetic eye. Every element in the poem has appeared in his work before, but is recast to jibe with the Dionysian, ecstatic quality which he imparts by the exclamatory phrase, rare for him: 'The gyres! the gyres!' and the repeated rhetorical question, 'What matter?' These interjections mitigate the oracular tone of many of the statements and are the main force in the confrontation of past, present and future. With fire and skill Yeats succeeds in transforming one's horror at the indifferent survival of evil as well as good into delight that good must survive as well as evil.

Yeats's ownership of his symbols is unchallengeable if we remember that the word 'gyre', and even 'cone' and 'vortex', did not appear originally in the automatic writing; there the word used was 'funnel'. Yeats did not like 'funnel' and set out to find a better term. He noted that the double cone occurred in Swedenborg's *Principia*, which he was reading in 1914, but it had no central place in the Swedenborgian system. A single cone appears as a principal symbol in Henry More's poem, *Psychathanasia*, which Yeats must have read; for More the cone represents the universe, with God as its base and the potentialities of matter as its point:

> Lo! here's the figure of that mighty Cone,
> From the straight Cuspis to the wide-spread Base
> Which is even all in comprehension.

Yeats sometimes, as in 'Sailing to Byzantium', employed a single gyre instead of a double one, profiting perhaps from More's example.

Many occult writers have made use of cones, gyres, or vortexes. The vortex also occurs from time to time in Blake, but in a different way. None of Yeats's 'worthies' brought the symbol home to him so directly, however, as did Ezra Pound. In 1916 Pound and the sculptor Gaudier-Brzeska set up a new esthetic movement to which they gave the name of 'Vorticism'. Vorticism, of which Pound told Yeats, was intended to move away from the neutral, opaque, motionless images which the Imagist movement had theoretically fostered with Pound's blessing a few years before, and to restore or implant dynamism in the image; a vortex, as Pound wrote John Quinn, was a 'whirlwind of force and emotion'. Pound's further explanation in his book on Gaudier presents the symbol more clearly:

> The Image is not an idea. It is a radiant node or cluster; it is what I can, and must perforce, call a VORTEX, from which, and through which, and into which, ideas are constantly rushing. In decency one can only call it a VORTEX. And from this necessity came the name 'Vorticism'.

Such remarks of Pound may well have emphasised to Yeats the sexual basis of the symbol, and he had studied comparative mythology to too good purpose to be ignorant that such symbols have the most staying power. They would also preserve him from the dangers of abstract geometry. Some of the lines which he wrote in 1923 in 'The Gift of Harun Al-Rashid', a thinly veiled autobiographical poem, may be taken literally as well as metaphorically:

> . . . The signs and shapes;
> All those abstractions that you fancied were
> From the great Treatise of Parmenides;
> All, all those gyres and cubes and midnight things
> Are but a new expression of her body
> Drunk with the bitter sweetness of her youth.

The more strange Yeats's symbols first appear, the more pains he takes to make them sound like household words. He surrounds the gyres with homely diction, often altering the more high-sounding names for them (gyres, cones, and vortexes) into a 'top', 'Plato's spindle', or 'bobbins where all time is bound and wound'; the winding movement is often represented as 'perning', a dialect word based on his recollection that at Sligo 'pern' was the spool on which thread was wound. Consequently, when he wrote in 'Demon and Beast' that he 'had long perned in the gyre, / Between my hatred and desire', or in 'Sailing to Byzantium' summoned the sages to 'perne in a gyre', that is, to whirl down from their more celestial part of the cone of the universe to his more natural part, he lightened esoteric symbolism by a word from peasant speech. That the peasant word was itself esoteric to his readers probably further endeared it to him.

He restated the symbol of the gyres and their transcending sphere in his second principal symbol, which was a representation of the opposition as between sun and moon. To avoid complications – and he was always trying to render the scheme as lucid as he could – Yeats put it entirely in lunar terms, with full moon and dark of the moon as the two contrary poles. These were depicted as phases fifteen and one respectively in the twenty-eight phases through which the moon passes each month. Any antinomial conflict can be registered in terms of the waning or waxing of the moon, just as it can be expressed in terms of the preponderance of one or the other gyre. Yeats preferred, however, to limit the lunar symbol to the description of the self as it shifts through a multitude of lives, in some of them tending towards the energetic personality, which Yeats calls 'subjectivity', of a Renaissance hero, and sometimes towards the sheering away of personality and the assertion of undistinguished equality, which he calls 'objectivity', of Christ or, he thinks, of Marx as well. One group exploits and extols the individual, and its counterpart suppresses and husks him. Self-fulfilment is related to the full moon and its neighbouring phases, while self-restraint is related to the dark of the moon. 'The typal man', Yeats writes in some early drafts of *A Vision*, 'lives through thirteen cycles, each of twenty-eight incarnations corresponding to the twenty-eight lunar mansions'; he later qualifies the statement by revealing that the two maximal phases when the moon is entirely full or dark are phases where the soul does not take on human form, but is a spirit in temporary refuge from the bustle of reincarnation:

> Twenty-and-eight the phases of the moon,
> The full and the moon's dark and all the crescents,
> Twenty-and-eight, and yet but six-and-twenty
> The cradles that a man must needs be rocked in:
> For there's no human life at the full or the dark.

The purpose of making the two extreme phases non-human was probably to keep the incompleteness of human life prominently displayed while at the same time demonstrating the nearness of supernatural life.

In the lunar symbol the equivalent of the sphere that transcends the gyres is the Thirteenth Cycle, sometimes known as the Thirteenth Cone or the Thirteenth Sphere. Here too reality inheres, and nothing can be known of it. Reality is also approximated, though not fully attained, in the four phases closest to full moon, where what Yeats (borrowing the phrase from his father) calls 'Unity of Being' is possible. In such unity the soul finds itself closest to its 'radical innocence'; it 'begins', he writes, 'to tremble into stillness, / To die into the labyrinth of itself!'[2] He develops the symbol most fully in 'The Phases of the Moon'. This is his most didactic poem, but even here he has none of *A Vision*'s dispassionateness. He introduces value judgements which give the poem its own colour; the soul's incarnations are a heroic 'discipline'; the spirits of the full moon are related to the lover's image of his beloved; the objective phases are disparaged; the poem is put in dialogue form, set in Galway, and its contents disingenuously represented as what the poet has not been able to discover.

The lunar symbol is more complex than that of the gyres. Moon and sun had been part of his early symbolism, but had occupied there a subordinate place. Yeats developed them steadily into greater prominence. In his *Autobiographies* he connected the symbolic meaning of solar and lunar with his work under MacGregor Mathers's tutelage in the Golden Dawn. ' "Solar", according to all that I learnt from Mathers, meant elaborate, full of artifice, rich, all that resembles the work of a goldsmith, whereas "water" meant "lunar" and "lunar" all that is simple, popular, traditional, emotional.' These correspondences might be varied; in 'Lines Written in Dejection' (1915) the moon is 'heroic' and the sun is 'timid'. He called attention to the moon's phases, and related them solipsistically to the states of mind of the beholder, in *The Cat and the Moon*, a little play written shortly before his marriage. Such reflections were evidently habitual with him. He united to them the theory of astral influence used by astrologers, according to which character is marked out by the relative influences of the dominant planets which have presided over the individual's birth. Yeats simplified the astrological scheme by excluding the planets and considering only the moon, and was thereby enabled to evaluate his acquaintances and the men of the past, as had been his inveterate custom all his life, according to a simpler and more workable system. The source of the Thirteenth Cycle, as well as of the other twelve, was a reminiscence, in either his mind or his wife's, of Christ and the Twelve Apostles. To give God so mechanical a title was to ensure that He would be discussed only as 'it', never as a personal deity, least of all as a Christian one. God became thereby a feature of the Yeatsian cosmogony which like other features the poet's symbolic vocabulary might grasp and include. And the embodiment of divinity in so unprepossessing a term as Thirteenth Cycle stood in ironic and urbane contrast to Yeats's claims for the cycle's unlimited powers, as if one were to say, 'Ah yes, I have given Almighty God the name of "Thirteenth Cycle" in my scheme'.

The other restatement of the gyres has two parts. The first, which receives less attention, is the contraposition of the self and its spiritual opposite or daimon. The daimon is a kind of anti-self or mask elevated, so to speak, to a plane beyond the human. The human being is partial in comparison with the daimonic fullness. In the second part, Yeats divided the self into two sets of symbolic opposites, Will and Mask, Creative Mind and Body of Fate. These may be roughly translated as Imagination and the Image of what we wish to become, and Intellect and the Environment. They are equivalent to fire and water, air and earth, in the early symbolic scheme, but have much more complexity here. Essentially their battle, for which Yeats had been writing the bulletins throughout his work, was between what we are and what we dream of becoming. According to this theme, first fully articulated in *The Player Queen*, a Caesar is buried in every hunchback, a lecher in every saint. It would be equally valid to say that every hunchback has a Caesar for his daimon, and every saint a lecher. The daimon's faculties are exactly opposite to those of his human counterpart. Since the combination of internecine war within the self, and foreign war with the daimon, made for impossible complications, Yeats was content in all except one chapter of *A Vision* to trace the quaternion of the soul and let the daimon fend for himself.

When the four faculties were in certain stages, when they were in harmony rather than at odds, they might attain the equilibrium of Unity of Being. In this respect they resembled Blake's Four Zoas, who in certain aspects could restore Albion, the fallen man, to life. Unlike Blake, Yeats avoided using his special terms in his verse, and instead of finding the nomenclature of the four faculties there, we find various contrasts which depend on them but have a fresher look. In 'Solomon and the Witch', a poem written in 1918, not long after the automatic writing began, some of Solomon's wisdom connects, at several removes, with *A Vision*:

> . . . 'A cockerel
> Crew from a blossoming apple bough
> Three hundred years before the Fall,
> And never crew again till now,
> And would not now but that he thought,
> Chance being at one with Choice at last,
> All that the brigand apple brought
> And this foul world were dead at last.
> He that crowed out eternity

Thought to have crowed it in again.
For though love has a spider's eye
To find out some appropriate pain –
Aye, though all passion's in the glance –
For every nerve, and tests a lover
With cruelties of Choice and Chance;
And when at last that murder's over
Maybe the bride-bed brings despair,
For each an imagined image brings
And finds a real image there;
Yet the world ends when these two things,
Though several, are a single light,
When oil and wick are burned in one;
Therefore a blessed moon last night
Gave Sheba to her Solomon.'

In love, Solomon is saying, the lover's dream of his beloved and her actual form are the same, and what he wills (Choice) is exactly what he gets (Chance). This marriage is the equivalent of the mystic marriage of *The Shadowy Waters*, but its physical aspect is much more conspicuous, and the notion of its ending the world is phrased as a witty conceit where the early play represented it as a genuine possibility. In this passage the Will, Mask, and Body of Fate may be fitted in if anyone wishes, but the theme antedates *A Vision* by many years.

With the four faculties, twenty-eight phases, and two gyres in the foreground, and the sphere looming mightily behind them, Yeats had the basic symbols for his book. There is no need to explore the ramifications of the scheme in greater detail; like most schematisations, it bulges at the seams, and Yeats has to knead history and human personality a good deal to make them stay where he wants them. The logical shortcomings of *A Vision* are not, however, of much consequence. The book ranged together a group of symbols which had in common what the earlier symbols, that clustered around a rose, lacked – a furious movement. Man, as seen in it, is a creature for ever turning around a wheel during a single lifetime, and around a larger wheel in the course of a cycle of reincarnations. Even the afterlife is nothing but a projection of tumult beyond the grave and into new cradles, or, as Yeats sometimes pictures it, an unwinding of a bobbin which winds up again during life. Each lifetime is the scene of a tug-of-war between four 'faculties' of the human mind, the daimon, the dead, certain miscellaneous spirits, the Thirteenth Cycle, and other forces. This contest is so intricate, and its outcome so unpredictable, that what starts out in the first part of *A Vision* and in some of Yeats's poems as a deterministic system is reframed by succeeding parts and other poems until it contains a large measure of free will. Yeats's father was accustomed to say that the poet should feel free to believe in marriage in the morning and not to believe in it in the evening, 'the important thing being not that he keep his mental consistency but that he preserve the integrity of his soul'; and his son felt similarly free to believe and disbelieve in free will until that Day of Judgement when chance would become one with choice at last.

The emphasis in *A Vision* falls heavily upon sublunary struggle, but from time to time it salutes translunar peace with the symbols of the sphere, the Thirteenth Cycle, and Unity of Being. Aware that he was no mystic and should not try to become one. Yeats also knew the importance of the furthest reaches of human experience or feeling, and felt that on four or five occasions of his life his 'body of a sudden blazed', and he had been released from conflict. And so his system, while its main allegiance is to Proteus, is also deferential to the god of stasis.[3]

Much of the argument of *A Vision* is clothed in a style more metaphorical than any used in English prose since the seventeenth century. If no reader has ever been converted to its doctrines, the reason is that one is never sure exactly what is being offered for acceptance or what attitude the writer wishes to elicit. Yeats varies greatly in the labels he applies to his book. It may be (1) direct revelation from remarkably loquacious spirits, imparted through his wife's automatic writing. This hypothesis is scarcely tenable, since he relentlessly doctored up the revelation, and since the spirits gave evidence of being well versed in his own earlier writings, and in books which he and his wife had read. Unconscious memory is a much less demanding explanation, and Yeats himself gradually relinquished the supernatural hypothesis. (2) It may be a system of historical and psychological classification. The difficulty here is that both history and psychology are over-simplified and stylised. As (3) a philosophy, its doctrines are often couched in too personal a language. Other labels lead in a different direction: it may be (4) 'a dream, and yet the nearest I can go to reality'; (5) a 'lunar parable'; (6) a myth or mythology; (7) a group of metaphors; (8) a symbolism or 'stylistic arrangement of experience'; or (9), in part at least, an 'exposition' of his poems. The title of the book does not help much in deciding among different labels, for the word 'vision' begs the question of whether a transcendental or merely a personal insight is involved.

A Vision can best be taken as a symbology, a study of symbols which sometimes stretches towards philosophy and at other times towards the condition of poetry. In so far as it was philosophical, Yeats felt compelled to apologise for it:

> This book records 'A Vision', and its writer like the writers of all similar books in the past, when he uses some abstract term or definition, knows that they are incidental and temporary. He is even persuaded that whatever is so defined is taken out of experience as water is when we describe it as two atoms of hydrogen and one of oxygen, in momentary ignorance of the fact that it uses a little sunlight, or sediment, a little duckweed or a fish or two, and that spiritual realities especially can only be known in the animation of experience. . . .

The best part of the book is not the explanation of the symbols, but their application to psychology and history, where the 'animation of experience' dominates abstract definition. What we really have in these sections is a series of moods comparable to those in his verse, to which Yeats fits certain well-known individuals and periods of time.

That *A Vision* has inconsistencies he tacitly admits half-way through it, when he describes the temperament of his own phase as one that will deal with images rather than with ideas, and will synthesise them 'in vain, drawing with its compass-point a line that shall but represent the outline of a bursting pod'. But the inconsistencies are of less importance than the powerful sense of tumultuous life, and of the struggle to transcend it, which the book conveys. In some unused notes for the second edition Yeats suggests the book's importance for him:

> I have now described many symbols, which seem mechanical because they are united into a single structure, and of which precisely because they are always the same story the greater number may have seemed unnecessary. Yet every symbol, except where it lies in vast periods of time and so beyond our experience, has brought me, as I think evoked for me, some form of human destiny, and the form once evoked appears everywhere, as my own form might in a room full of mirrors, for there is but one destiny.

It was his most splendid attempt to bring his mind to the state which Stendhal in another connection calls 'crystallisation'. . . .

SOURCE: extract from the chapter on 'Symbols and Rituals in the Later Poetry', in *The Identity of Yeats* (London, 1954; 2nd edn, 1964), pp. 149–64.

NOTES

[Reorganised and renumbered from the original – Ed.]

1. The closest parallel in literary history is the *tables tournantes* on the island of Guernsey, which helped Victor Hugo in 1853 to consolidate his poetic scheme, and seemed to provide supernatural sanction for it. Yeats's experience did not quite match Hugo's, for the 'spirits' who seemed to be communicating through Mrs Yeats often adopted the names of household pets (such as cats), while Hugo's extramundane visitants were Dante, Racine, Hannibal, 'and other heroes of that kidney'.

2. He shows little interest in that approximation of reality which occurs at phase one, presumably because it is the state of 'nothingness' of the saint rather than the state of 'everythingness' of the artist.

3. In so prominent a place as the end of the introduction to the first edition of *A Vision*, Yeats admitted that there might be nothing for man but endless becoming: '. . . I murmured, as I have countless times, "I have been part of it always and there is maybe no escape, forgetting and returning life after life like an insect in the roots of the grass". But murmured it without terror, in exultation almost.'

Yvor Winters   'Yeats's Silly Ideas'   (1960)

We have been told many times that we do not have to take the ideas of Yeats seriously in order to appreciate his poetry; but if this is true, Yeats is the first poet of whom it has ever been true. We need to understand the ideas of Donne and of Shakespeare in order to appreciate their works, and we have to take their ideas seriously in one sense or another, and it is possible to take their ideas seriously much of the time. A great deal of scholarly work has been done on their ideas, and some of this work has contributed to our appreciation of what they wrote. A great deal of scholarly work has been done on Yeats in recent years; unfortunately, the better one understands him, the harder it is to take him seriously. . . .

. . . I will try to summarise the principal ideas which motivate

Yeats's poetry. All good comes from the emotions, and even madness is good. *Wisdom* is a pejorative term; *ignorance* is the reverse. In Yeats's later work *lust* and *rage* become increasingly prominent and they represent virtues. Sexual union is equated with the mystical experience or at least participates in the mystical experience in a literal way. This is not the same thing as the analogy of sexual union which is sometimes used by the Christian mystics. The Christian mystics tell us that the mystical experience is absolutely different from any human experience and thus cannot be described in language, but that the experience can be suggested by analogy. This leads, I think, to a more or less fraudulent poetry, for the poet is dealing with an ineffable experience by dealing with something irrelevant to it; but the fraud is, in a sense, an honest one, for the rules of the procedure are known. But for Yeats the two experiences are of the same kind, the only difference being that the sexual experience is less nearly pure than would be the experience of disembodied spirits: we are given the pure experience in 'Ribh at the Tomb of Baile and Ailinn', in which Ribh reads his book by the pure light given off by the orgasm of the disembodied lovers.

Yeats's concept of what would be the ideal society is also important. Such a society would be essentially agrarian, with as few politicians and tradesmen as possible. The dominant class would be the landed gentry; the peasants would also be important, but would stay in their place; a fair sprinkling of beggars (some of them mad), of drunkards and of priests, would make the countryside more picturesque. The gentlemen should be violent and bitter, patrons of the arts and the maintainers of order; they should be good horsemen, preferably reckless horsemen (if the two kinds may exist in one); and they should be fond of fishing. The ladies should be beautiful and charming, should be gracious hostesses (although there is a place for more violent ladies – videlicet Mrs French in 'The Tower'), should if possible be musicians, should drive men mad, love, marry and produce children, should not be interested in ideas, and should ride horseback, preferably to hounds. So far as I can recollect, the ladies are not required to go fishing. What Yeats would have liked would have been an eighteenth-century Ireland of his own imagining. He disliked the political and argumentative turmoil of revolutionary Ireland; he would scarcely have thought that the order which has emerged was sufficiently picturesque to produce poetry. . . .

. . . I will turn to the principal poems related to the theory of the historical cycles.

'Leda and the Swan' describes the rape of Leda by Zeus in the form of a swan: a rape which led to the birth of Helen, the destruction of Troy, and the disintegration of early Greek civilisation. The rape introduced the next cycle of Greek civilisation, which ended with the collapse of 'Platonic tolerance', 'Doric discipline', and ultimately the Roman Empire.

'Two Songs from a Play' describe the end of the second Greek cycle and the beginning of the Christian.

'The Second Coming' prophesies the imminent end of the Christian cycle.

Each of these works deals with violence, for every cycle begins and ends in violence. Yeats admires violence in general and has little use for Platonic tolerance, Doric discipline or the civilisation produced by Christianity. This fact is especially important when we come to read 'The Second Coming'.

'Leda and the Swan'

The account of the rape in the first eight lines . . . is very impressively done, but an account of a rape in itself has very limited possibilities in poetry. The important thing here is this: that the rape is committed on a mortal girl by Zeus. In the significance of this fact will reside the power or weakness of the whole poem. In the first portion of the sestet we are told that the swan has engendered the fall of Troy and the death of Agamemnon, but there is nothing about the historical cycles: this has to be read in from what we know of Yeats's theories – which are, after all, ridiculous. The greatest difficulties reside in the remainder of the sestet. 'Did she put on his knowledge with his power?' The question implies that she *did* put on his power, but in what sense? She was quite simply overpowered or raped. She did not share his power, unless we understand a mystical union in the sexual act, which I think is implied. And what about his knowledge? Was this the knowledge of the fall of Troy and the death of Agamemnon? Was it the knowledge that a new cycle was about to begin (in spite of the fact that there is no reference to the cycles in the poem)? Or was it the omniscience of the god, resulting from the sexual union, a knowledge which would include the two other forms of knowledge? I suspect the last, but I would have difficulty in proving it.

Next, we have to consider 'the brute blood of the air'. The swan as such is a brute and flies through the air. Zeus may be thought of as living in the air and descending from the air. But Zeus as such was not a brute in Greek mythology, and his animal disguises were 'disguises'; nevertheless he often appeared in brute forms. The brute form here would appear to be connected with the identification of sexual union with the mystical experience. Satan, however, was referred to in the Middle Ages as the Prince of the Air, and he and his demons were said to live 'in darkened air'. I do not recollect that Yeats has mentioned this fact anywhere, but the fact is easily available, and it seems to me unlikely that Yeats would have overlooked it. Yeats was fascinated with the concept of demonic possession as a form of the mystical experience and with the possibility of obtaining supernatural knowledge from such possession. In 'The Gift of Harun Al-Rashid', the young wife is possessed by a Djinn, apparently as a result of sexual awakening, and in her sleep she communicates the knowledge which her husband desires. This is a pretty fantasy, I suppose, but one can scarcely take it seriously. But we return to the question: is Zeus a god or a demon, or does it make no difference? It should make a difference if we are to adjust our emotions to the motive, for what is the motive?

Then there is the difficulty that the poem ends with a question. A question, if it is really a question, is a weak way in which to end a poem, for it leaves the subject of the poem unjudged. But this question may be, as I suspect it is, a rhetorical question: in this case the answer should be either *yes* or *no*.

This brings us to the final difficulty: the vehicle of the poem is a Greek myth, and there is no harm in this if the tenor is serious; but the tenor is a myth of Yeats's private making, and it is foolish. That is, if we are to take the high rhetoric of the poem seriously, we must really believe that sexual union is a form of the mystical experience, that history proceeds in cycles of two thousand years each, and that the rape of Leda inaugurated a new cycle; or at least we must believe that many other people have believed these things and that such ideas have seriously affected human thinking and feeling. But no one save Yeats has ever believed these things, and we are not sure that Yeats really believed them. These constitute his private fairy tale, which he sometimes took seriously and sometimes did not. I see no way to make up one's mind about this poem except to decide that it is one of two things: an *aboli bibelot d'inanité sonore* or *an aboli bibelot de bêtise sonore*. I feel sure that it is the latter, but I wish it were the former, for the former would at least be inscrutable and would call for greater skill on the part of the poet. The sonority is real, and I can appreciate it as well as the next man, but it takes more than sonority to make a great poem. Pure sonority eventually comes to seem pompous and empty. . . .

'The Second Coming'

[Here] the difficulties are similar . . . . In line six, the expression 'the ceremony of innocence' is misleading and awkward. By reading 'A Prayer for My Daughter', which follows, one discovers that the phrase means the ceremonious life in which innocence flourishes; but as one comes to it in the poem, it would seem to indicate some kind of ceremony, perhaps baptismal, perhaps sacrificial, perhaps some other.

Otherwise, the first eight lines are very impressive if one takes them phrase by phrase: the adjective *mere* in the fourth line, for example, is a stroke of genius. But what do the lines mean? One who has lived through the last thirty years and who has not observed the date of the poem (the volume was published in 1921) may feel that Yeats was writing about the growth of fascism, nazism or communism:

> . . . the worst
> Are full of passionate intensity.

But the first two are impossible and the third is unlikely. 'The best' are the Irish aristocrats; 'the worst' are the Irish engaged in politics, who were trying to establish a constitutional democracy and who eventually succeeded. The poem is an attack on civilised government made by a man who felt an immense dislike for democracy and the political activity without which democracy cannot survive – a dislike which was due in part to his native temperament but largely, I fear, to the fact that Maud Gonne was more interested in politics than in Yeats; by a man who, during much of his later life, was often tempted in the direction of fascism.

The first four and a half lines of the second section are an example of Yeats's high rhetoric, but for their effect they depend upon our belief in his notion of the Spiritus Mundi. From there on we have his description of the beast, which is a fine description. But the account of the beast is not pure description. If we are to take it as seriously as Yeats's language indicates that we should, we must again accept his theory of the gyres as in some way valid. And if we do this we must face the fact that Yeats's attitude toward the beast is different from ours: we may find the beast terrifying, but Yeats finds him satisfying – he is Yeats's judgement upon all that we regard as civilised. Yeats approves of this kind of brutality.

When we consider all of these complications, it becomes very difficult to arrive at an acceptance of the poem, an acceptance both rational and emotional. I do not deny that civilisation may be coming to an end – there is no way of knowing, although I think that the chances of its surviving for a long time are fairly good. But if we are to have a poem dealing with the end of civilisation, and one that we can suppose to be great, the poem must be based on something more convincing than a home-made mythology and a loose assortment of untenable social attitudes. . . .

'Among School Children'

[This], like the poems which I have already discussed, is regarded as among the greatest. The first stanza is quietly and effectively descriptive. The second stanza opens with one of his personal clichés, 'a Ledaean body': the body is Ledaean because it is the body of Helen, daughter of Leda – that is to say, of Maud Gonne. But none of us has ever seen Leda or Helen, and in a few more years there will be no one who has ever seen Maud Gonne, and the portraits of Maud Gonne which I have seen are not very convincing. This is a somewhat pretentious way of saying 'a very beautiful body', but it is not description – it is easy allusion.

What we have is an overtone from the Greek myth and from the Yeatsian myth, both very thin. Helen destroyed the civilisation of her time and was thus heroic. Yeats believed that Maud Gonne was destroying the civilisation of her time, and he longed to see it destroyed (although he regretted her personal part in the destruction). Therefore the two women were similar, not merely in their beauty but in their action. But Maud Gonne played a real, though minor, part in establishing a civilised government in Ireland, and her son Sean MacBride played his part also. If Maud Gonne was really heroic (I am not a specialist in Irish history nor an aficionado of the Irish temperament), it was in a way that Yeats was incompetent to understand. Maud Gonne was neither Helen nor Deirdre; she was a vigorous and practical (albeit Irish) woman. She may have been beautiful and she may have had faults and virtues which are irrelevant to this discussion, but Yeats did not understand what she was doing. As Mrs Yeats is reported to have said, Yeats simply did not understand people. One can find additional testimony to the same effect in the letters of Ezra Pound – letters written when Pound was young and still a pretty shrewd observer. This may seem to be too much talk about a mere phrase: the point is that Yeats regularly employed mere phrases. Other clichés in these lines are 'I dream' and 'bent above a sinking fire'.

In the sixth line [of the second stanza] the sphere contains the idea in a general way, but not with the precision that would have been possible with abstract language or a better figure; the egg adds nothing to the significance of the sphere and is comical in itself.

The third stanza introduces fewer and less troublesome difficulties; but such phrases as 'fit of grief or rage' and 'daughters of the swan' are mechanical, and 'my heart is driven wild' is stereotyped melodrama of a sort to which I have already objected and shall object again. The fourth stanza is composed almost wholly of similar clichés and concludes with Yeats's favorite, that of the scarecrow.

Stanzas five and six are of much the same kind: shoddy diction, carelessly violent diction, and further exploitation of the scarecrow. The two lines about Plato are passable but scarcely profound; the two lines about Aristotle are ridiculous without being witty; the lines about Pythagoras mean nothing, except that they raise a curious question about the mechanics of fiddling, an art with which Pythagoras was not acquainted. The seventh stanza seems to be the beginning of an important statement, but unfortunately it is part of a statement which is continued in the final stanza.

The final stanza is one which I can understand in terms of the pseudo-mysticism and anti-intellectualism of the past two hundred and fifty years, but I cannot grasp it imaginatively – that is, in terms of human life as I know human life. The word *labour* seems to me to mean fruitful labor, or ideal labor. But where does this kind of labor exist, except, perhaps, in the life of a tree? The body is always bruised to pleasure soul; wisdom is always born out of midnight oil or out of something comparable. The diction in these lines is abominable: the first two lines are bad enough, but the third and fourth are as bad as Keats's 'Here where men sit and hear each other groan'. The question addressed to the tree is preposterous: the tree is obviously more than the leaf, the blossom or the bole, but these all exist and can be discussed, and it is because of this fact that we have words for them –

the implication of the passage is that the tree is an inscrutable unit, like the Mallarméan poem. The diction of the seventh line is as bad as that of the third and fourth. The last line is similar to the fifth and sixth. When we watch the dancer we may not discriminate, although a choreographer could; but if the dancer and the dance could not be discriminated in fact, the dancer could never have learned the dance. Precisely the same idea will be found in Emerson's *Blight*, a small affair but somewhat better written. . . .

SOURCE: extracts from *The Poetry of W. B. Yeats* (Denver, Col., 1960), pp. 3, 5, 7–8, 9–10, 12–14.

Thomas Parkinson (1964) 'Rhyme and Stanza'

. . . The proper ratio of naturalness to formality cannot be fixed in any rigorously systematic manner, but Yeats was constantly seeking the unique and intuitively felt ratio that would endow each poetic structure with its appropriate form. His rhymes reflect his preoccupation, for they are rhymes, clearly enough, but often very imperfect. One poem ['The Mother of God'] has the following rhyme pattern in its three stanzas:

A	flare	A	shows	A	pains
A	ear	A	knows	A	sustains
B	room	B	walk	B	stop
A	bore	A	clothes	A	bones
B	womb	B	talk	B	up

This is far from atypical of a rhyming habit that can produce such combinations as 'gone–stone–sun', 'intent–point', 'house–luminous', 'thought–begot', 'on–man–Lane' – all in one very formal poem. Because of his intent concern with meaning, and because his rhyme words often controlled meaning and established tone, his persistent assonance does not seem forced. Professor Wimsatt has discussed the novelty generated by Pope's refusal to rhyme noun with noun or verb with verb, so that the expected rhyming sound continued surprising through centuries of couplets. Yeats achieved the opposite effect by upsetting the ear's expectancies and fulfilling the emotional currents of meaning:

> The light of evening, Lissadell,
> Great windows open to the south,
> Two girls in silk kimonos, both
> Beautiful, one a gazelle.
> . . .
>
> ['In Memory of Eva Gore-Booth and Con Markiewicz']

Here the off-rhyme of 'both' with 'south' is rhetorically predictable by the antecedent 'Two girls', and when the full rhyme comes, it does not clang heavily because the carry-over of the preceding line holds the gazelle in its web. I do not mean by this that the rhymes are to be unnoticed, merely that they are to be seen as part of the line. The importance of this linear unity is engrossed by Yeats's tendency to present his matter in a long and overriding period. The result is a great deal of rhetorical repetition within a given stanza, fortified and at times undercut by the poetics, the insistence on linear form rather than periodic. In the reminiscent poems this is especially evident, and when in his commemorative poem for Eva Gore-Booth and Con Markiewicz he returns to the initial image of the two girls in silk kimonos, the repetition is qualified by the use of off-rhyme:

> . . .
> Many a time I think to seek
> One or the other out and speak
> Of that old Georgian mansion, mix
> Pictures of the mind, recall
> That table and the talk of youth,
> Two girls in silk kimonos, both
> Beautiful, one a gazelle.

As with all his refrains, this repetition is so changed by its context that its meaning has shifted, in this instance, from the original exaltation to muted sadness. The development of the poem has been a major force, and the rhyme of 'recall–gazelle' merely fortifies the resigned imperfection of life so far presented. And since the initial image of the girls at the south window has been revised and qualified by the overlay of their later experience, the term 'recall' implies effortfulness in evocation, and what was so sweetly and spontaneously present initially has by now become soiled and darkened by the irrelevancies of life. The imperfect rhyme is consonant with the imperfections of experience that have led from the prized recollection to this hesitant attempt to bring back to mind what had once occurred without conscious thought.

But Yeats's off-rhymes were not justified by one specific motive. Frequently they did exhibit an imperfection in the experience treated:

> . . . the children's eyes
> In momentary wonder stare upon
> A sixty-year old smiling public man.
>
> ['Among School Children']

This presentation of his own image as comical is matched by the awkwardness of 'upon–man', but the same sort of self-deprecation is, later in the poem, presented in perfect rhyme:

> . . .
> Better to smile on all that smile, and show
> There is a comfortable kind of old scarecrow.

Not every sardonic statement occurs in off-rhyme, though many do:

> But the torn petals strew the garden plot
> And there's but common greenness after that.
>
> ['Meditations in Time of Civil War']

The justification of off-rhyme comes not in any single relation between tone and rhyme, but in the appropriateness to line and stanza. No irony is intended in the first stanza of 'Crazy Jane and Jack the Journeyman' when 'bone' is rhymed with 'gone', and when two-thirds of the rhymes in the very carefully written 'Coole Park, 1929' are imperfect, that is no reason for suspecting a self-deprecating intent.

We do not, in reading Yeats's later poems, think of the off-rhymes as violations of perfection. They are too normal, too pervasive in the poetry's texture, to come as violations of expectation. When he rhymes (in 'Sailing to Byzantium',) 'young' with 'song' and 'dress' with 'magnificence' and 'soul' with 'animal', no principle is violated, no convention flaunted. The rhymes require no more justification than do perfect rhymes, for they are striking only in their appropriateness.

With these provisos, it is still possible to see Yeats's off-rhymes as indices to his state of mind. In his early poems, the extremely rare off-rhymes asked to be forgiven, and this was easy enough to do on the infrequent occasions when charity required it. They were simply the sort of thing that is, at times, necessary. After the 1903 volume, the frequency of off-rhyme increased until off-rhyme became a predictable part of the expectations of any reader of Yeats's verse. But like all the technical changes in Yeats's verse, this major shift was tightly bound up with the changes in the quality of experience that he took to be poetically admissible. The off-rhymes are comic not in the conventional sense but in the Yeatsean sense that they admit the presence of a world of divided imperfection, and the language of that world. They were part of his refusal to be ingratiating, and they were means of indicating the precedent claims of fullness. And these off-rhymes were not mere failures, second-best choices that he used only after he had tried unsuccessfully to make perfect rhymes. One of his habits in composing was to establish his possible rhymes and write to them, fill out the design thus offered. The rhyming of 'bough' with 'dew' in the second part of 'Vacillation' was established early in the manuscript drafts, and when he wrote out a set of rhymes for this stanza, he accepted the rhyme without trouble:

bough
leaf
dew
chief
anew
belief
grief

And though he changed 'anew' to 'renew' and altered 'leaf', 'chief', and 'belief', he accepted 'bough' and 'dew'. He was not deterred by their obvious imperfection.

He did not say, 'Well, let's rough it up a bit here and make it awkward there; that will make it seem mussed and *real*'. The truth was that the off-rhymes were to his mind normal, not violations of convention but in effect the establishment of patterns that were in themselves valid. They made his already tightly linked – by internal sound pattern, by syntax – poems more linear. The assonant rhymes of Wilfred Owen, by contrast, do not make the poems linear but instead call attention, by their insistent harshness, to themselves. With Owen, we are always aware that the poems are rhyming very oddly; with Yeats, we know that they rhyme, but we see the rhyme, important as it is, as part of a general interweaving of sound and assertion. One virtue of his prosody is its insistence on the line as unit, and off-rhyme was a device strengthening this insistence.

His stanzaic habits are also rather fixed. He wrote only two sonnets in his later years, and in his lyrics he wrote practically no free verse. One of his favorite stanza forms ('Sailing to Byzantium', 'Among School Children', parts II and III of 'Vacillation') was the *ottava rima*, which he handled with extraordinary skill. Some of his stanza forms were taken from minor earlier writers, as the form of 'In Memory of Major Robert Gregory' was taken from Cowley's 'Ode on the Death of Mr William Hervey' and used again in 'A Dialogue of Self and Soul' and part II of 'The Tower'. The stanza form of 'The Mother of God' also came from Cowley, for under his first notes on the poem's subject appears a brief description of the stanza used by Cowley in the lyric from his 'Essay on Solitude':

5 feet good
4 " wood
4 " rejoice
5 " voice
3 " food[1]

Yeats evidently meant by 'feet' stresses, as his finished poem shows:

The threefold terror of love; a fallen flare
Through the hollow of an ear;
Wings beating about the room;
The terror of all terrors that I bore
The Heavens in my womb.

In this one poem, and in no other, he followed the pattern of rhymes and of line length established by Cowley's lyric. Other stanza forms, like the elaborate form of part III of 'Nineteen Hundred and Nineteen', were evidently invented for the occasion. He frequently, especially in the short lyrics, wrote in quatrains. He preferred stanzaic form that was fairly elaborate and compelled him to feats of self-discipline. Characteristically in his manuscripts he wrote out the rhyme scheme in ABC form, and he often wrote the rhymes for a stanza (altering as he went along) before writing all the lines.

The general design of his later prosody suggests that his primary aim was to effect a passionate syntax that would allow the voice to move in proximity to authentic patterns of speech. His steady use of off-rhyme is one indication of this motive, as is his occasional departure from the linear norm established in the poem, the use of an extra stress in a stress line, the occasional redundant syllable in a syllabic line. The off-rhymes indicated his primary interest in getting the semantics of a poem right, and his use of stanza forms that require repeated rhyme (notably the ottava rima) permitted him to use off-rhyme without obvious insistence. Within the elaborate stanza form, the off-rhymes were separated by intervening lines, and Yeats's special urge toward making stanza and sentence coincide made the stanza a more naturally fluent structure.

Stanzaic formality was necessary to him for many reasons, but chiefly he required it as discipline for the passionate syntax that he accepted as a norm. In his prosody as in his iconography he qualified his motives in dramatic terms. In the only recently published preface to the projected 1936 edition of his poems he talks at some length about his sense of prosody and characteristically prefaces his comments with notes on lyric dramaturgy[2] . . . [Parkinson quotes the passage reproduced above in Part One, section 1, under the caption 'On Style' (p. 32); his excerpt concludes with: 'If I spoke my thoughts aloud they might be as angry and as wild.' – Ed.]

But anger and wildness were not the end product of poetry, and the function of traditional meters was to qualify, condition and purify these originating motives. The powerful syntax that he thought desirable would be formalised by stanzaic pattern, and out of the tension of pattern and passion would come a permanent joyful poetry . . . [Parkinson continues to quote from the passage reproduced above (page 33), beginning with: 'It was a long time before I had made a language to my liking . . .'; and concluding with: 'I must choose a traditional stanza, even what I alter must seem traditional.'[3] – Ed.]

This passage suggests the theoretical justification of his practice that Yeats came to at the close of his career. It suggests also the main motive of this chapter, to explore through printed and manuscript versions of Yeats's later poems the way in which he established a prosody at once traditional and innovative, flexible to his extremely varied needs as poet, and capable of endowing his passionate articulations with a form that would make them '. . . all men's speech'. . . .

SOURCE: extract from the chapter on 'The Passionate Syntax' in *W. B. Yeats: The Later Poetry* (Berkeley, Cal., 1964), pp. 194–202.

NOTES

1. Unpublished MS.
2. *Essays and Introductions* (London, 1961), p. 521.
3. Ibid., pp. 521–2.

Hugh Kenner (1956) The Sacred Book of the Arts

> The way out is via the door, how is it no one
> will ever use this method? (Confucius)

1. CATECHISM

Q. In 'Among School Children' we read of a 'Ledaean body'. Where are we to seek information about that?

A. Not from the mythological dictionary, but as everybody knows, from the poem 'Leda and the Swan'.

Q. And where is this poem to be discovered?

A. On the previous page.

Q. Very good. You are on the way to noticing something. Now consider the last stanza of 'Among School Children'. After an apostrophe to 'self-born mockers of man's enterprise' we read:

> Labour is blossoming or dancing where
> The body is not bruised to pleasure soul,
> Nor beauty born out of its own despair,
> Nor blear-eyed wisdom out of midnight oil.
> O chestnut-tree, great-rooted blossomer,
> Are you the leaf, the blossom or the bole?
> O body swayed to music, O brightening glance,
> How can we know the dancer from the dance?

That 'where' is by its placing in the line made very emphatic. Its gesture implies a place or a state intensely real to Yeats. Does he print lines elsewhere that might be taken as descriptive of that place or state?

A. He does; in 'Colonus' Praise', after invoking 'immortal ladies' who 'tread the ground / Dizzy with harmonious sound' (which invocation of course we are meant to connect with 'O body swayed to music'), he goes on,

> And yonder in the gymnasts' garden thrives
> The self-sown, self-begotten shape that gives
> Athenian intellect its mastery,
> . . .

the self-born no longer a mocker, body and intellect thriving in unison, neither bruised to pleasure the other; and the miraculous olive-tree that, as he goes on to tell us, symbolises that perfection, is to be connected with the domestic 'chestnut-tree, great-rooted blossomer' of the famous peroration.

Q. Excellent, excellent. And now tell me where, in relation to 'Among School Children', this song in praise of Colonus is to be found.

A. On the following page.

Q. You are answering today with admirable point and economy. Now tell me: were the three poems you have mentioned as bearing upon one another written, as it were, simultaneously?

A. I find by the chronology at the back of Mr Ellmann's *Identity of Yeats* that the first was written nearly four years before the last. I notice furthermore that the arrangement of the poems in the volume we are discussing, *The Tower*, is far from chronological. 'Sailing to Byzantium' (26 Sept. 1926), with which it begins, was written *after* 'Among School Children' (14 June 1926), which is located two-thirds of the way through the book. In between there are poems dating as far back as 1919, and the volume ends with 'All Souls' Night', 1920.

Q. We should be lost without these American scholars. You would say, then, that the arrangement of poems within the volume was deliberate rather than casual or merely chronological?

A. I would indeed. But wait. I have just noticed something else. In 'Sailing to Byzantium', at the beginning of the book, the speaker has abandoned the sensual land of 'dying generations' and is asking the 'sages standing in God's holy fire' to emerge from it and be his singing-masters. At the end, in 'All Souls' Night', he announces that he has 'mummy truths to tell' and would tell them to some mind that, despite cannon-fire from every quarter of the world, can stay

. . .
Wound in mind's pondering
As mummies in the mummy-cloth are wound;
. . .

In the former poem he was calling forth sages to teach him; throughout 'All Souls' Night' he is calling up ghosts to hear. Pupil has become master.

Q. How often must I enjoin precision on you? It is the land of sensual *music* he has left: bird-song, love-songs. 'All Souls' Night' opens, by contrast, with the formal tolling of 'the great Christ Church bell', like the 'great cathedral gong' that dissipates 'night walkers' song' in 'Byzantium'. Furthermore, there is a calling-up of ghosts near the beginning of the book too, in the poem called 'The Tower', where he summons them not (as later) to instruct them but to ask a question. What else have you noticed?

A. Why, it gets more and more deliberate as one examines it. He began the volume by renouncing his body; he ends it in the possession of disembodied thought:

Such thought – such thought have I that hold it tight
Till meditation master all its parts,
. . .
Such thought, that in it bound
I need no other thing,
Wound in mind's wondering
As mummies in the mummy-cloth are wound.

Earlier he had expected to need the body of a jewelled bird. Through that volume, *The Tower*, runs a dramatic progression if ever I saw one. And the presence of such a progression, once it is discerned, modifies all the parts. Now I have a theory . . .

Q. Stop, you grow prolix. Write it out, write it out as an explanation that I may read at my leisure. And please refrain from putting in many footnotes that tire the eyes.

2. EXPLANATION

'Among School Children', to begin with that again, is as centrifugal a major poem as exists in the language. Whoever encounters it out of the context Yeats carefully provided for it – for instance in an Anthology Appointed to be Taught in Colleges – will find himself after twenty minutes seeking out who Leda was and what Yeats made of her, and identifying the daughter of the swan with Maud Gonne (excursus on her biography, with anecdotes) and determining in what official capacity, through what accidents of a destiny sought and ironically accepted, the poet found himself doubling as school inspector. So true is this of the majority of his major poems, that the anthologists generally restrict themselves to his minor ones, his critics practise mostly a bastard mode of biography, and his exegetists a Pécuchet's industry of copying parallel passages from *A Vision* (first and second versions), from letters and diaries, from unpublished drafts, and occasionally from other poems. Even Dr Leavis [see excerpt in Part Two, above – Ed.] calls his poetry 'little more than a marginal comment on the main activities of his life'. Occasionally someone feels that Yeats's poems need to be reclaimed for the modern critic's gallery of self-sufficient objects, and rolling up his sleeves offers to explain 'Two Songs from a Play' without benefit of *A Vision*. This requires several thousand words of quasi-paraphrase. The least gesture of unannounced originality on a poet's part suffices to baffle critical presupposition completely, and the two regnant presuppositions of the mid-twentieth century – the old one, that poems reflect lives and announce doctrines, the new one, that poems are self-contained or else imperfect – are rendered helpless by Yeats's most radical, most casual, and most characteristic maneuver: he was an architect, not a decorator; he didn't accumulate poems, he wrote books.

It would have been surprising if he had not, preoccupied as he was with sacred writings. When he functioned as a critic, as in his essay on Shelley or his useful generalisations on Shakespeare, it was the oeuvre, not the fragment, that held his attention.

The place to look for light on any poem is in the adjacent poems, which Yeats placed adjacent to it because they belonged there. And the unit in which to inspect and discuss his development is not the poem or sequence of poems but the volume, at least from *Responsibilities* (1914) to *A Full Moon in March* (1935).[1] This principle is sometimes obvious enough; anyone can see that the six songs following 'The Three Bushes' belong in its entourage, or that 'The Phases of the Moon' incorporates the half-dozen poems appended to it. Such obvious instances are, however, slightly misleading; one is apt to think of the main poem as not quite completed, ravelling out into lyrical loose ends, or not quite definitive in scope, making shift to appropriate, like a handful of minnows, lesser foci of energy that ought to have been brought within its sphere at the time of composition. In the Age of Eliot, the poet is supposed to gather his interests and impulses and discharge them utterly in a supreme opus every so often, and evades this responsibility at the price of being not quite a major poet. Those weren't the terms in which Yeats was thinking; we misread him if we suppose either that the majority of the poems are casual or that in each he was trying for a definitive statement of all that, at the time of composition, he was.

'Men Improve with the Years' looks like an attempt of this kind; it cuts off, of course, too neatly. The poet was once young, and a lover; now he is a monument, and no lady will love him. The quality of the rhetoric is impeccable, but the poem, on some acquaintance, appears to reduce itself to its mere theme, and that theme so simple-minded as to invite biographical eking out. The unspoken premise of Yeats criticism is that we have to supply from elsewhere – from his life or his doctrines – a great deal that didn't properly get into the poems: not so much to explain the poems as to make them rich enough to sustain the reputation. It happens, however, that 'Men Improve with the Years' has for context not Yeats's biography but two poems about a man who did not undergo that dubious improvement: at the climax of 'In Memory of Major Robert Gregory' we read,

> Some burn damp faggots, others may consume
> The entire combustible world in one small room
> As though dried straw, and if we turn about
> The bare chimney is gone black out
> Because the work had finished in that flare.
> Soldier, scholar, horseman, he,
> As 'twere all life's epitome,
> What made us dream that he could comb grey hair?

Dried straw, damp faggots; in 'Men Improve with the Years' we discover a 'burning youth' succeeded by water:

> . . .
> A weather-worn, marble triton
> Among the streams.

Major Robert Gregory, 'all life's epitome', concentrated all in an instantaneous conflagration; the speaker of 'Men Improve with the Years' has advanced serially through phases one can enumerate to the condition of a statue. Statues, of course, have their immortality, their nobility of arrested gesture. Yeats isn't being picturesque in specifying the kind of statue; tritons blow their wreathèd horns, and a marble one would be puffing soundlessly at a marble trumpet, like an official Poet; not even in the open sea, but amid the fountains of Major Gregory's mother's garden. The poem isn't a small clearing in which Yeats sinks decoratively to rest, it is a counter-rhetoric to the rhetorical memorial poem. It doesn't come quite on the heels of that poem, however; between the two we hear the dry tones of the Irish Airman ('soldier, scholar, horseman') himself:

> . . .
> Those that I fight I do not hate,
> Those that I guard I do not love;
> . . .

Midway between Yeats's contrasting rhetorics, Gregory ('An Irish Airman Foresees His Death') hasn't a rhetoric but a style. He wasn't exhilarated by the prospect of consuming 'the entire combustible world'; 'a lonely impulse of delight' redeems from calculation the decision born of an explicit disenchantment:

> . . .
> I balanced all, brought all to mind,
> The years to come seemed waste of breath,
> A waste of breath the years behind
> In balance with this life, this death.

Those are the words from which we pass to these:

> I am worn out with dreams:
> A weather-worn, marble triton
> Among the streams;
> . . .

– the traditional sonorities, the diction ('my burning youth!'), the conventional elegances of cadence evoking (while just evading) a 'literary' tradition against which is poised the next poem in the volume: 'The Collarbone of a Hare'.

> Would I could cast a sail on the water
> Where many a king has gone
> And many a king's daughter,
> And alight at the comely trees and the lawn,
> The playing upon pipes and the dancing,

> And learn that the best thing is
> To change my loves while dancing
> And pay but a kiss for a kiss.

This live rhythm quickens a remote, folkish idiom, unsonorous and wry. 'Men Improve with the Years' seems in retrospect heavier than ever. In this pastoral kingdom not only are there no marble tritons (its tone has nothing in common with that of the Land of Heart's Desire where the Princess Edain was 'busied with a dance'), but the newcomer's characteristic gesture is to look back through 'the collarbone of a hare' and laugh at 'the old bitter world where they marry in churches' with a lunatic peasant slyness. The symbol of trivial death proffers a peephole or spyglass; it doesn't, as death is reputed to do, open vistas. You can squint with its aid at the old world, from fairyland. Yeats is trying out different arrangements of a poetic universe with the blunt fact of death in it. In the next poem ('Under the Round Tower') he reverses the situation and rearranges the perspective. Stretched for nonchalant slumber 'On great grandfather's battered tomb', Beggar Billy sees the dancing-world: not

> . . . the comely trees and the lawn,
> The playing upon pipes and the dancing,
> . . .

but

> . . . a dream
> Of sun and moon that a good hour
> Bellowed and pranced in the round tower;
>
> . . .
>
> That golden king and that wild lady
> Sang till stars began to fade,
> Hands gripped in hands, toes close together,
> Hair spread on the wind they made;
> That lady and that golden king
> Could like a brace of blackbirds sing.

This is the celebrated music of the spheres; and Beggar Billy decides that 'great grandfather's battered tomb' that educes such noisy and energetic visions is no place for him. So the book, having degraded its initial persona to beggardom (there are curious analogies with *Lear*) and preoccupied itself with themes and images of death until it has set the celestial boiler shop going, takes leave of this theme for a time and turns to quieter matters like the dead lovers Solomon and Sheba.

That initial persona now wants looking at. The volume we are examining, *The Wild Swans at Coole*, began not with the Gregory elegy – that is its second poem – but with 'The Wild Swans at Coole' itself: an image of personal dejection ('And now my heart is sore') that uses the permanent glory of the swans to silhouette the transience attending human beings who must keep their feet on the ground and try to assimilate the 'brilliant creatures' by counting them.

> . . .
> All's changed since I, hearing at twilight,
> The first time on this shore,
> The bell-beat of their wings above my head,
> Trod with a lighter tread.
>
> Unwearied still, lover by lover,
> They clamber in the cold
> Companionable streams or climb the air;
> Their hearts have not grown old;
> . . .

'All's changed' is a mood, not a summary of presented facts; this initial poem confines itself to a wholly familiar *Angst*, a setting documented in a spare but traditional manner –

> The trees are in their autumn beauty,
> The woodland paths are dry,
> . . .

– a specified month and time of day, a poet who does and thinks and feels nothing unusual, verbs no more than inert copulas, and swans that are scarcely more than swans. We are in the presence of a mind reflecting nature and then reflecting Locke-wise upon what it reflects: tantalised – not teased, but undergoing the pangs of Tantalus – because it must undergo change while nature – the swans – remains other, 'unwearied still'. Though none of the great Romantics could have written it with such economy and directness, the poem remains within, say, the Coleridgean orbit of experience.

It is upon experience resignedly ordered in this plane that the brilliant death of Major Robert, the Irish Airman, impinges; he took wing like the swans; his heart has not grown old; he demonstrated that it lay within human capacity to

> . . . consume
> The entire combustible world in one small room
> As though dried straw, . . .

This death and the contemplation of the poet's impotent middle age ferment and interact throughout the volume, entoiling other materials, discovering unexpected resonances in the pastoral mode ('Shepherd and Goatherd') and in the lingering end of Mabel Beardsley ('Upon a Dying Lady'), never for long oblivious of the piercing hypothesis that maximum human intensity coincides with human extinction. What is arrived at is an extinction not of the person but of his natural context. At the end of the volume (in 'The Double Vision of Michael Robartes') October water no more mirrors a natural sky:

> On the grey rock of Cashel the mind's eye
> Has called up the cold spirits that are born
> When the old moon has vanished from the sky
> And the new still hides her horn.

The mind's eye, no longer the Newtonian optic; and that moon isn't nature's moon. Nor does the mind's eye see swans that fly away, but calls up three arresting figures – one a sphinx – observed not in placidity but in active intensity:

> . . .
> Mind moved but seemed to stop
> As 'twere a spinning-top.
>
> In contemplation had those three so wrought
> Upon a moment, and so stretched it out
> That they, time overthrown,
> Were dead yet flesh and bone.

The poem – and the volume – closes on a note of triumph; Yeats tells us he 'arranged' – deliberate word – his vision in a song –

> . . .
> Seeing that I, ignorant for so long
> Had been rewarded thus
> In Cormac's ruined house.

The poles of this volume are its first and last poems, 'The Wild Swans at Coole' and 'The Double Vision of Michael Robartes', as the poles of *The Tower* are 'Sailing to Byzantium' and 'All Souls' Night'.

Between the observation of the swans and the vision of the sphinx passes the action of the book. The crisis occurs when, in 'Ego Dominus Tuus' (which immediately follows the account of the Dying Lady's heroic arrogance), '*Ille*'[2] determines to 'set his chisel to the hardest stone' and forget about the kind of self-fulfillment envisaged by people who tell us that men improve with the years. Immediately a long poem devotes itself to the moon, the faded cliché of a thousand mewling nature poets; and examining it not as they do in the Irish sky but by way of the sort of diagram one discovers in a penny astrology book, sets the stage for the double vision of Michael Robartes.

The Wild Swans at Coole is a book about death and the will. A component poem like 'Men Improve with the Years' will no more pull loose from it than the 'foolish fond old man' speech will pull loose from *King Lear*. It is a radical mistake to think of Yeats as a casual or fragmentary poet whose writings float on a current discoverable only in his biographable life. How much time does he not spend telling us that he has carefully rendered the mere events of his life irrelevant!

SOURCE: extract from the essay, 'The Sacred Book of the Arts', *Sewanee Review*, LXIV, 4 (1956); reproduced in Kenner's *Gnomon* (New York, 1958), pp. 9–22.

NOTES

1. It isn't clear how much, if any, of *Last Poems* was arranged by Yeats himself.

2. 'Willy', commented Ezra Pound.

2. STUDIES ON SPECIFIC POEMS

Donald Stauffer On 'The Wild Swans at Coole' and the Swan Image in Yeats (1949)

. . . Since the achievement of poetry marks the worth of poetic theory, let us turn to a single lyric poem and read it in the light of Yeats's thought. Consider 'The Wild Swans at Coole' (1919) . . . [Stauffer quotes the whole poem – Ed.]

Like all the luckiest poems, this can be read with enjoyment on any of many levels. Often it gets into the anthologies, where readers may legitimately consider it as a pleasing poem on a pretty subject. The technical analysts and metrists may savor the contrasts between its feminine and masculine line-endings, may speculate on the uses of its two pairs of half rhymes, and above all may be delighted by the unanalysable rhythm of its lines.

Those who believe a poem is self-sustaining and explicable only in its own words and form will also find rewards in 'The Wild Swans' – in Yeats's cunning and almost invariable linking of each stanza to its predecessor by some repeated word or thought which modifies into a new development. They will note that the poem begins with the swans upon the lake, shifts to the images of the swans in the air, and returns to the swans on the lake – a perfect round. They will find structure in the antitheses between the swans and their beholder, and between the beholder now and the beholder nineteen years ago. And they will note (let us hope) that the essential pattern is not built in time[1] but in a contrast between moods, and that since only mortal man in this poem feels such contrasts, the founding antithesis is between transient man and eternity.

Those who like comparative judgements may occupy themselves profitably in the parallels between the building of this poem and of, for instance, Keats's 'Ode to a Nightingale'. In structural devices for meditative poems of about this length, Keats and Yeats are as similar as their names.

And in this manner we might continue to invent little games of criticism, and new, or conventional, or fashionable approaches.

But what does the poem say? Everyone knows that paraphrases are inadequate. Yet a paraphrase of a poem by Yeats seems particularly thin to anyone who has read him for more than a couple of hours. Let us try it for this lyric.

In a particular place at a particular time a particular poet sees a particular number of swans. He first counted them nineteen years earlier, when they rose into the air almost before he had numbered them. He has looked upon the swans and he is sorrowful – the two statements are joined with an 'and', so that he is not forcing the reader to make a causal connection if the reader doesn't care to. But at any rate, when he first heard them rise from the water, he was made happier. The swans, however, do not change. Like the 'self-same song' of Keats's nightingale, the paddling or climbing of the swans goes on still; in all their wanderings, they are symbols of 'passion or conquest' – or more boldly in Yeats's thought, passion and conquest are servants of the swans. Returning to the original picture of the swans drifting upon the lake in autumn, Yeats finds them mysterious as well as beautiful, and wonders whom they will delight at some future day.

Such a prose statement verges upon travesty. Yet within the strict limits of the poem it could not be built up, so long as ingenuity played fair, to the pitch of intensity which this poem rightly assumes among Yeats's other works. In structure, the poem points away from self-sufficiency: it begins with the most precise particularised stanza; by the time the next-to-the-last stanza is reached, the realm is general speculation; and the final stanza opens out, like a rich horn, into mystery, questioning, and the future.

Almost anything that is said within the formal strictures of the poem takes on more significance if Yeats's thought elsewhere is known more fully. The first two words are 'The trees', and though it is of no great importance here, a whole essay might be written on Yeats's brilliant use of the tree as symbol. Criticism may be made by critics like me, but only Yeats can make a tree into the 'great rooted blossomer' of 'Among School Children' or into the 'half all glittering flame and half all green / Abounding foliage' of the poem 'Vacillation'.

The second line speaks of 'paths', but we shall not be carried aside to ask the possible relevance of the straight path of the intellect and the winding path of intuition. The paths are 'dry', and perhaps that is of importance to see how earth, air and water give structure to the poem; only the fourth element is neglected – unless the lyric itself has the simplicity of fire. We know that Yeats speculated on the meaning of the four elements and ordinarily used them with consistency. It is more than just natural history, it is symbolism, that in this poem Yeats associates the swans with water and with air. And it is more than photographic realism that Yeats is standing on the shore, the swans drifting on the water. An essay on 'water' imagery in Yeats, and on 'stone' imagery in opposition, would illuminate such a line as

> Upon the brimming water among the stones,

but will not be written here.

The admirer of Yeats is tempted to connect the flight of the swans, 'wheeling in great broken rings', with his spiral imagery, or with the falcon turning and turning in the widening gyre; he is tempted by 'the bell-beat of their wings' to run off into speculation as to why Yeats (who alludes so frequently to music yet who admits he has no ear) limits his usual references to specific musical instruments so strangely to bells and gongs. He may not be able to read the line 'Among what rushes will they build', without thinking of Yeats's volume *The Wind Among the Reeds* (1899), besides a dozen other near-relevancies and associations that might possibly turn into explanations that make lines clearer.[2]

Another almost unescapable approach is the filling in of biography; the question is naturally roused by the poem, and only the pure theorist will brush it aside in petulance. Where is Coole? What is Yeats doing there? How did he come there nineteen years ago? Why is his heart now sore? Yeats knew, and knew when he wrote the poem. Should not the reader?

I do not think it would do the reader any harm, but I am not writing a biography of William Butler Yeats. I shall choose for detailed attention a subject only relatively less complicated than the poet himself – his swans.

Nineteen years earlier, he had first seen the swans. Fifteen years earlier, in 1904, he had published a poem called 'The Withering of the Boughs'.[3] It is a 24-line three-stanza poem, with a refrain that insists

> . . .
> No boughs have withered, because of the wintry wind;
> The boughs have withered because I have told them my dreams.

The loose irregularly flowing pentameters carry with ease the sleepy leafy dreamy faery mood. There are swans in the poem; but what is more remarkable is the ganglion of associated words and images in that poem and in 'The Wild Swans'. Just as Shakespeare had his own sets of unexpected associations, from which according to Caroline Spurgeon it is even possible to deduce in part his personality and his experiences, so does Yeats make special patterns. The pressure is not great enough in many of them to lend them symbolic importance, but they contribute in repeated minute touches to the general texture and even to the structure, as the small *pointilliste* dots of paint in a Seurat finally add up to the outlines and massed planes of the whole painting. There are 'paths' in both poems, and 'streams', and a 'lake', and drifting. Both are muted to the meditative mood: it is 'twilight' in one, while in the other 'The honey-pale moon lay low on the sleepy hills', and 'the light grows cool'. The contrasted ideas of wandering and of permanence are in both poems. The 'mysterious' of 'The Wild Swans' is matched by the 'secret smile' in 'The Withering of the Boughs'. The 'great broken rings' of the swan's flight in the later poem are present in the earlier, where the 'swans fly round', and where the gyrating notion is played with variants in the 'spindles of wool' of witches, or in the fairy folk who 'wind and unwind dancing' on the island lawns.

The later poem is infinitely more certain and subtle. 'The Withering of the Boughs' vacillates between the unconvincing fairyland of witches with crowns of pearl, and the sharp touches of curlew and peewit crying. The swans sing, whereas in the more mature poem it is the bell-beat of their clamorous wings that fires Yeats's thought. In the apprentice poem, the swans fly round somewhat embarrassingly 'coupled with golden chains'; the same idea is better ordered in the later Yeats when we hear that

> Unwearied still, *lover by lover*,
> They paddle in the cold
> *Companionable* streams, or climb the air;
> . . .

And the founding emotional contrast of 'The Wild Swans' between the present, when the poet's heart is sore, and the past, when he trod with a lighter tread, is present in 'The Withering of the Boughs', not only in the title but in the final stanza:

> I know of the sleepy country, where swans fly round
> Coupled with golden chains, and sing as they fly.

> A king and a queen are wandering there, and the sound
> Has made them so happy and hopeless, so deaf and so blind
> With wisdom, they wander till all the years have gone by;
> . . .

Although these lines are fuzzily allegorical, they help in their rumpled way toward an understanding of the cold stillness of the more nearly perfect lyric. And this early poem, written so close to the original experience, may show that Yeats too creates his best poetry not in the heat of passion but in recollection long years after.

If slow maturing stamps this particular poet, then later poems as well may cast light upon 'The Wild Swans at Coole'. The most important are 'The Tower', Part III, 'Nineteen Hundred and Nineteen', Part III, 'Leda and the Swan', 'Among School Children', and 'Coole Park and Ballylee, 1931'. Since these are among his best poems, it is safe to assume that Yeats in crucial moments reverted to the swan as a center for his thought, a focal symbol.

Because its subject is the cyclical theory of history, or the unforeseen consequences of the moment of intense passion, 'Leda and the Swan' may be dismissed here, although Zeus as the swan is the most powerful image Yeats ever developed for his 'passion or conquest'.

'The Tower', written in 1926, is Yeats's house and home, restored for himself and his wife; it is also the symbol of himself in his lonely pride and introspection. The short first section, with a kind of petulant disgust, admits old age; the second tries to find compensation in images and memories of the past; the third and final section concerns us here. It is Yeats's testament. He bequeaths to young upstanding men his faith and his pride. The passage on the swan is the longest and the culminating image to describe reckless, generous, open-handed 'pride', and immediately precedes his declaration of 'faith' in man as creator of the cosmos. These are the words:

> . . .
> Pride, like that of the morn,
> When the headlong light is loose,
> Or that of the fabulous horn,
> Or that of the sudden shower
> When all streams are dry,
> Or that of the hour
> When the swan must fix his eye
> Upon a fading gleam,

Float out upon a long
Last reach of glittering stream
And there sing his last song.
. . .

The section is of such importance that Yeats calls attention to it in a note:

In the passage about the Swan in Part III I have unconsciously echoed one of the loveliest lyrics of our time – Mr Sturge Moore's 'Dying Swan'. I often recited it during an American lecturing tour, which explains the theft.

THE DYING SWAN

O silver-throated Swan
Struck, struck! A golden dart
Clean through thy breast has gone
Home to thy heart.
Thrill, thrill, O silver throat!
O silver trumpet, pour
Love for defiance back
On him who smote!
And brim, brim o'er
With love; and ruby-dye thy track
Down thy last living reach
Of river, sail the golden light –
Enter the sun's heart – even teach,
O wondrous-gifted Pain, teach thou
The god to love, let him learn how.[4]

Defiance, love, death, pain, heart-stricken song, blood, brilliance – these elements in Sturge Moore's poem are all of use to Yeats in his appropriated image. And though the swan singing before death is one of the commonest of the beast fables or vulgar errors, it chimes so perfectly with Yeats's conception of pride that he manages to make it seem new-minted and intense.

The swan returns in that most powerfully bitter and desolating of all his poems, 'Nineteen Hundred and Nineteen'. The First World War is past; violence is upon the roads in Ireland, and the bloody guerrilla warfare of Black-and-Tans and Irish Republicans shows 'the weasel's twist, the weasel's tooth'. Imbedded in the heart of these sections devoted to mockery and destruction, the third section uses the swan again as a symbol for the artist's pride, now coupled with the idea of solitude in the face of death and approaching night.

> Some moralist or mythological poet
> Compares the solitary soul to a swan;
> I am satisfied with that,
> Satisfied if a troubled mirror show it,
> Before that brief gleam of its life be gone,
> An image of its state;
> The wings half spread for flight,
> The breast thrust out in pride
> Whether to play, or to ride
> Those winds that clamour of approaching night.

Then follows a stanza developing more directly a man's own secret meditation, his triumph and solitude, before the last stanza where the return to the swan image satisfies Yeats's bitterness at the crack-pated dream of mending the world:

> The swan has leaped into the desolate heaven:
> That image can bring wildness, bring a rage
> To end all things, to end
> What my laborious life imagined, even
> The half-imagined, the half-written page;
> . . .

The image is growing in intensity and complexity, so that now, as with all of his symbols, Yeats can use it as a kind of shorthand, which will bring up for him and for 'those few people who have read all that I have written' unexpressed emotions. In 'Among School Children' (1926), for instance, though the swan is mentioned directly only once, it dominates in imagery three of the eight stanzas, associated with ideas of wildness and wind, of rage and pride and unsatisfied desire. Above all, the idea of a union between perfect beauty and divine strength – passion *and* conquest – in the half-expressed image of Leda and the swan. These are the shorthand fragments:

> I dream of a Ledaean body, bent
> Above a sinking fire, . . . [stanza II]
>
> . . .
> For even daughters of the swan can share
> Something of every paddler's heritage –
> . . . [stanza III]
>
> . . .
> And I though never of Ledaean kind
> Had pretty plumage once – . . . [stanza IV]

The imagery is so strong that it colors and shapes other images, as in the first fragment quoted above it colors and shapes a recollection from Ronsard (which elsewhere Yeats has adapted as an entire poem).[5] Similarly, the same fragment within its own stanza impinges upon Yeats's comparison drawn from Aristophanes' fable of the separated halves of lovers seeking reunion, and unexpectedly shapes it by attraction into an image governed by the thought of the eggs from which Leda's children by Zeus were born:

> . . . it seemed that our two natures blent
> Into a sphere from youthful sympathy,
> Or else, to alter Plato's parable,
> Into the yolk and white of the one shell.

And finally, 'Coole Park and Ballylee, 1931'. The year is part of the title: Yeats is now in his late sixties. The October twilight is gone; the season is winter and the mood is winter. The first stanza follows the course of the stream darkening underground as it flows from Yeats's Thoor Ballylee, where he writes the poem, to the lake at Coole Park.

> What's water but the generated soul?

In the second stanza, Yeats again is standing on that lake shore, this time under a wintry sun; the wood is all dry sticks; Nature is in a tragic mood that mirrors his own; then the swan passage:

> . . .
> At sudden thunder of the mounting swan
> I turned about and looked where branches break
> The glittering reaches of the flooded lake.
>
> Another emblem there! That stormy white
> But seems a concentration of the sky;
> And, like the soul, it sails into the sight
> And in the morning's gone, no man knows why;
> And is so lovely that it sets to right
> What knowledge or its lack had set awry,
> So arrogantly pure, a child might think
> It can be murdered with a spot of ink.

The succeeding stanzas meditate on Lady Gregory's house at Coole Park. Again he can use shorthand, for in so many of his stately reflective lyrics – 'Coole Park, 1929', 'Meditations in Time of Civil War', 'A Prayer for My Daughter', 'Shepherd and Goatherd', 'In

Memory of Major Robert Gregory', 'To a Friend Whose Work Has Come to Nothing' – he has fingered in many modulations his worship of family, tradition, honor, dignity, so frequently that he can assume that a single impressionistic phrase ('a last inheritor', 'ancestral trees') will conjure up Custom and Ceremony as a refuge for the artist, as Lady Gregory was a protection and a haven for the wracked young Yeats more than thirty years before. But in the modern world of fashion and fantasy and fanaticism, man is homeless as a Bedouin – 'all that great glory spent'.

Then the last stanza with its elegiac lament for tradition, beauty, the simplicity of the folk and the elevation of art, and its return to the symbol of the swan drifting upon the waters in a darkening world:

> We were the last romantics – chose for theme
> Traditional sanctity and loveliness;
> Whatever's written in what poets name
> The book of the people; whatever most can bless
> The mind of man or elevate a rhyme;
> But all is changed, that high horse riderless,
> Though mounted in that saddle Homer rode
> Where the swan drifts upon a darkening flood.

I do not wish to murder Yeats's swan with a spot of ink by glossing his lines at too great length, though it may be fair to mention that of this particular swan Yeats wrote his wife on February 3, 1932: 'a symbol of inspiration I think'[6] And it is fair also to suggest that for Yeats 'The Wild Swans at Coole' is but a part of a continuous experience of living, that the poignancy of that one sharp experience is increased if the reader is simultaneously aware of the similar experience reflected in part fifteen years before in 'The Withering of the Boughs', and of the reenacting of the experience twelve years later in 'Coole Park and Ballylee, 1931'. Then 'The Wild Swans' becomes the central portion of a three-part symphony, to which other poems also contribute auxiliary motifs.

And although the phrases come from other poems, 'The Wild Swans at Coole' may be more fully realised when we know that a king and queen wandering in the sleepy country were made 'happy and hopeless' by their song; that a swan sings his last song while floating out 'upon a long last reach of glittering stream'; that in the proud swan, breast thrust out and wings half spread for flight, the solitary soul may see 'an image of its state'; that its 'feathered glory', its 'white rush', 'its stormy white', its 'sudden thunder' as it mounts to ride the clamorous winds, its leap 'into the desolate heaven' – are merely the intense poetic visions that catch its arrogant purity. Yeats's poems respond to – indeed, they compel – a knowledge of his other poems.

His symbols also presuppose or compel knowledge of their complementary or opposed symbols. The swan can be better understood if one is aware of his opposites, particularly of the phoenix and the eagle or hawk. If anyone approves of books with such titles as 'Animal Imagery in Shakespeare' or 'Milton's Knowledge of Horticulture', a long one could be written on birds in Yeats. It would include the peacock and the heron, the owl, the daws and the linnet, the stare or starling, bats, cattlebirds, the cock and cockerel (a long chapter), gulls (another long chapter), geese and wild geese and the barnacle goose, cuckoos, ravens, rooks, jackdaws, the peewit, the curlew, the sea-mew, lapwings, swallows, parrots and crows. Not to mention 'an absurd / Portly green-pated bird' on which Yeats furnishes no more specifically ornithological information. The imaginary book should have a long chapter on Yeatsian birds in general – particularly on his fascinated dwelling upon bird-song. The cry of birds, like his symbol of the gong or bell, seems to be an emblem of instinctive passionate unthinking life that breaks the trance of eternity. In his *Last Poems*, the birds definitely become symbols: they are not particularised, but appear as 'a long-legged bird, / A symbol of longevity' ['Lapis Lazuli'], or 'A great black ragged bird' ['The Pilgrim']. Those 'bird-like things' among the shrouds end the poem 'Cuchulain Comforted' on the eery line:

> . . .
> They had changed their throats and had the throats of birds.

And his last play, *The Death of Cuchulain*, comes to its epilogue as the crow-headed Morrigu stands motionless upon a darkening stage: 'There is silence and in the silence a few faint bird notes.'

But this chapter will not turn into a parliament of fowls, nor will it guarantee that the roll call is complete. The design has been merely to look for Yeats's theory of the lyric – the cold, hard, brave, proud pattern, intense with passion, all its strength and sweetness rolled up into one ball, not dynamic or kinetic but static in its lyric purity. As such, the lyric is not to be judged by criticism that insists upon standards essentially dramatic or ironic. A poem, even a poem by Yeats, is legitimately self-contained to the extent that it should be judged, at some point in a criticism, by its own standards – by what it is trying to do. And Yeats is not trying to be dramatic or ironic in the common meanings of those words. Drama and irony would break the trancelike ecstasy Yeats tries to evoke and maintain. His drama, such as it is, is the quarrel of a man with himself, and he sees this not as a changing movement but as a fixed design, like a mask, a hawk painted upon a curtain, a bronze head, a statue, an Eastern city, a horoscope, a tower above a stream, a six-pointed star. As for irony, his characteristic nearest approximation is in his antitheses and antinomies, and these are in such sharp opposition that the pattern and the effect are broken and lost if one term is taken for the other.

Nor should Yeats be judged by the literary theory of the self-contained poem. He pours his whole personality, increasingly coherent and consistent, into every poem, so that the poem is self-contained only in the sense that it contains all of Yeats's own self. Nor is he a self-contained man, but a part of all that he has met. In theory, he believed that much of his work came even from sources over which he had no conscious control and of which he had no conscious knowledge. By a series of echoes and allusions and repetitions from poem to poem, he gave rich texture and underpainting to even his shortest lyrics. As a line from a tragedy or epic lives with added vigor because of its great context, so a lyric of Yeats gains part of its force from its being one of many related lyrics. By this device of repetition, applied with unparalleled persistence and passion, Yeats elevated the possibilities of the lyric to hitherto unrealised heights. In the history of poetry this may eventually be counted as his greatest achievement.

As a demonstration of his method, 'The Wild Swans at Coole' was selected because of its surface simplicity. It has not been 'analysed', for to do so would be to defeat Yeats's intention and achievement. But the most important related material from other poems has been set forth to suggest that the swan, *though it should be experienced as an indivisible single image*, is rich in thought and complex in passion.

This, then, was the dilemma of the lyric poet: to give simultaneously the variety of actual life and the intensity of art. The multiplicity of the waters, of fish, flesh and fowl, and yet the simplicity of fire. Complexity and compression at the same time. Yeats confronted the antinomies and triumphed as an artist. All of the birds and all of the bird-songs are transmuted into the golden nightingale.

Always compression, greater and yet greater compression. No one but Yeats could have written his own epitaph. An earlier version had yet one more line which, in the cutting of this agate, Yeats finally found unnecessary:

Cast a cold eye
On life, on death.
Horseman, pass by! ['Under Ben Bulben']

SOURCE: extract from 'The Reading of a Lyric', ch. 4 in *The Golden Nightingale* (New York, 1949), pp. 64–79.

NOTES

[Reorganised and renumbered from the original – Ed.]

1. Yeats's poems, even his plays, seem deliberately to avoid strict consciousness of time. This his theories would lead us to expect. Time, for Yeats as for Shakespeare, is the envious and calumniating robber who crams his rich thievery up; and thus may be felt as an antagonist. Positively, time is that medium within which an artist's convictions become clearer, his joy therefore greater, and his choices more his own. But since it intensifies the individual's awareness of his own accidental and consequently almost trivial state, poetry should try to disregard time or at most to blur its tyranny. In 'The Wild Swans', for instance, careful reading is necessary to see that the second and third stanzas are laid primarily in the past, the final stanza in the future. How does Yeats know there are fifty-nine swans? On the evidence of the poem, I would say because he counted them nineteen years ago; but the second stanza is so cunningly wrought that it allows the reader almost to believe that the swans take flight 'now', while Yeats looks at them. The third stanza is 'now' and nineteen years ago. The fourth stanza is any time – it is the nature of the wild swans, still, unwearied still. And the last stanza is 'now' and 'some day' in the future. Since only the first stanza is laid in a single moment, and the rest are either double in time or disputable, Yeats has done his deliberate best to take the swans out of time without diminishing their precise and believable nature as 59 particular swans at Coole Park.

2. Two examples: The first time Yeats saw the swans, he 'trod with a lighter tread'. The illogical hidden sexual reference here to the treading of male swans may seem more legitimate if one remembers Yeats's 'Leda and the Swan', or if one reads over again 'Quarrel in Old Age', in which 'that lonely thing', his beloved in her youth, 'trod like Spring'. Then one may turn to 'His Phoenix' to learn of 'that sprightly girl trodden by a bird'.

'The still water' of the last stanza will suggest the Psalms without further help from Yeats; within the poem, the reader may catch the use here of 'still' for 'placid', and in the previous stanza for 'yet', as Keats uses 'still' with a double, perhaps a triple, ambiguity in 'Thou still unravished bride of quietness'. But the reader must go outside the poem to feel the full importance for Yeats in the fourth stanza of 'still' to suggest continuing or permanent 'passion or conquest', an example of his characteristic 'lyrical stasis' or ecstasy.

3. To avoid bewildering bibliographical details, I use here, as elsewhere, the dates given in Yeats's *Collected Poems*. Actually, the Cuala Press edition of *The Wild Swans at Coole* was published October 10, 1917, and the Dun Emer edition of *In the Seven Woods*, which contains 'The Withering of the Boughs', was published July 16, 1903.

4. A poet must be most punctilious to feel such an indebtedness should be acknowledged: 'last reach' is the only verbal debt, plus the image of the long glittering river-track, for the idea of the dying swan is common property. More interesting, Sturge Moore's 'brim, brim o'er' possibly governs 'the brimming water' in the earlier 'The Wild Swans at Coole'.

5. 'When You Are Old', in *The Rose* (1893).

6. Joseph Hone, W. B. Yeats (2nd edn, London, 1962), p. 425.

C. K. Stead On 'Easter 1916' (1964)

. . . 'Easter 1916', written to commemorate the 1916 rising against the British occupation of Ireland, is one of Yeats's public poems. It is a complete poem which, more than illustrating Yeats's achievement of objectivity by means of the dramatic 'mask', uses the terms of drama in order to stylise and objectify the world of political fact which is its subject. In the writing of this poem literary problems have become, for Yeats, analogues for the problems of living: 'Life' and 'Art' interact and merge into a single image.

The first three sections of the poem look backward to a 'comic' world that has been left behind – a world of restless individuality, of mutability, subject to death and regeneration. The fourth section points forward to a world of tragic stasis, achieved by those killed in the rising. Thus the movement of the poem – from the temporal to the timeless – and the intermediate position of Yeats's persona in that movement, make the poem a forerunner of the more famous 'Sailing to Byzantium'.

The opening lines of the poem present the 'comic' Dublin scene before the Easter rising:

I have met them at close of day
Coming with vivid faces
From counter or desk among grey
Eighteenth-century houses.
I have passed with a nod of the head
Or polite meaningless words,
Or have lingered awhile and said
Polite meaningless words,
. . .

These, whom Yeats met 'at close of day', are the Irish patriots, shaped in the world of modern commerce ('from counter or desk') which came into being with 'grey eighteenth-century' reason. Dublin is part of the civilisation that followed when 'the merchant and the clerk / Breathed on the world with timid breath' ['At Galway Races'] – a fragmented society, where 'polite meaningless words' serve in place of collective spiritual enterprise. 'Doubtless because fragments broke into ever smaller fragments', Yeats writes in his *Autobiographies* (p. 192), 'we saw one another in a light of bitter comedy.' The 'vivid faces' of the patriots could never, it seemed, assume the static mask of tragedy. So the persona of this poem recalls his certainty

. . . that they and I
But lived where motley is worn:
. . .

But we are warned:

. . .
All changed, changed utterly:
A terrible beauty is born.

Comedy, Yeats suggests in an essay, accentuates personality, individual character; tragedy eliminates it in favour of something universal: 'Tragedy must always be a drowning and breaking of the dykes that separate man from man, and . . . it is upon these dykes comedy keeps house.'[1]

The second section of the poem sketches the personalities of some of the nationalists before their destruction in the Easter rising. One, beautiful when young, had spoiled her beauty in the fervour of political agitation; another was a poet and schoolteacher; a third had shown sensitivity and intellectual daring; a fourth had seemed only 'a drunken vainglorious lout'. But the 'dykes that separate man from man' have now been broken. Each has

> . . . resigned his part
> In the casual comedy;
> . . .
> Transformed utterly:
> A terrible beauty is born.[2]

So far the change seems all achievement: the petty modern comedy has given way to tragic beauty. But this is also a '*terrible* beauty', beauty bought only at the expense of life:

> Hearts with one purpose alone
> Through summer and winter seem
> Enchanted to a stone
> To trouble the living stream.
> The horse that comes from the road,
> The rider, the birds that range
> From cloud to tumbling cloud,
> Minute by minute they change;
> A shadow of cloud on the stream
> Changes minute by minute;
> A horse-hoof slides on the brim,
> And a horse plashes within it;
> The long-legged moor-hens dive,
> And hens to moor-cocks call;
> Minute by minute they live:
> The stone's in the midst of all.

This third section is a general image of the world subject to time and death ('minute by minute they live') – an image which implies another, kindlier way of seeing the Dublin street before the rising. The nationalists have transcended the mutable word, but only by the destruction of normal human values, by a single-mindedness that turns the heart to stone. The movement of this section imparts the joy of life, which throws a new light on the 'terrible beauty', emphasising terror over beauty. The events are thus presented with an ambiguity which does justice to their complexity.

'Nations, races, and individual men', Yeats tells us

> are unified by an image, or bundle of related images, symbolical or evocative of the state of mind which is, of all states of mind not impossible, the most difficult to that man, race or nation; because only the greatest obstacle that can be contemplated without despair rouses the will to full intensity.[3]

The 'most difficult' image which the nationalists have contemplated 'without despair' is that of a united, independent Ireland. But there is another way of looking at their aspirations:

> We had fed the heart on fantasies,
> The heart's grown brutal from the fare;
> . . . ['Meditations in Time of Civil War']

Approval and disapproval, delight and disappointment, lie behind the poem. Out of the tensions in Yeats's own mind a complex image is generated. We know from what Maud Gonne has written that Yeats hated in her the passionate intensity that turned the heart to stone.

> Standing by the seashore in Normandy in September 1916 he read me that poem ['Easter 1916']; he had worked on it all the night before, and he implored me to forget the stone and its inner fire for the flashing, changing joy of life.[4]

But it was Yeats as a man who urged her to abandon her patriotic intensity. As a poet his task was more difficult; to make an image that would encompass the event, transcending mere 'opinion' – his own, and that of others. To achieve this he must transcend himself, giving up his personality as the revolutionaries gave up life, in order to achieve the mask of tragedy. At this level the writing of the poem becomes an analogue for the event which is its subject. Yeats is caught up in the play, and must move with it. He can no longer take pleasure in 'a mocking tale or a gibe' at the nationalists' expense, for he is no longer 'where motley is worn'. Nor can he pass judgement: 'That is heaven's part.' 'Our part' is only that of chorus –

> . . . our part
> To murmur name upon name,
> As a mother names her child
> When sleep at last has come
> On limbs that had run wild.
> . . .

At whatever human expense, a new symbol of heroism has been created. For good or ill

> . . .
> MacDonagh and MacBride
> And Connolly and Pearse
> Now and in time to be,
> Wherever green is worn,
> Are changed, changed utterly:
> . . .

The Irish mind carries a new symbol, and Irish literature a new poem: there is a new stone resisting the flow of the stream. Such an achievement constitutes a defeat over the mutable world. The personalities of principal actors and chorus – of all those whose interaction created the play – are irrelevant to the effect. The world is, for the moment in which the event is contemplated, 'transformed utterly'.

Yeats stands alone among English-speaking poets of this century in his ability to assimilate a complex political event into the framework of a poem without distortion of the event or loss of its human character in abstraction. It will be worth keeping 'Easter 1916' in mind when we come to consider the English poets of the First World War. Of them, the patriots are absurdly partisan, abstract and rhetorical; while the disillusioned soldier poets – though more admirable than the patriots because their poems come from honest feeling and particular experience – are too closely involved in the destruction to be capable of transforming these things, as Yeats transforms them, into a universal image. It is . . . a matter of establishing a correct distance between the poet and his subject. The soldier poets stand too close to their subject, the patriots at too great a distance. Yeats's dramatic 'mask' is a means of holding himself at a correct distance.[5] He had pored long enough over the slow fires of his own and others' art, to know that death in itself is a commonplace; but that particular death, transformed in poetry to an object of contemplation, becomes a symbol – a way of understanding and expressing the human condition.

In 'Easter 1916' Yeats has already achieved a solution – one solution – to a problem which had bedevilled poetry for many years: the problem of how a poem could enter the public world without losing itself in temporal 'opinion'. 'Easter 1916' is not a pure Symbolist poem, for it is capable of discursive paraphrase; but no paraphrase can use up the poem's life. The event which is its subject is not described, but re-fashioned. There is no question of simply praising heroism or blaming folly. The men of the poem are all dead – 'all changed, changed utterly' – no longer men at all but symbols that take life in the mind. Yeats leaves his personality, his opinions, behind. He puts on the mask of tragic chorus, and out of the slow impersonal contemplation of a particular event in which idealism, folly, heroism and destructiveness were intermixed, fashions an image which stands for all such events in human history. . . .

SOURCE: extract from the chapter, 'W. B. Yeats, 1895–1916', in Stead's *The New Poetic* (London, 1964), pp. 35–40.

NOTES

[Reorganised and renumbered from the original – Ed.]

1. *Essays and Introductions* (London, 1961), p. 241.
2. Cf. *Autobiographies* (London, 1955), p. 195: 'I had seen Ireland in my own time turn from the bragging rhetoric and gregarious humour of O'Connell's generation and school, and offer herself to the solitary and proud Parnell as to her anti-self, buskin followed hard on sock. . . .'
3. *Autobiographies*, pp. 194–5.
4. *Scattering Branches*, ed. Stephen Gwynn (London, 1940), pp. 31–2.
5. Cf. Yeats writing of two of his contemporary poets in *The Boston Pilot*, 23 April 1892. 'The din and glitter one feels were far too near the writer [John Davidson]. He has not been able to cast them back into imaginative dimness and distance. Of Mr Symons' method . . . I have but seen stray poems and judge from them that, despite most manifest triumphs from time to time, he will sometimes fail through gaining too easily that very dimness and distance I have spoken of. He will, perhaps, prove to be too far from, as Mr Davidson is too near to, his subject.' *Letters to The New Island*, ed. Horace Reynolds, reprinted (London, 1970), p. 147.

Daniel A. Harris On 'The Tower' (1974)

It is the natural consequence of Yeats's mode of dramatic lyric – 'I study every man I meet at some moment of crisis'[1] – that 'The Tower' should test so incisively the resolution gained in 'Meditations. . .':

> What shall I do with this absurdity –
> O heart, O troubled heart – this caricature,
> Decrepit age that has been tied to me
> As to a dog's tail?
> . . . [I]*

* Author's note: for poems which Yeats divided into sections by Roman numerals, I have used lower-case Roman numerals to indicate the stanza within the section – e.g., [II xi].

The 'ageing man' becomes a thing of hatred. If the speaker can 'shut the door' on military violence, he cannot so easily block out nature, his bodily image. '*Daemonic* images', remote, do not 'suffice'. As he withers into skeleton, his imagination gains in passionate fecundity: the discrepancy appals, disgusts him.

Yeats had handled the irreconcilable conflict between sexual potency and imaginative capability in 'Pardon, Old Fathers', the middle poems about Maud [Gonne], and elsewhere; his Nobel Prize medal had rekindled the obsession: 'It shows a young man listening to a Muse, who stands young and beautiful with a great lyre in her hand, and I think as I examine it, "I was good-looking once like that young man, but my unpractised verse was full of infirmity, my Muse old as it were; and now I am old and rheumatic, and nothing to look at, but my Muse is young".'[2] This account of psychological antinomies, as in Blake's 'The Mental Traveller' and *A Vision*, dooms the poet to perpetual quest, unrequited desire. But its most damaging consequence, as the anguished speaker of 'The Tower' knows, is that the Muse, a *belle dame sans merci*, may turn termagant and mock her helpless lover. Because the imagination works through concrete sensuous embodiment, not 'abstract things', it constantly exposes the particulars of human form, however debilitated. In 'Sailing to Byzantium' (1926, but placed before 'The Tower'), Yeats evaded this dilemma by creating a realm where the imagination, encased in 'gold enamelling', could dwell immune from the tortured self-consciousness of decrepitude yet still freely sing the temporal world. 'The Tower' rejects that solution as cowardly, meretricious and sterile. The choice is not between an art which accepts the body and an art which ignores it, but between an art which accepts the body and no art at all:

> . . .
> It seems that I must bid the Muse go pack,
> Choose Plato and Plotinus for a friend
> Until imagination, ear and eye,
> Can be content with argument and deal
> In abstract things; or be derided by
> A sort of battered kettle at the heel. [I]

These alternatives, spat out with such colloquial, sardonic bitterness,[3] both require enormous sacrifice. To break off the treacherous affair with the Muse is to conquer death by making nature 'but a spume that plays / Upon a ghostly paradigm of things' ['Among School Children']; yet this perverse alchemy insists that he surrender what he has barely salvaged from 'Meditations . . .', his vocation and identity. Conversely, if he affirms the imagination he must endure humiliation, self-contempt in the world of matter. The *tertium quid* of the conclusion, the imagination's capacity to make death palatable, is not yet visible on the poem's horizon.

The quandary shows Yeats's purpose: 'The Tower', taking sight of all personal follies wrought in the history of the Rising, the Black and Tans, and the civil war, is Yeats's most self-demanding revaluation of the imagination. The temptation to alter the tower's ancestry – from '*Il Penseroso's* Platonist', the questing poet, to the Plato of the *Ion* and *Republic* – renders the traditional philosophical debate in terms of the territorial myth. Despite his exuberant, Wordsworthian sense that the 'fantastical' imagination (I) both perceives and half creates its universe, the speaker seriously entertains Plato's charge that imagination, imitating an imitation, distorts truth. If imagination produces only illusion, why pursue its lures? 'Nineteen Hundred . . .' and 'Meditations . . .' have caustic comments on its falsehoods:

> . . .
> O what fine thought we had because we thought
> That the worst rogues and rascals had died out.
>
> A man in his own secret meditation
> Is lost amid the labyrinth that he has made
> In art or politics;
> . . . ['Nineteen Hundred . . .', I ii; III ii]
>
> Mere dreams, mere dreams! . . .
>
> We had fed the heart on fantasies,
> The heart's grown brutal from the fare;
> . . . ['Meditations . . .', I ii; VI iv]

After that last condemnation, 'fantastical' is a risky praise of imagination's virtue. If the speaker in section II of 'The Tower' sometimes appears to grant Plato everything, his torrential outburst is also a defiant defense of imagination's splendor, climaxing in the firm declaration of faith (III). Between these two extremes, puzzlement: Was it liquor *or* poetry which maddened Mary Hynes's brawling lovers (II iv)? Was Hanrahan drunk *or* sober when, crazed, he sought Mary Lavelle's ghost (II vi–viii)?[4] The strained ambivalence, the wildly rocking vacillations between wry wit and desperation signify his persistent questioning: is the imagination worth affirming?

Failure to perceive the pressing reality of this debate will obscure the poem's structure.[5] In contrast to 'Meditations . . .' (VII), the speaker neither flees experience nor suffers uncontrolled vision. He deliberately ascends to the tower-top, a place of energetic defiance ('battlements' against the battering 'kettle' of age), and organises his mortal world. With the panoramic perspective his promontory offers,[6] he stares upon a landscape whose psychic legacy he will compel to yield him guidance (II i). Craving some community with whom to share his isolate pain, he will ask, when his historical imagination has provided 'Images and memories' with new bodies,

> Did all old men and women, rich and poor,
> Who trod upon these rocks or passed this door,
> Whether in public or in secret rage
> As I do now against old age?
> . . . [II xi]

But the structural complexity of section II is that, as in the opening portraits of 'In Memory of Major Robert Gregory', the spectres serve a thematic function quite different from what the speaker initially purposes. The summonings focus not on the 'absurdity' of 'Decrepit age' (as section I and the question of section II xi might suggest),[7] but on the nature of the imagination. The specifically aesthetic concerns of section I cannot be repressed; each episode becomes a miniature version of the problem of fantasy. The second, more crucial question;

> Does the imagination dwell the most
> Upon a woman won or woman lost?
> . . . [II xiii]

is one which the speaker initially has no intention of asking: evolving subconsciously and spontaneously from the meditation itself, it constitutes a structural refutation of abstract 'argument'.

The spectres reveal a world where imagination and fact are perpetually confounded, sunlight outshone by the moon. Thus, the metaphorical language of Mrs French, a type of the poet, sparks victimisation (II ii): 'I wish the fellow's ears were cut off! that might quiet him'[8] Unlike Salome, whom she distantly resembles, she does not intend her wish fulfilled; but the sly, devoted 'serving-man' imaginatively interprets her outburst literally. The speaker's wry, understated tone contains this explosive anecdote with fine dramatic tension yet leaves his response obscure. As the arch ironies show, he delights in the outrageous admixture of passion and courtesy, the intrusion of grotesque, barbaric comedy upon late eighteenth-century Anglo-Irish ceremony. But, ominously, he is not only spectator but vicarious actor in his literary memory: as a poet, unable to control the consequences of his language, he too must 'make men mad' (II v). Beyond that nagging ethical concern, he senses an affinity with Mrs French's victim. What if *he* lost his 'ears' – the metaphorical ears by which the poet perceives and half creates? Obliquely, 'deafness' links the double threats of decrepitude and waning imaginative power.

The mythic plot of this anecdote is reiterated in the Raftery and Hanrahan episodes (II iii–v; II vi–viii). Its basic form describes the magic and madness of art: the poet, sitting at a table where liquor is served, creates a poem or metaphor so captivating that its hearers, their 'wits astray', confuse aesthetic illusion with reality; they quest after the subject of the poem; disaster, however comically treated, follows. The superimposition of narratives demonstrates the homogeneous experience of aristocrat, peasant and poet which the tower's inhabitant inherits by reviving. What holds his attention, as he explores a legend of poetic fame all but carved on the stones of Thoor Ballylee, is Raftery's vision of the peasant Mary Hynes, as mythical as Homer's of Helen: an emblem of unobtainable beauty and sexual fulfilment. The poet's song, living beyond his death, binds the community in a frenzy which is also the tower's foreboding legacy. Mary Hynes, because she exists only in the imaginative illusion created by blind poets, must always lure her lovers in vain pursuit: 'one was drowned in the great bog of Cloone'. Like Hanrahan possessed by the 'horrible splendour of desire' (II vi), they must return tormented to a deathly world whose 'prosaic light of day' can no longer illumine. This is why the speaker, despite his gauged comic detachment, suddenly speculates on 'the tragedy' and affirms an archetype indigenous to Western culture, local history and private biography alike: 'And Helen has all *living* hearts betrayed'. Implicitly, he names himself a victim, and not simply Maud's. The lover's sexual anguish mirrors the poet's desire for his Muse: he may envisage but not possess her. Like Coleridge's mariner, the speaker now knows the dark suffering his vocation entails. Tormented by his Muse, he must, whether he seeks catharsis or displaced revenge, create images which inflict his anguish upon others. The passionate cry –

> . . .
> O may the moon and sunlight seem
> One inextricable beam,
> For if I triumph I must make men mad. [II v]

– voices the harrowing plea that poetry be other than it is.[9]

Thus, amalgamating sadistic pride and hideous self-loathing, the speaker proclaims his creation of Hanrahan, acknowledges his self-compensatory cruelty. The Hanrahan episode, gleaned from the speaker's past, not from history or public legend, is possibly Yeats's most complicated allusion anywhere. In the *Stories of Red Hanrahan* (1897), Yeats had saddled Hanrahan with his passion for Maud [Gonne] and projected that turmoil upon the territory around Thoor Ballylee. Announcing his proprietary role in elaborating the tower's mythology by alluding to those tales, the speaker simultaneously recovers an earlier phase in his consciousness, the 'barren passion' which memory of the stories enables him to examine from the dual perspectives of youth and age. But he seemingly cannot recall much of what he has written (II viii). What does his apparent lapse of memory mean?

In an episode which encompasses autobiography and present drama, ancient myth and allegory of the daemonic intricacies of the imagination, the speaker takes all parts at once. Despite his tirade against ageing, his focus is not Hanrahan's 'curse on his own head because it withers grey',[10] but the re-enactment of his own unrequited passion. As the *Stories* indicate, a ghostly trickster from the faery Sidhe of Celtic mythology hypnotises Hanrahan from his earthly love of Mary Lavelle and sends him off in dizzy pursuit of an immortal beauty he scarcely knows exists. Bewitching fact into phantom, the trickster is a poet; his 'juggleries' are indistinguishable from the present (and past) machinations of the self-mocking, self-recognising speaker. The interfusion is clear:

> And I myself created Hanrahan
> And drove him drunk or sober through the dawn
> From somewhere in the neighbouring cottages.
> Caught by an old man's juggleries
> He stumbled, tumbled, fumbled to and fro
> . . . [II vi]

Hanrahan is essentially victimised by his own imagination, symbolised by the poet-trickster figure; in the *Stories* Hanrahan confuses him with 'his own shadow'. Hanrahan, 'the learned man and the great song-maker', makes a poem 'in praise of Venus and of Mary Lavelle',[11] modelled on Raftery's vision of Mary Hynes as Helen. The poem, seductive, tempts him to make his life imitate his art. As he mistakes his poem for reality, an uncontrollable passion compels him to seek – not Mary Lavelle, but the metaphor he has made for her – Venus. His quest derives from the Grail legend. If, when he enters the 'shining house' of the Otherworld,[12] he can ask the proper questions about the Grail symbols, he will win the love of Echtge – the spiritual form of Mary Lavelle. In learning the mystery, he will gain the self-completing understanding of Pleasure, Knowledge, Courage and Power, redeem himself from death, and inhabit – not merely 'dream' – 'Translunar Paradise' (III). But Echtge's supreme loveliness paradoxically terrifies Hanrahan the poet into muteness. The vision breaks; he awakes into mortality and soon ages into madness. Failure to complete the quest haunts him until death.

This whole adventure underlies the tremendous crisis which explodes when the speaker dramatically truncates his narrative:

> . . .
> Hanrahan rose in frenzy there
> And followed up those baying creatures towards –
> O towards I have forgotten what – enough!
> I must recall a man . . .
> . . .
> [II vii–viii]

This is too impassioned, the 'enough!' too desperately willed, the excursus too deliberate for anyone to believe that the speaker has really forgotten the goal of Hanrahan's quest.[13] He knows, but *will not* remember beyond the journey's beginning, as if full verbal expression could itself entail some terrible consequence. By repressing Hanrahan's confrontation with Echtge and his subsequent derangement, the speaker hopes to dissociate himself from Hanrahan's fate. He shrinks from vicariously reliving his own anguished, 'horrible splendour of desire' for Maud, recoils from renewed knowledge of failure. In this intricate symbiosis between creator and creation, what Hanrahan does or thinks commits the speaker to virtually identical behavior. The creator, now nearly his creation's slave, can wrest his freedom from a doom which appals him only by denying that the main substance of Hanrahan's quest – and his own – ever occurred.

The denial is a crucial rejection of the imagination's odyssey toward beauty and wisdom. Without quite choosing 'Plato and Plotinus for a friend', he turns from 'a great labyrinth' (II xiii) to the more tangible landscape of the tower, grasping the ignoble but honest consolation that his disaster hardly matches the unending calamity of its mid-nineteenth-century tenant:

> . . .
> I must recall a man that neither love
> Nor music nor an enemy's clipped ear
> Could, he was so harried, cheer;
> . . . [II viii]

Despite its bleakness, the memory subtly counterbalances the negative interpretation of the imagination. The 'master of this house', though he *became* 'fabulous', lacked the delight in fable, aesthetic distance, which would have eased his misery;[14] his true bankruptcy was imaginative. The notion that the imagination can 'cheer', heal as well as maim, is the speaker's first positive judgement on art since his praise of Raftery's song (II iii); his vacillation, following so suddenly his dissociation from Hanrahan's quest, measures a new detachment from his trepidations. Behind it lies the faith of 'Lapis Lazuli': the imagination, for all its horrors, can also transfigure raw suffering into aesthetic shape and thus permit a transcendental gaiety.

Rejecting a life untouched by art, the speaker returns to his Anglo-Norman heritage (II ix): resilient earth-bound warriors whose clanking ascent of the 'narrow stairs' warns him that, in pacing 'upon the battlements' (the metaphorical extension of their movements), he has symbolically committed himself to mortal struggle. Even more cautionary, in a poem which values so highly the conscious power to summon spirits, are the 'men-at-arms'

> . . .
> Whose images, in the Great Memory stored,
> Come with loud cry and panting breast
> To break upon a sleeper's rest
> While their great wooden dice beat on the board. [II ix]

As in 'Meditations . . .' (VII), these spirits come uncalled. The dead, not done with life, intrude into the unconscious mind; their imaginations mingle with those of the living.[15] To 'choose' Plato and Plotinus is a metaphysical and psychological impossibility; to exclude the Muse, an indulgence in pernicious fiction. In that unspoken recognition of the independence of the imagination the speaker will ultimately discover his freedom.

To the tower the speaker now summons directly the spectres he has meditated into being (II x). The postponed question (II xi), coming in tense fury, is painfully rhetorical. The cumulative *genius* of his territory condemns him not only to imagination's thraldom but to a bitter ageing. Imperiously, yet with sympathy for the spectres he has forced to relive their rage, he releases all but Hanrahan, his own image.

The spontaneously generated, climactic questioning of Hanrahan (II vii–xiii) is an excruciatingly transparent self-judgement. Unlike Hanrahan at the end of the Grail quest, the speaker is not mute in confronting his own purgatorial 'shadow':

> Does the imagination dwell the most
> Upon a woman won or woman lost?
> . . .
> [II xiii]

The question *is* the answer. Through it the speaker 'remembers' what he had 'forgotten', accepts his own experience: the 'woman lost', Maud, Hanrahan's quest for Echtge. The courageous act of remembrance commits him, irrevocably, to imaginative quest, however dreaded. But the risks of *not* questing are as dangerous: the energetic lechery of Hanrahan's old age is but a surrogate activity designed to assuage the violent remorse of his failure;[16] the pain of unfulfilled desire, as the warriors' 'loud cry' implies (II ix), does not end with death. Thus, the self-castigating speaker attacks his double:

> . . . admit you turned aside
> From a great labyrinth out of pride,
> Cowardice, some silly over-subtle thought
> Or anything called conscience once;
> . . .
> [II xiii]

By way of displaced accusation the speaker encompasses not only his guilt about Maud, but, with stunning critical insight, his withdrawal from imaginative quest in section I: the Hamlet-like vacillations, the cowardice masking as compliance with natural law, the vain fear of decrepitude, the casuistic belief that imagination could be satisfied with 'abstract things'. In this ruthless stripping away of masks, the speaker breaks loose from his haunting 'near-identity with Hanrahan',[17] frees himself to prevail where Hanrahan failed. As in 'Little Gidding' (III), 'This is the use of memory: / For liberation'. The speaker thus becomes Theseus, seeking to liberate himself, the trapped Daedalus of 'Nineteen Hundred . . .', the creator of the *Stories* caught in his own artifice. The labyrinth through which he must wander, armed with nothing but imagination, is the symbolic body of the Muse. Passionate pursuit of the Muse and battle against death's tyranny have become one: 'only an aching heart / *Conceives* a changeless work of art' ('Meditations . . .', III). The metaphor of mystical sexual union, as in the 'Crazy Jane' sequence, here reconciles the realms of body and imagination. But the quest's conclusion remains ambiguous: the conflation of the Grail legend with the Theseus myth makes plain that the figure at the center may be either 'a woman, the most beautiful the world ever saw',[18] or the chthonic, devouring minotaur.

Having accepted mortality, the speaker accomplishes by design the surrender which time will require:

> It is time that I wrote my will;
> I choose upstanding men
> That climb the streams until
> The fountain leap, and at dawn
> Drop their cast at the side
> Of dripping stone; . . .
> . . . [III i]

Imagery and diction from section I emphasise his decision: he 'chooses' not 'Plato and Plotinus' but 'upstanding men' who will continue the quest he began in 'boyhood'. His shrewd pun on 'upstanding' saves this powerful naming of heirs from sentimentality – and compactly defines his visionary men: they are 'upright' physically, as well as morally and intellectually; they neither drown 'in the great bog of Cloone' (II iv) nor, like Hanrahan, stumble on 'broken knees' (II vi).[19] Mr Bloom has questioned the fishing imagery as being 'inappropriate if not silly',[20] but its symbolic value is plain from the allusions to 'The Song of Wandering Aengus' (1893), 'The Fisherman' (1914), and the Grail legend, as well as from the link between fishing and apocalyptic vision (I). The fishermen are Yeats's aristocrats: indomitably searching for beauty and perfection, intent upon 'contact with the soil', skilled in *sprezzatura* – the effortless flick of the wrist. Yeats, having learned in 'Meditations . . .' that the 'abounding glittering jet' cannot truly 'leap' amidst artificed gardens, has moved it to a lonelier, less accessible terrain. His speaker does not say 'until *they see* the fountain leap'; the omission, together with the subjunctive mood, makes the landscape visionary. The fountain is the internal joy which the climbing, the quest itself causes. These seekers alone are fit to receive the speaker's pride.

> . . .
> The pride of people that were
> Bound neither to Cause nor to State,
> Neither to slaves that were spat on,
> Nor to the tyrants that spat,
> The people of Burke and of Grattan
> That gave, though free to refuse –
> Pride, . . .
> . . . [III i]

All this departs radically from the preceding sections. Expansive joy replaces a morbid fascination with victims. From possessing nothing but a 'caricature' (I), the trick of 'mocking Muses' (II x), he now knows himself the 'rich inheritor' of an autonomous aristocratic culture whose values he can transmit without the fear of corrosion evident in 'Meditations . . .' (IV). The confidence, matched by no other 'tower' or Coole Park poem, reflects more than the liberation from Hanrahan. While vacillating between Plato and the Muse, he gradually recognises the cultural synthesis his territory embodies; his awareness confers new strength. What had been a dramatic background for the debate now becomes foreground. Mrs French, Raftery, the Anglo-Normans and the rest – studied as examples of the imagination's intricacy, *not* as symbols of the imagination in a particular historical epoch – now epitomise 'that one Irish century that escaped from darkness and confusion'. Many critics, confounding Yeats with his speaker, have seen the speaker consciously reconstructing his eighteenth-century world; but the poem does not support the interpretation. The speaker inhabits an Anglo-Irish landscape only after he accidentally makes it; its identity is not fully known until he utters the triumphant, collectivising epithet, 'the *people* of Burke and of Grattan'. Typically, Yeats chose to define his territory not by presenting conclusions but by dramatising a revelation.

Through the revelation Yeats countered the debacle of 'Meditations . . .', with its frank admission of modern Anglo-Irish enervation, and buttressed his mythology by revising his poetic approach to the eighteenth century. 'Meditations . . .' judges Augustan and

Georgian greatness partly by its consequences: barren inheritors sapped by its genius. In 'The Tower' that standard vanishes: the speaker celebrates the genesis of his tradition for its own sake. Yeats also discarded his concern with the radiant creative *moment* which, like the 'symbolic rose', dies as it flowers: the speaker can thus dwell unrestrained upon the imaginative richness of an extended period more completely fleshed out in panorama than any other in Yeats's poetry. And because contemporary history does not darken his mind, he feels no compulsion to assert the present 'stamina', social and political, of the Anglo-Irish tradition. Although his language recalls the Divorce Speech, his meaning differs. Instead of claiming present class-power by association ('We *are* the people of Burke . . .'), 'The Tower' specifically turns its back on modern Anglo-Ireland and extols 'people that *were* / *Bound* neither to Cause nor to State'.[21] Less parochial than the speech, the poem dispenses with political and religious warfares. It suffices both Yeats and his speaker that they have internalised their eighteenth-century heritage, brought that world in procession before the tower, and implicitly pronounced the West of Ireland the place of its most characteristic – and last – expression.

Nor is the speaker's cultural synthesis exclusively Anglo-Irish. Its epic spectrum includes the tower's Anglo-Norman founders, Protestants, Catholics, pagans, aristocrats and peasants alike. The history encapsulated extends explicitly back to the fourteenth century and implicitly back to Homer. It is Ireland 'Before that ruin' (II ix) of O'Connell's cheap, demagogic nineteenth century, and Western culture before

> Locke sank into a swoon;
> The Garden died;
> God took the spinny-jenny
> Out of his side. ['Fragments', I]

Yeats, in his introduction to *The Words Upon the Window-pane*, sought from the Anglo-Irish eighteenth century 'an image of the modern mind's discovery of itself'[22] to oppose that mechanistic catastrophe; but the conceptual design of 'The Tower' differs. The speaker, like Yeats in his earlier understanding of the Renaissance, finds in Burke and Grattan not something new but the florescence of the old: their 'written tradition . . . has been established' on the customary, imaginative, oral culture of the countryside;[23] their self-possessed dedication to liberty, their magnanimity bred of Roman and Renaissance decorum are the grave public counterparts to its flamboyant and spontaneous independence.

This legacy the speaker has received directly from his ancestors. The word 'Pride' (III, line 14) is *either* apposite to 'my pride' (line 7) *or* the direct object of the verb 'gave' (line 13). The marvelous syntactic ambiguity embodies his deep Burkean faith in cultural continuity. His understanding is not merely intellectual; he has been given his 'pride' personally, in the course of the meditation, by 'the people of Burke and of Grattan' – who have reached out from history to name him heir, as he in turn chooses 'upstanding men'. This pride is not the arrogance of a powerful minority but the exuberant sense of creative activity in history. It has the purity of natural fruition and the disinterest of courtesy. It is described in similies whose very cleanness of diction radiates, in perfectly blended fusion, amplitude and sanctity:

> . . .
> Pride, like that of the morn,
> When the headlong light is loose,
> Or that of the fabulous horn,
> Or that of the sudden shower
> When all streams are dry,
> Or that of the hour
> When the swan must fix his eye
> Upon a fading gleam,
> Float out upon a long
> Last reach of glittering stream
> And there sing his last song.
> . . .
> [III i]

This vibrant, sensuous chiaroscuro, imitating the organic cycle of the entire poetic artifice, culminates in the swan's artless artistry. The speaker becomes what he beholds: a selfless creator, knowing death imminent, in love with the productions of time, singing. At the poem's end he will seek to emulate the serenity he images: the swan no longer leaps 'into the desolate heaven' ('Nineteen Hundred . . .', III iii).

Anyone privileged to perform this poem must pause, as the speaker certainly does, before beginning afresh. Exhilaration and elegy, tragic joy, subside momentarily into a delicate object-less reverie. The dramatic recovery, thus accentuated, follows:

. . .
And I declare my faith:
I mock Plotinus' thought
And cry in Plato's teeth,
Death and life were not
Till man made up the whole,
Made lock, stock and barrel
Out of his bitter soul,
Aye, sun and moon and star, all,
And further add to that
That, being dead, we rise,
Dream and so create
Translunar Paradise.
[III i]
. . .

The passage resonates with full humanism. As the speaker chants his spiritual regeneration, the capacious and ever-generating human mind replaces God as the organising center of experience. Matter is real; yet its particularities are real in that they are symbolic emanations of human passion and psychology, as Yeats thought Berkeley (despite his orthodoxy) had discovered. Only the human imagination, independent, even wayward, can transmute these material reflections of dreams into the 'Mirror-resembling dream' of art and thus confer Edenic release from 'Dull sublunary lovers' love' – even if the art it creates, 'makes up', is an emblem of its own violence, a rifle. The fall into matter and time is not only necessary but fortunate; as Stevens has it, 'Death is the mother of beauty' ('Sunday Morning').

The rhapsodic affirmation ebbs in tranquil reconciliation to mortality. For the first time since section II, the speaker focusses on the tower, his own 'proud stones' (III i) that will outlast his death:

As at the loophole there
The daws chatter and scream,
And drop twigs layer upon layer.
When they have mounted up,
The mother bird will rest
On their hollow top,
And so warm her wild nest. [III ii]

The movement from anxiety to serenity and the construction of a natural house (as in 'To a Wealthy Man . . .') mirror the speaker's own evolution, harmonising it with cyclical regeneration in nature.

The construction counterbalances both the bitter awareness of 'ruin' (II i; ix) and the swan's death; an earthly answer to the cry for transcendental sweetness in 'Meditations . . .' (VI), it symbolically rebuilds the 'broken stone' battlements in 'Meditations . . .' (VII i). The imagery of ascent, fused by pun with the fishermen's quest ('Climbing the *mount*ain-side'; 'When they have *mount*ed up'), produces a cluster of values nearly Jonsonian: imaginative excellence, consummate physical control, architectural wholeness.

These concrete physical images remind the speaker of his waning stamina. Nostalgic envy tinges his last, almost involuntary bequest to 'young upstanding men'. The metrical weakness of 'I leave both faith and pride' and the slack word 'leave' make the regret unmistakable. For an instant, as self-pity tempts him, he wavers in his new faith that imagination may triumph over death; the exasperated turbulence of section I nearly erupts afresh. The vacillation, like the *pianissimo* preceding a Beethoven *finale*, intensifies the flat resolve to master bitter experience:

> Now shall I make my soul,
> Compelling it to study
> In a learned school
> . . . [III iv]

This is no appeal to 'sages standing in God's holy fire' nor an attempt to cast off 'bodily form' ('Sailing to Byzantium', III–IV) but a hard testing of his rhetorical claim: 'Death and life were not / Till man made up the whole.' His intellect remains too muscular to succumb to Plato and Plotinus. The schoolmaster is his autonomous imagination, teaching natural passion to obey; the 'learned school', his mortal world;[24] the end of education, the transmutation of death's slow agony into aesthetic beauty. The gruff irony in 'a learned school', acknowledging the difficulty of disciplining the recalcitrant heart to disinterested vision, slyly debunks philosophy's vaunted superiority by dressing the Muse in academic garb. If the phrase misses the lightness of the 'grammar school of courtesies', it is because the stakes are higher, not because the intent of fundamentally revising the self has changed.

The packed, appropriately entropic subordinate clause which completes the speaker's self-command is one of Yeats's finest bravura performances. One by one the speaker summons the disasters of old age – and then neutralises them all with a placidity which scarcely seems possible. That he even magnifies his impending ruin, seeks the most difficult confrontation – '*wreck* of the body', '*Slow* decay', '*Testy* delirium', the death 'Of *every* brilliant eye' – makes the imagination's triumph all the more spectacular. If this victory appears meretricious, compare the exactly reversed relation between fact and metaphor in 'Easter 1916':

> . . .
> What is it but nightfall?
> No, no, not night but death.
> . . .

The final metaphors in 'The Tower' are not escapist euphemisms[25] but mirroring emblems permeated by the sensation of oncoming death. As aesthetic beauty transfigures experience, fact and metaphor mingle inextricably – without distortion, without engendering madness. What the speaker sees from the tower – 'the day's declining beam' (II i), 'the clouds of the sky / When the horizon fades' (III iv) – are indistinguishable from the 'fading gleam' on which 'the swan must fix his eye' (III i); the swan's 'last song' (III i), the 'sleepy cry' (III iv) of the 'mother bird' (III ii) and the poem's end are the same. The entire landscape, for all the speaker's visionary perception, is but reality observed, the spiritualised world of the tower accurately delineated. Such observation, like the self-transcending gaiety in 'Lapis Lazuli', comes from the courteous discipline to become spectator of oneself. This saving capacity to conceive experience as aesthetic drama is precisely what the 'ancient bankrupt master' – and the speaker remembering Hanrahan – lacked. It is also the death of selfhood from which Hanrahan turned aside and the darkness which the speaker now accepts: 'detachment / From self and from things and from persons', as Eliot has it.[26] Finally, within time, time collapses: the speaker's goal of creating the soul's future peace is what he achieves now. Having gathered history into the present world of the tower, he thus completes the process of eternising that mutable landscape by fusing the language of prophecy with that of perception. For a moment of tragic exaltation, he realises the dream of 'A Tower on the Appenines': the poet is 'not, as we say of many a one, speaking in metaphor, but as this were Delphi or Eleusis'.[27] He sings 'Of what is past, or passing, or to come', and they are the same.

SOURCE: extract from the chapter, 'An Acre of Stony Ground', in *Yeats: Coole Park and Ballylee* (Baltimore, Md., 1974), pp. 184–200.

NOTES

[Reorganised and renumbered from the original – Ed.]

1. *The Letters of W. B. Yeats*, ed. Allan Wade (London, 1954), p. 675. Yeats went on to add, in a mood similar to that which closes *Reveries*: 'I alone have no crisis.' The poems seek to show otherwise.

2. *Autobiographies* (London, 1955), p. 541.

3. Cf. Daniel Albright, *The Myth Against Myth: A Study of Yeats's Imagination in Old Age* (London, 1972), p. 10: 'This descent into abstraction is surely a last resort for a poet, especially for a poet with Yeats's intense hatred of abstraction; but it is all treated with good humour, almost too gently to be the gallows humour of old age.'

4. Cf. Sarah Youngblood, 'A Reading of *The Tower*', in *Twentieth Century Literature*, 5 (1959), pp. 77–8. Youngblood, speaking of the 'drunken admirers who are betrayed by their excited imaginations', obscures the question. Cf. also Albright, op. cit., pp. 15–16.

5. Cf. Donald Torchiana, *W. B. Yeats and Georgian Ireland* (Evanston, Ill., 1966), p. 305: the speaker is '*pretending* to abandon poetry' for philosophy (italics mine). See Albright, op. cit., p. 13.

6. Youngblood, op. cit., pp. 78–9, argues that the tower (as a physical emblem) has little prominence in this poem because it is a 'phallic symbol *manqué*'. Quite apart from that distressingly mixed metaphor, it seems plain that the real reason for Yeats's lack of direct attention to Thoor Ballylee is that he was concerned with its function, not its nature.

7. Cf. Albright, op. cit., p. 12: 'By summoning the images of the old, Yeats is summoning his own rage against old age'. Harold Bloom – *Yeats* (London, 1970), p. 350 – apparently thinks that the speaker intends both questions from the very beginning. Thomas Whitaker – *Swan and Shadow* (Chapel Hill, N.C., 1964) – thinks that the 'question' [II i] leads only to II xi.

8. Sir Jonah Barrington, *Sketches of His Own Times*, 3rd edn. (London, 1871), I, p. 17. He cites the episode as proof of 'the devotion of servants in those days to their masters'.

9. Cf. Albright, op. cit., p. 18.

10. *Mythologies* (London, 1959), p. 243.

11. Ibid., pp. 219, 216, 215.

12. Ibid., p. 220.

13. Youngblood – op. cit. (note 4 above), p. 76 – has reached the same conclusions about the psychological implications of the language.

14. Cf. Whitaker – op. cit. (note 7 above), p. 195 – who argues that the 'ancient bankrupt master' is 'parallel to the speaker himself, save that he has

"finished his dog's day" '. More important is the speaker's gradual self-differentiation from this unimaginative creature who is beyond 'cheer'.

15. See *A Vision* (London, 1962), pp. 221, 228–9, 233–4.

16. See *Mythologies*, p. 239.

17. Bloom, op. cit. (note 7 above), p. 351.

18. *Mythologies*, p. 220.

19. See also the 'half-mounted man' [II x]. Torchiana, op. cit., p. 306, n. 42, citing Jonah Barrington – *Recollections of Jonah Barrington* (Dublin, n.d.), p. 90 – restricts the meaning of 'half-mounted' to a designation for the lowest category of gentry; but Yeats was doubtless wittily aware of other and more visually dramatic implications in the phrase.

20. Bloom, op. cit., p. 351.

21. Both Torchiana (op. cit., p. 308) and Whitaker (op. cit., p. 198) assume that the prose – *Senate Speeches of W. B. Yeats*, ed. Donald Pearce (London, 1961), p. 99 – and the poetry carry the same meaning.

22. *Explorations* (London, 1962), p. 345.

23. *Essays and Introductions* (London, 1961), p. 6.

24. Whitaker – op. cit., p. 202 – observes that 'The speaker approaches Keats's view that the world is the "vale of soul-making", a "School" in which each soul learns its "Identity" '; cf. *The Letters of John Keats*, ed. Hyder Edward Rollins (Cambridge, Mass., 1958), II, p. 102 (21 April 1819). Torchiana (op. cit., p. 310), however, believes that the speaker capitulates to philosophy.

25. Bloom, op. cit., p. 352.

26. 'Little Gidding', III, in *Four Quartets*.

27. *Essays*, p. 291. Whitaker (op. cit., p. 202) writes that 'as the metaphors suggest, with them ["evil and loss"] fades all that is temporal'. But the content of the metaphors seems ultimately to contribute less to this fading of time than Yeats's method of spinning out his subordinate clause to such lengths that, by the end, the crucial conjunction denoting future time ('Till') has been forgotten.

Thomas R. Whitaker On 'Meditations in Time of Civil War' (1964)

. . . The dialogue between self and shadows – whether antiselves or projections of the self – produced in 'Meditations in Time of Civil War' a rich orchestration of personal and historical conflicts. The poem is a complex act of creation and self-judgement in the realm of the spiritualised soil.

'Surely . . .' – the dialogue enters with that stress on the very first word, as the speaker yearningly considers 'Ancestral Houses'. Already the opening sentence contains the seeds of its own negation:

> Surely among a rich man's flowering lawns,
> Amid the rustle of his planted hills,
> Life overflows without ambitious pains;
> . . .

Gradually the image of the fountain emerges, establishing the correspondence of spirit and soil which underlies the entire poem. But the pale abstractness of the setting, in which the fountain alone 'rains down life', already calls into question the reality of that social ideal. The retort is deserved: 'Mere dreams, mere dreams!' But a surprising counterassertion follows:

> . . . Yet Homer had not sung
> Had he not found it certain beyond dreams
> That out of life's own self-delight had sprung
> The abounding glittering jet; . . .
> . . .

It is the intuition of a radical self-sufficiency and vitality, which has been too hastily projected into the inadequate landscape of ancestral houses. The allusion to Homer suggests the reason for the inadequacy: sweetness must come from strength. Life cannot merely overflow 'without ambitious pains'; the 'abounding glittering jet' results from a pent-up force that can surmount obstacles. The dream must be revised: it is precisely the ambitious pains of violent and bitter men that

> . . . might rear in stone
> The sweetness that all longed for night and day,
> The gentleness none there had ever known;
> . . .

Instead of an effortless fountain, a monumental synthesis of opposites: but though 'in stone', such a synthesis is momentary, a historical climax which bears the seeds of its own destruction. The eighteenth-century elegance, mimed in the verse itself, renders ambitious pains unnecessary and dries up the fountain:

> . . .
> O what if levelled lawns and gravelled ways
> Where slippered Contemplation finds his ease
> And Childhood a delight for every sense,
> But take our greatness with our violence?

Where then may the speaker himself seek the transfiguration of the fallen world? He turns from the world dreamed of to the world possessed, from 'Ancestral Houses' to 'My House'. At the time he was writing this sequence, 1921–22, Yeats was relating the 'sense of possession' he had felt in Sligo to his concept of 'Unity of Being':

> All that moves us is related to our possible Unity; we lose interest in the abstract and concrete alike, only when we have said, 'My fire', and so distinguished it from 'the fire' and 'a fire', does the fire seem bright. Every emotion begins to be related, as musical notes are related, to every other.[1]

In the 'My House' section we see a measure of historical continuity, but also strength and even violence:

> An ancient bridge, and a more ancient tower,
> A farmhouse that is sheltered by its wall,
> An acre of stony ground,
> Where the symbolic rose can break in flower,
> Old ragged elms, old thorns innumerable,
> The sound of the rain or sound
> Of every wind that blows;
> . . .

Isaiah had prophesied the spiritualisation of a soil very like this stony ground: 'The wilderness and the solitary place shall be glad for them; and the desert shall rejoice, and blossom as the rose.' Blake had envisioned in such a place the marriage of Heaven and Hell:

> Roses are planted where thorns grow,
> And on the barren heath
> Sing the honey bees.[2]

But in the harsh Yeatsian landscape even the symbolic rose must *break* in flower.

Here the speaker does not inherit the glory of the rich; he re-enacts the founding of a house:

> Two men have founded here. A man-at-arms
> Gathered a score of horse and spent his days
> In this tumultuous spot,

Where through long wars and sudden night alarms
His dwindling score and he seemed castaways
Forgetting and forgot;
And I, that after me
My bodily heirs may find,
To exalt a lonely mind,
Befitting emblems of adversity.

The isolated modern poet's need to forge his own tradition may itself be a condition of great achievement: his spiritual inheritance is that of adversity, with its attendant opportunities. Yet the comparison of founders ominously reduces the man-at-arms to the speaker's own proud and introverted isolation. Such was not the condition of those violent, bitter men who could rear in stone the sweetness and gentleness that all had longed for. In a wilderness where art is divorced from power and communion, the symbolic rose threatens to be more dream than reality.

That lurking conflict is already evident in the first stanza of 'My House'. This is a poem of interior landscapes, one in which 'familiar woods and rivers . . . fade into symbol'. The speaker might say with Wordsworth,

. . . bodily eyes
Were utterly forgotten, and what I saw
Appeared like something in myself, a dream,
A prospect in the mind . . .

– or feel with Coleridge that the object of Nature is 'the dim awaking of a forgotten or hidden truth of my inner nature.'[3] Hence, as we move from 'Old ragged elms, old thorns innumerable,' to

. . .
The stilted water-hen
Crossing stream again
Scared by the splashing of a dozen cows;
. . .

we should suspect an ironic self-image, as yet unexplored. The second stanza takes up that stilted isolation, presenting as another spiritual ancestor Milton's Platonist, atop his winding stair, in his 'chamber arched with stone', withdrawn from the crude traffic of the world:

. . .
Benighted travellers
From markets and from fairs
Have seen his midnight candle glimmering.

The ironic parallels are as yet but implicit; the speaker has not allowed himself to examine his proud isolation in full daylight.

Asking why such blindness is possible, we note a further implication in the Platonist who, the speaker imagines,

> . . . toiled on
> In some like chamber, shadowing forth
> How the daemonic rage
> Imagined everything.
> . . .

Both he and his spiritual heir, though lonely creators of emblems, castaways from the world of markets and fairs, are yet at home in a lighted chamber, communing with the world soul, while others are 'benighted'. But they do not commune with the 'holy calm' that overspread Wordsworth's soul and caused him to see the landscape as a prospect in the mind. The demiurgic power as this speaker experiences it is a 'daemonic rage', the transcendental corollary of his own bitter violence and of the 'long wars and sudden night alarms' that isolate him as they once isolated the first founder in this spot. Again the poem's complex theme modulates from reassuring unity to division and fragmentation. But the conflicts in 'My House' are submerged, apparent only because the speaker is shadowing forth more complete emblems of his own condition than he yet admits.

He turns now, in 'My Table, to another possession: the table whereon he shadows forth that daemonic rage. Into his world of adversity, isolation, and cyclical change comes 'Sato's gift, a changeless sword', placed by pen and paper

> . . .
> That it may moralise
> My days out of their aimlessness.
> . . .

But for a poet aware of the virtues of change as well as its dangers, that is a vexing symbol:

> . . . In Sato's house,
> Curved like new moon, moon-luminous,
> It lay five hundred years.
> Yet if no change appears
> No moon; only an aching heart
> Conceives a changeless work of art.
> . . .

Though a world of tortured change needs an image of the changeless, does not that image itself imply a fallacious ideal, a static culture, empty and unproductive?[4] No, the speaker surmounts his objection by imagining in the East an unchanging tradition maintained by centuries of mental alertness, inspired by transcendental longings:

> . . .
> Soul's beauty being most adored,
> Men and their business took
> The soul's unchanging look;
> For the most rich inheritor,
> Knowing that none could pass Heaven's door
> That loved inferior art,
> Had such an aching heart
> That he, although a country's talk
> For silken clothes and stately walk,
> Had waking wits; it seemed
> Juno's peacock screamed.

There, in contrast to the milieu of 'Ancestral Houses', the grandson was no 'mouse', the 'inherited glory of the rich' was not an empty shell, the peacock did not merely stray 'with delicate feet upon old terraces' while Juno was ignored by the 'garden deities'.

But is that peacock scream, that apocalyptic annunciation,[5] more than another illusion? Whether dream or past reality – and it is slightly distanced by the ironic diction of this section – it can now do no more than stimulate this speaker's aching heart. Is that not function enough?

An ambiguous answer emerges in the next section, 'My Descendants'. Returning to the cyclical world of the West, to the lunar inheritance which for better or worse he must enjoy and transmit, the speaker presents himself as one who 'must nourish dreams' – but is he obligated or condemned to do so? And are they unsubstantial fantasies or symbolic roses, evasion or transfiguration of life?

> Having inherited a vigorous mind
> From my old fathers, I must nourish dreams
> And leave a woman and a man behind
> As vigorous of mind, and yet it seems
> Life scarce can cast a fragrance on the wind,
> Scarce spread a glory to the morning beams,
> But the torn petals strew the garden plot;
> And there's but common greenness after that.

But if his descendants should lose that ambiguous flower, he would, enraged, hasten the very cyclical destruction that haunts him:

> . . .
> May this laborious stair and this stark tower
> Become a roofless ruin that the owl
> May build in the cracked masonry and cry
> Her desolation to the desolate sky.

No longer dare he hope that his 'bodily heirs' may find, to their advantage, 'Befitting emblems of adversity'. He may be both founder and last inheritor –

> The Primum Mobile that fashioned us
> Has made the very owls in circles move;
> . . .

– and he will therefore take consolation only in the goods of the moment:

> . . .
> And I, that count myself most prosperous,
> Seeing that love and friendship are enough,
> For an old neighbour's friendship chose the house
> And decked and altered it for a girl's love,
> . . .

Though still unable to refrain from adding another phrase which contemplates at least some bare monument to the present –

> . . .
> And know whatever flourish and decline
> These stones remain their monument and mine

– in his minimal optimism he has now abandoned even the immortality of the 'changeless work of art'. Surely here at least the speaker may find the self-sufficiency for which he longs: no mere dream, but the reality of 'life's own self-delight'.

Yet in glimpsing the depths of his isolation, he has begun to reach outward: 'Seeing that love and friendship are enough'. That evocation of a sweetness and gentleness not 'in stone', as in ancestral houses, but memorialised by these 'stones', translates the entire problem to a different plane. The isolation itself called into question, the speaker turns from house and descendants to 'The Road at My Door'.

An affable Irregular,
A heavily-built Falstaffian man,
Comes cracking jokes of civil war
As though to die by gunshot were
The finest play under the sun.

He turns from lunar tragedy to solar comedy, from lofty poetic isolation to the gay cameraderie of a modern man-at-arms – or (in terms of what Yeats called Shakespeare's dominant myth, and was one of his own) from that porcelain vessel, Richard II, saluting his native soil with ostentatious sentiment and telling sad stories of the death of kings, to those vessels of clay, Falstaff and Prince Hal, with their rough humor and affection.[6] Adversity and violence need not imply isolation, nor can the poet dismiss this comedy as trivial:

A brown Lieutenant and his men,
Half dressed in national uniform,
Stand at my door, and I complain
Of the foul weather, hail and rain,
A pear tree broken by the storm.

It is not a symbolic rose that has broken, and the contrast of persons recalls the unacknowledged difference in 'My House' between the introverted speaker and the first founder in that tumultuous spot. By night the Platonist in his tower had seemed romantically superior to the travellers; by day the retiring and complaining poet becomes a half-comic, half-pathetic pastoral foil to the new military hero.[7] He is, in fact, like that 'shadow' noted earlier, the stilted water-hen 'Scared by the splashing of a dozen cows'.

I count those feathered balls of soot
The moor-hen guides upon the stream,
To silence the envy in my thought;
And turn towards my chamber, caught
In the cold snows of a dream.

What dream has been nourished? In this solitary place what narcissus has broken in flower?

The implied answer is developed in 'The Stare's Nest by My Window', and it will lead, in 'I See Phantoms . . .', beyond the humility of perception to a new reconciliation: an ironic acceptance of the poet's vocation.

> The bees build in the crevices
> Of loosening masonry, and there
> The mother birds bring grubs and flies.
> My wall is loosening; honey-bees,
> Come build in the empty house of the stare.

He no longer imagines a sweetness that bitter men might rear in stone, nor does he hope defiantly for the destruction of his tower and for owls to 'build in the cracked masonry'. He now sees that sweetness may reside in the very loss he had feared – the very loosening of his wall. This is an inevitable discovery – or rather, rediscovery, for the breaking of protective walls, the nakedness before the winds of heaven, had long been known to Yeats as a prerequisite of poetic vision. Although the invoked honey bees recall those in Porphyry's cave of the nymphs – souls who are 'eminently just and sober' and who, 'after having performed such things as are acceptable to the gods', will reascend from the world of generation[8] – they also, and perhaps more importantly, recall those which Blake imagined as singing on the barren heath, on the desert that blossoms as the rose. Yeats had once read that prophecy thus: 'Freedom shows beauty like roses, and sweetness like that given by the honey of bees, in the road where morality had only revealed a desert or a heath.'[9] Given Blake's understanding of negative and restrictive morality (a disguise for the impulse to tyrannise, to wall others in or out), the sweetness which comes with the abandonment of such morality is not opposed to that ('both cathartic and preservative'[10]) produced by Porphyry's bees. For the speaker of this poem such sweetness can come only with freedom from his own self-confinement. Though able, in Shelley's symbolic language, to imagine his tower as contrary in meaning to a dark cave,[11] he now sees that the cloistered permanence of his 'chamber arched with stone' is what it always was, the cavern of the mind of which Blake had written: 'For man has closed himself up, till he sees all things thro' narrow chinks of his cavern.'[12] As this speaker states it, now fusing visions of himself and of society:

> We are closed in, and the key is turned
> On our uncertainty; somewhere
> A man is killed, or a house burned,
> Yet no clear fact to be discerned:
> Come build in the empty house of the stare.

He shares Eliot's waste land –

We think of the key, each in his prison
Thinking of the key, each confirms a prison
Only at nightfall, aethereal rumours
Revive for a moment a broken Coriolanus

– and the waste land of Claudel's Coufontaine:

Là-bas on dit qu'il y a eu je sais quoi,
Les villes de bois qui brûlent, une victoire vaguement
gagnée. L'Europe est vide et personne ne parle sur la terre.[13]

But the besieged dynastic house or prison is not, from this speaker's humbled position, the abbey of Coufontaine or even 'some marvellous empty sea-shell'; it is an empty starling's nest.

Not through coincidence or mere rhetorical artifice does he fuse here the isolation and vastation sprung from his own mind and those imposed by violence from without. He has moved from a romantic parallel between poet and man-at-arms to a humiliating acknowledgment of their differences, and now to an agonised perception of their moral identity:

A barricade of stone or of wood;
Some fourteen days of civil war;
Last night they trundled down the road
That dead young soldier in his blood:
Come build in the empty house of the stare.

We had fed the heart on fantasies,
The heart's grown brutal from the fare;
More substance in our enmities
Than in our love; O honey-bees,
Come build in the empty house of the stare.

The poet's barricade of self-sufficiency and his consequent self-brutalisation are, in his introverted realm, equivalent to the nationalist-inspired civil war that rages about him. 'Was not a nation . . . bound together by this interchange among streams or shadows . . . ?' His fantasies that bitterness and violence might bring sweetness, his glorying in adversity, and his rage against his descendants have earned his indictment. But the indictment itself is a partial release from the prison: hence the initial statement, in the first person singular, 'My wall is loosening', leads to community in isolation, 'We are closed in', and then to a perception of shared guilt, a moral identification of self and those beyond all barricades, 'We had fed the heart on fantasies . . .'. In the final cry to the honeybees the arrogant dream of self-sufficiency is transcended; the perception that 'love and friendship are enough' has flowered, purged of its complacency.

The poet can now climb his winding stair, not to a chamber arched with stone, but to the top of a *broken* tower, where he is possessed by a vision ('I See Phantoms . . .'):

> I climb to the tower-top and lean upon broken stone,
> A mist that is like blown snow is sweeping over all,
> Valley, river, and elms, under the light of a moon
> That seems unlike itself, that seems unchangeable,
> A glittering sword out of the east. A puff of wind
> And those white glimmering fragments of the mist sweep by.
> Frenzies bewilder, reveries perturb the mind;
> Monstrous familiar images swim to the mind's eye.

Every 'Space that a Man views around his dwelling-place / Standing on his own roof . . . is his Universe'. But as the animating wind makes clear, this universe is no longer a confining mental chamber. The speaker is naked to the winds of heaven. He leans upon the very ruin of self-sufficiency; sweeping over the landscape are the 'cold snows of a dream' shared by those beyond the broken barricades. Though he sees by a light whose ominously unchangeable source is a bizarre transmutation of his own earlier ideal, 'A glittering sword out of the east', and though the 'monstrous' images that come are also damningly 'familiar', this is no private fantasy but a vision based upon his own complicity in the engulfing horror.

The first group of phantoms objectifies the brutality and hatred he has just recognised:

> 'Vengeance upon the murderers', the cry goes up,
> 'Vengeance for Jacques Molay'. In cloud-pale rags, or in lace,
> The rage-driven, rage-tormented, and rage-hungry troop,
> Trooper belabouring trooper, biting at arm or at face,
> Plunges towards nothing, arms and fingers spreading wide
> For the embrace of nothing; . . .
> . . .

But he is no longer a lofty Platonist, shadowing forth the 'daemonic rage'; he glimpses the abyss within himself:

> . . . and I, my wits astray
> Because of all that senseless tumult, all but cried
> For vengeance on the murderers of Jacques Molay.

The next group, phantoms of the 'heart's fullness', provides an emotional antithesis:

> Their legs long, delicate and slender, aquamarine their eyes,
> Magical unicorns bear ladies on their backs.
> The ladies close their musing eyes. No prophecies,
> Remembered out of Babylonian almanacs,
> Have closed the ladies' eyes, their minds are but a pool
> Where even longing drowns under its own excess;
> Nothing but stillness can remain when hearts are full
> Of their own sweetness, bodies of their loveliness.

But this is not an ethical antithesis: these apparitions are not the invoked honeybees. Here one aspect of the self-sufficiency and self-delight which the speaker first projected into the fountain of 'Ancestral Houses' achieves final definition: not a fountain but a pool, not an abounding jet of life but an eternal stillness of self-contemplation. However beautiful, it is the deathly goal of Narcissus. For the living speaker these ladies and unicorns can image not a solution but one term of a predicament.

Indeed, they are strangely similar to their antitheses, the rage-driven troop: 'even longing drowns under its own excess'. Because the vision has moved from one blindness to another – from the ravenous imperception of Breughel's blindmen careering into the abyss to the closed eyes of Moreau's narcissistic women and unicorns[14] – it can now move easily, through an inversion of details further stressing that affinity, to a harshly empty synthesis:

> The cloud-pale unicorns, the eyes of aquamarine,
> The quivering half-closed eyelids, the rags of cloud or of lace,
> Or eyes that rage has brightened, arms it has made lean,
> Give place to an indifferent multitude, give place
> To brazen hawks. . . .
> . . .

Predatory rage and static self-satisfaction merge in a yet more terrible blindness:

> . . . Nor self-delighting reverie,
> Nor hate of what's to come, nor pity for what's gone,
> Nothing but grip of claw, and the eye's complacency,
> The innumerable clanging wings that have put out the moon.

Such is the consummation the speaker envisions in modern history, such the consummation of his own ethical dialectic. Yet, though inescapably of his time, he is partly freed by the vision itself. He does not fully yield to the rage of the avenging troop, and he cannot now adopt the transcendent narcissism of aquamarine or closed eyes. The poem renders a precarious solution: not the imagined escape from the prison of self through freedom in love, but the open-eyed self-recognition of the half-trapped poet.

> I turn away and shut the door, and on the stair
> Wonder how many times I could have proved my worth
> In something that all others understand or share;
> But O! ambitious heart, had such a proof drawn forth
> A company of friends, a conscience set at ease,
> It had but made us pine the more. . . .

The 'ambitious pains' which vexed him at the beginning of the poem cannot be escaped. The dialogical movement here as throughout the meditation – 'But O! ambitious heart' – renders the speaker's alertness to the continual temptations to self-containment. It renders, therefore, his actual if momentary freedom from such self-containment. Because all images of fulfilment carry their own irony, he must accept the problematic human state, with its attendant guilt and dissatisfaction. And if life cannot in any facile way be self-delighting –

> . . . The abstract joy,
> The half-read wisdom of daemonic images,
> Suffice the ageing man as once the growing boy.

The irony of 'suffice', which has led critics to comment upon Yeats's vacillation between action and contemplation or upon his 'unfortunate' dabbling in the occult, can be fully weighed only in the context of this rich meditation on what may and what may not suffice the heart. That irony implies no dismissal of the poetic task as 'mere dreams'. Nor is the speaker now Shelley's 'visionary prince' priding himself, through romantic irony, on 'mysterious wisdom won by toil' ['The Phases of the Moon']. He is rather the fortunate victim of the 'daemonic images' we have just seen, which are for him the burden of self-knowledge. He no longer strives for the goal of action or that of fantasy – a substitute for action.

. . .
The rhetorician would deceive his neighbours,
The sentimentalist himself; while art
Is but a vision of reality.
. . . ['Ego Dominus Tuus']

The complex irony in that 'but', as in the 'suffice' of this poem, partly answers any objection that 'Meditations in Time of Civil War' does not move to a clear ethical transcendence of the speaker's problem, as glimpsed in 'The Stare's Nest at My Window'. A willed vision of what the honeybees might bring would be factitious; the poet can realise only what he is. The rest may come of its own accord when, through being perceived, the psychic walls begin to crumble. Ribh would say, 'He holds him from desire' – and, indeed, the final section of this poem has rendered just such a 'symbolical revelation received after the suspension of desire' as 'What Magic Drum?' describes. 'Does not all art come', Yeats wrote, 'when a nature, that never ceases to judge itself, exhausts personal emotion in action or desire so completely that something impersonal . . . starts into its place, something which is as unforeseen, as completely organized, even as unique, as the images that pass before the mind between sleeping and waking?'[15] Such are the 'daemonic images' of this last section; such, in a larger sense is the entire poem.

Despite Yeats's frequently quoted remarks about virtue as dramatic, the wearing of a mask,[16] this poem renders his understanding of the fact that attention is the mother of virtue as it is of art. Though the speaker wears various masks of poetic or moral ambition, engages in the deceits of rhetorician and sentimentalist, he closely watches the self that does so. From that watching, that attention, spring both the ethical development of the speaker and the poem itself. For the poem, the 'vision of reality', is of that mask-wearing self, and it is therefore, like the poems of Villon, finally 'without fear or moral ambition' though decidedly ethical in its substance. In 1905, arguing against didactic art, art composed with the intent to persuade, Yeats had said:

If we understand our own minds, and the things that are striving to utter themselves through our minds, we move others, not because we have understood or thought about those others, but because all life has the same root. Coventry Patmore has said, 'The end of art is peace', and the following of art is little different from the following of religion in the intense preoccupation that it demands. Somebody has said, 'God asks nothing of the highest soul except attention'; and so necessary is attention to mastery in any art, that there are moments when we think that nothing else is necessary, and nothing else so difficult.[17]

Yeats clearly understood another of Patmore's statements: 'Attention to realities, rather than the fear of God, is "the beginning of wisdom" . . .' Given the bold prophetic note sounded by his art, we can see that he also might say with Patmore: 'Indeed, it is difficult to say how far an absolute moral courage in acknowledging intuitions may not be of the very nature of genius and whether it might not be described as a sort of interior sanctity which dares to see and confess to itself that it sees, though its vision should place it in a minority of one.'[18]

In 'Meditations in Time of Civil War', as in the apocalyptic romances of the nineties, a partial yielding to the daemonic voice enables the poet to perceive and judge those powers within him which, unconsciously obeyed, would lead and have led to historical catastrophe. But this poem of dramatic experience shows more clearly the complex interior dialogue through which suffering moves toward illumination, as the daemonic is incorporated into the precarious equilibrium of personality – and so transformed. The last sentence of the poem, ironically echoing Wordsworth's 'Ode on the Intimations of Immortality',[19] reinforces this conclusion. Wordsworth had said:

Shades of the prison-house begin to close
    Upon the growing Boy,
But He beholds the light, and whence it flows,
    He sees it in his joy; . . .

And in compensation for the complete loss of that light, Wordsworth had found 'soothing thoughts that spring / Out of human suffering', a 'faith that looks through death', a 'philosophic mind'. But the Yeatsian speaker, aware of the Wordsworthian atrophy so rationalised, ironically affirms in his own life a lack of change, and so points to a more genuinely continuing growth:

. . .   The abstract joy,
The half-read wisdom of daemonic images,
Suffice the ageing man as once the growing boy.

Though his continuing joy is 'abstract', an inevitable limitation arising from his turning inward to the source of daemonic images, the light shining through those images has led him to perceive the existence of his own prison-house, his chamber arched with stone, and to prevent it from closing upon him irrevocably. It has led him also to see that the 'philosophic mind', with *its* 'eye's complacency' is another form of the spiritual atrophy that tempts through every image that asks to be taken as a final truth, another phantom illustrating the multiform blindness which he precariously escapes. Perception must 'suffice', and full perception warns that our wisdom is momentary and but 'half-read'.

The symbolic rose, which here *breaks* in flower so diversely, cannot be forced. It must bloom in the midst of civil war: a unity of being that maintains the abounding jet of life must arise from the perception of disunity. No individual may complacently possess that fountain of life's self-delight. He may know it only through continuing openness, continuing vulnerability. Yeats had recognised as much, in a passage of 1917 which foreshadowed this poem:

> A poet, when he is growing old, will ask himself if he cannot keep his mask and his vision without new bitterness, new disappointment . . . .
>
> Surely, he may think, now that I have found vision and mask I need not suffer any longer. He will buy perhaps some small old house, where, like Ariosto, he can dig his garden, and think that in the return of birds and leaves, or moon and sun, and in the evening flight of the rooks he may discover rhythm and pattern like those in sleep and so never awake out of vision. Then he will remember Wordsworth withering into eighty years, honoured and empty-witted, and climb to some waste room and find, forgotten there by youth, some bitter crust.[20]

And the speaker of 'Meditations in Time of Civil War' had guessed as much, near the beginning of the poem: 'Homer had not sung . . .' . The *Iliad* offers no Goethean assurance of the eternal harmony of existence; indeed, Homer taught Goethe that in our life on earth we have, properly speaking, to enact Hell. The rose, finally, is the meditation itself, the spiritualisation of that tragic soil, the vision of that state. For both the poet and the man, Yeats was discovering, the 'peace' of that vision is the paradoxically active means of transfiguring the wheel of destiny.

SOURCE: extract from ch VIII, 'The Spiritualised Soil', in *Swan and Shadow* (Chapel Hill, N.C., 1964), pp. 171–87.

NOTES

[Reorganised and renumbered from the original – Ed.]

1. *A Vision*, 1st edn (London, 1925), p. 61.

2. *Isaiah*: 35 i; William Blake, *Complete Writings*, ed. Geoffrey Keynes (London, 1957), p. 148.

3. William Wordsworth, *The Prelude*, II 349ff.; Samuel Taylor Coleridge, *Animae Poetae* (1895 edn), p. 115.

4. For an earlier description (1916) of Eastern traditionalism ('the painting of Japan, not having our European moon to churn its wits . . .'), see *Essays and Introductions* (London, 1961), p. 225.

5. Cf. *A Vision*, rev. edn (London, 1962), p. 268.

6. Dated 1901: see *Essays* . . ., pp. 103–9. There, as in this poem, Yeats has an eye for the tragic ironies in both porcelain and clay. A simpler use of the metaphor appeared in *The Countess Cathleen* (1899; 1912): in *Collected Plays*, rev. edn (London, 1952), p. 46.

7. Yeats's use of such a foil comes, of course, from literary tradition as well as from personal experience. He used it more simply for romantic pathos in *The Countess Cathleen*, as Cathleen says of the gardener – *Poems* (London, 1895), p. 98 –

> Pruning time,
> And the slow ripening of his pears and apples,
> For him is a long, heart-moving history.

In *L'Otage* by Paul Claudel (Paris, 1911), p. 14, amidst the breaking of the nations occurs this dialogue:

> Coufontaine: Il était temps de nous mettre à l'abri.
> Je reconnais le vent de mon pays
> Sygne: Quel dommage! Les pommiers etaient si beaux!
> Il ne restera pas un pépin sur l'arbre.

8. Porphyry's cave quotation (1900 essay): see *Essays* . . ., p. 84; and cf. *Selected Works of Porphyry*, trans. Thomas Taylor (London, 1823), p. 185.

9. *The Works of William Blake*, ed. E. J. Ellis and W. B. Yeats, 3 vols (London, 1893): I, p. 61.

10. *Selected Works of Porphyry*, p. 181.

11. Quotation from Shelley (1900 essay): see *Essays* . . ., p. 87.

12. Blake, *Complete Writings*, p. 154.

13. Claudel, *L'Otage*, p. 54.

14. For a more explicit image of the blindmen, see 'A Dialogue of Self and Soul' or 'On a Political Prisoner'. For Yeats's possession of Moreau's 'Women and Unicorns', see *The Letters of W. B. Yeats*, ed. Allan Wade (London, 1954), p. 865.

15. *Autobiographies* (London, 1955), p. 332.

16. Ibid., p. 469.
17. *Plays and Controversies* (London, 1923), p. 161.
18. Coventry Patmore, *Principle in Art, and Religio Poetae*, 1-vol. edn (London, 1913), pp. 244, 290.
19. As Richard Ellmann has suggested, in *The Identity of Yeats*, 2nd edn (London, 1964), p. 223.
20. *Mythologies* (London, 1959), p. 342.

Thomas R. Whitaker On 'Nineteen Hundred and Nineteen' (1964)

. . . Because the title of 'Nineteen Hundred and Nineteen' reminds us of the Black-and-Tan terrorising of the Irish countryside, we know at the outset that the panoramic perspective of the first stanza cannot be objective but must be shaped by the speaker's awareness of his own situation:

> Many ingenious lovely things are gone
> That seemed sheer miracle to the multitude,
> Protected from the circle of the moon
> That pitches common things about. There stood
> Amid the ornamental bronze and stone
> An ancient image made of olive wood –
> And gone are Phidias' famous ivories
> And all the golden grasshoppers and bees.

He points to Phidian Athens with a familiarity of tone born of his own sense of intimacy and even 'possession' – but also with a strange note of deprecation that is not simply aristocratic nonchalance. We see the ideal harmony of Doric and Ionic or European and Asiatic: the strength and solidity of 'bronze and stone' and the brilliance and intricacy of ivory and gold. But the Asiatic qualities of 'ingenious lovely things' are dominant. Bronze and stone are 'ornamental'; 'ivories' hardly suggests the monumental quality of the chryselephantine Zeus or Athene; and the 'golden grasshoppers and bees', yet more delicate, provide the climax. The golden honeycomb of Daedalus, according to Pater, symbolises the Asiatic element in the Greek synthesis; the golden grasshoppers, according to Thucydides, are symptomatic of the Athenians' degeneration from Spartan to Ionic qualities, as they laid aside their arms and adopted the luxurious ways of peace.[1] In this speaker's retrospective view, then, Athenian art seems to indicate a self-deceptive and effete ornamental culture. In the second stanza the basis for that departure from the vision of 'Dove or Swan' emerges, as a bitter irony erupts:

> We too had many pretty toys when young:
> A law indifferent to blame or praise,
> To bribe or threat; habits that made old wrong
> Melt down, as it were wax in the sun's rays;
> Public opinion ripening for so long
> We thought it would outlive all future days.
> O what fine thought we had because we thought
> That the worst rogues and rascals had died out.

Something like Thucydides' critique is being sharply directed at modern British culture:

> All teeth were drawn, all ancient tricks unlearned,
> And a great army but a showy thing;
> . . .

– but no genuinely peaceable society had emerged:

> . . .
> What matter that no cannon had been turned
> Into a ploughshare? Parliament and king
> Thought that unless a little powder burned
> The trumpeters might burst with trumpeting
> And yet it lack all glory; and perchance
> The guardsmen's drowsy chargers would not prance.

The taste for military display suggests that violence had merely gone underground, had hidden in the deeper recesses of the self. But now the fragile and the frivolous have been swept away, and with them the facile and self-deceptive dreams of wisdom and beauty. The drawn teeth have been sown again; the seemingly drowsy psychic forces lurking below the consciousness have erupted:

> Now days are dragon-ridden, the nightmare
> Rides upon sleep: a drunken soldiery
> Can leave the mother, murdered at her door,
> To crawl in her own blood, and go scot-free;

> The night can sweat with terror as before
> We pieced our thoughts into philosophy,
> And planned to bring the world under a rule,
> Who are but weasels fighting in a hole.

With that last line, the uglier subliminal forces have been admitted even within the speaker and his fellows. The sinister shadow – 'that dark portion of the mind which is like the other side of the moon' and which has prepared for 'anarchic violence'[2] – has become dominant: 'the nightmare / Rides upon sleep'. The speaker is aware through direct experience of the destructive riding or treading of that *mara* (whether horse, fate, Lamia, or terrible mother) which, as vehicle of the erupting adverse unconscious forces, may assume social as well as individual form.[3]

The speaker of 'The Gyres' will be able to cry, 'What matter though numb nightmare ride on top . . .?' This earlier speaker, though finding no such clear 'tragic joy', takes at least a step toward that exultation known when all falls in ruin:

> He who can read the signs nor sink unmanned
> Into the half-deceit of some intoxicant
> From shallow wits; who knows no work can stand,
> Whether health, wealth or peace of mind were spent
> On master-work of intellect or hand,
> No honour leave its mighty monument,
> Has but one comfort left: all triumph would
> But break upon his ghostly solitude.

Here, as later in 'Meditations in Time of Civil War' and 'Coole Park and Ballylee, 1931', the word 'break' has a strange richness, suggesting both temporal loss and a partial transcendence of that loss. But how firm is that 'ghostly solitude'? Is it a citadel upon which the waves of triumph would beat ineffectually, upon which the sword of triumph would be shattered – or a more fragile sanctuary which would be easily disturbed by triumph? Instead of answering such questions, the speaker immediately doubts the adequacy of his enigmatic comfort and retreats to despair:

> But is there any comfort to be found?
> Man is in love and loves what vanishes,
> What more is there to say? . . .
> . . .

But even that attempt at laconic acceptance does not quite succeed: there *is* more to say. The voice of a bitter disillusionment must add, pointing to an Athens that now carries the significance of modern Ireland as well:

> . . . That country round
> None dared admit, if such a thought were his,
> Incendiary or bigot could be found
> To burn that stump on the Acropolis,
> Or break in bits the famous ivories
> Or traffic in the grasshoppers or bees.

The worst having been faced if not accepted, the speaker turns in Part II to a richer image than 'the circle of the moon' to render the movement of history. For a moment he rises above the dramatic situation into the realm of panoramic vision alone:

> When Loie Fuller's Chinese dancers enwound
> A shining web, a floating ribbon of cloth,
> It seemed that a dragon of air
> Had fallen among the dancers, had whirled them round
> Or hurried them off on its own furious path;
> So the Platonic Year
> Whirls out new right and wrong,
> Whirls in the old instead;
> All men are dancers and their tread
> Goes to the barbarous clangour of a gong.

When historical flux is seen as artistic form, then, as in 'Dove or Swan', change may be accepted and fate may be creatively danced. But though this speaker entertains such a possibility, for him the sense of coercion by the whirling dragon is still dominant. And in the last line his vision of the human dance lapses easily into an image of gong-tormented life.

The 'dragon of air' becomes, in Part III, the wind of night and of winter. But after the brief contemplation *sub specie aeternitatis*, the speaker has a quiet detachment. Comfort is again in sight; he offers, in effect, a definition of 'ghostly solitude',

> Some moralist or mythological poet
> Compares the solitary soul to a swan;
> I am satisfied with that,
> Satisfied if a troubled mirror show it,
> Before that brief gleam of its life be gone,

An image of its state;
The wings half spread for flight,
The breast thrust out in pride
Whether to play, or to ride
Those winds that clamour of approaching night.

In the world of stormy flux the dialogue with the 'troubled mirror' of history may at least bring self-knowledge, an image of the soul's 'state'. Turning on the ambiguity of that word, the stanza evokes now a condition of nobility, the easy yet defiant stateliness of the swan's 'play' and its rising to meet and 'ride' the opposing winds. No longer 'ridden' by dragon or nightmare, the soul uses adversity to further its own flight. As hinted earlier ('He who can read the signs nor sink unmanned . . .'), adversity may bring greater vitality than do the 'ingenious lovely things' of a supposedly ideal era. The speaker is now holding down *hysterica passio* at sword's point. Triumph would but 'break' upon his solitude both because it is relatively weaker and because it would calm the winds which aid the soul's flight. But, as 'To a Friend Whose Work Has Come to Nothing' warns, this 'harder thing / Than Triumph' is 'of all things known / . . . most difficult'. Because of that difficulty, in the next two stanzas the 'ghostly solitude' is progressively redefined and finally overwhelmed.

A man in his own secret meditation
Is lost amid the labyrinth that he has made
In art or politics;
Some Platonist affirms that in the station
Where we should cast off body and trade
The ancient habit sticks,
And that if our works could
But vanish with our breath
That were a lucky death,
For triumph can but mar our solitude.

The solitary soul is not solitary enough. Like Milton's fallen angels, it is 'in wandering mazes lost', its hell the Blakean Satanic labyrinth of this life. Even death may not dissipate those self-created complexities to which it mistakenly clings, those ironically triumphant triumphs which now 'can but mar' (no longer 'break upon') its solitude. The sense of present self-sufficiency is waning. In a similar situation an earlier Yeatsian speaker could imagine a dreamy leap from the Satanic 'nets' into a 'grey twilight' where 'God stands winding His lonely horn' ['Into the Twilight']. But here:

> The swan has leaped into the desolate heaven:
> That image can bring wildness, bring a rage
> To end all things, to end
> What my laborious life imagined, even
> The half-imagined, the half-written page;
> . . .

The swan is riding the winds of the storm, but its heaven is desolate. This is not detachment or even solitary triumph but that converse of clinging which masks the continuing impulse to cling: a destructive rage born of frustration.

Hence, though the image suggests that terrible yet ecstatic hour in 'The Phases of the Moon' when 'all is fed with light and heaven is bare', or that moment when Forgael can cry, 'I plunge in the abyss',[4] the mood remains close to that of the owl in 'Meditations in Time of Civil War', who will cry her 'desolation to the desolate sky'. The speaker exhibits what Rachel Bespaloff has seen in Achilles, a Dionysian 'passion for destruction growing out of a hatred for the destructibility of all things'.[5] Instead of an acceptance of suffering and an attendant joyous freedom, the speaker knows a desire for annihilation, for the Buddhistic negation of the will which Nietzsche considered the most dangerous temptation for the Dionysian man.[6] Hence this very stanza relapses into the self-mockery that has colored the entire poem:

> . . .
> O but we dreamed to mend
> Whatever mischief seemed
> To afflict mankind, but now
> That winds of winter blow
> Learn that we were crack-pated when we dreamed.

The attempt at transcendence a failure, the poem subsides in Parts IV and V into the exhaustion of that mood. The speaker develops the implications of the earlier perception – from which he had turned away in desiring to contemplate a nobler image of his 'state' – that he and his fellows are like 'weasels fighting in a hole': they themselves 'Shriek with pleasure' if they show the 'weasel's twist, the weasel's tooth'. Like Petrie, who had mocked the learned 'child who could not understand the winter' of the historical cycle,[7] he mocks the great, the wise ('They never saw how seasons run'), and the good; but he concludes by reducing himself to a status lower than that of the incendiary and bigot who 'traffic in the grasshoppers or bees':

Mock mockers after that
That would not lift a hand maybe
To help good, wise, or great
To bar that foul storm out, for we
Traffic in mockery.

The 'troubled mirror' of the historical moment is now showing the soul a mocking, raging, destroying image that cannot be denied. The dancers of history seem no longer mere victims of dragon or barbarous gong but accomplices. Despite its slighter drama, 'Nineteen Hundred and Nineteen' contains an ethical and psychological dialectic very like that of 'Meditations in Time of Civil War': a thrust and counterthrust of assertion and painful recognition that leads toward an understanding of the soul's true state. That is why, personal emotions exhausted, self-complicity in the cultural failure acknowledged, the speaker has the impersonal vision of Part VI. Again 'a nature, that never ceases to judge itself, exhausts personal emotion in action or desire so completely that something impersonal . . . starts into its place, something which is as unforeseen, as completely organized, even as unique, as the images that pass before the mind between sleeping and waking . . .'[8]

Dragons, nightmare, soldiery, and dancers are caught up in a visionary coda:

Violence upon the roads: violence of horses;
Some few have handsome riders, are garlanded
On delicate sensitive ear or tossing mane,
But wearied running round and round in their courses
All break and vanish, and evil gathers head:
Herodias' daughters have returned again,
A sudden blast of dusty wind and after
Thunder of feet, tumult of images,
Their purpose in the labyrinth of the wind;
And should some crazy hand dare touch a daughter
All turn with amorous cries, or angry cries,
According to the wind, for all are blind.
. . .

Though these images recall Symons's 'The Dance of the Daughters of Herodias',[9] both literary reference and meaning are richer than that echo implies. Symons's poem itself relies upon a Yeatsian, and European, convention:

Is it the petals falling from the rose?
For in the silence I can hear a sound
Nearer than mine own heart-beat, such a word
As roses murmur, blown by a great wind.
I see a pale and windy multitude
Beaten about the air . . .

That apocalyptic multitude had already been envisioned in Yeats's 'The Hosting of the Sidhe':

. . .
The winds awaken, the leaves whirl round,
Our cheeks are pale, our hair is unbound,
. . .

Like Symons's daughters of Herodias, the Sidhe embody the fatal lure of immortal passion and beauty, present also in the 'great wind' of Yeats's 'The Secret Rose'. Yeats had long known of their millennial connotations: 'Sidhe is also Gaelic for wind . . .', he said in 1899. 'They journey in whirling winds, the winds that were called the dance of the daughters of Herodias in the Middle Ages, Herodias doubtless taking the place of some old goddess.'[10] Yeats was often deliberately vague in his prose notes, and he probably knew then what he did not write until 1934: that Wilde's *Salome* partly derives from Heine's depiction of Herodias in *Atta Troll*, which in turn may derive from 'some Jewish religious legend for it is part of the old ritual of the year'.[11] Directly or indirectly, he might have met this Aradia, Habundia or Diana as described by Jacob Grimm or Charles Leland.[12] In any case she entered his own myth of the tri-form goddess who is mother, mistress and murderess of the solar hero. Now Herodias's daughters return as the frenzy of destructive passion, the collective nightmare, that ever brings the fall of a civilisation. Loie Fuller's dancers (who had presented a Salome dance)[13] become the Sidhe; the dragon of air becomes a dusty wind.

Such images are also prophetic. 'When I think of the moment before revelation', Yeats would write in 'Dove or Swan', 'I think of Salome . . .'[14] And Pater had written of Leonardo's women, in whom Yeats found the lunar beauty of the Sidhe:

Daughters of Herodias, . . . they are not of the Christian family. . . . They are the clairvoyants, through whom, as through delicate instruments, one becomes aware of the subtler forces of nature, and the modes of their action, all that is magnetic in it. . . . Nervous, electric, faint always with some inexplicable faintness, these people seem to be subject to exceptional conditions, to feel powers at work in the common air unfelt by others, to become . . . the receptacle of them, and pass them on to us in a chain of secret influences.[15]

Here the daughters lead to a macabre revelation:

> . . .
> But now wind drops, dust settles; thereupon
> There lurches past, his great eyes without thought
> Under the shadow of stupid straw-pale locks,
> That insolent fiend Robert Artisson
> To whom the love-lorn Lady Kyteler brought
> Bronzed peacock feathers, red combs of her cocks.

The blind life-denying passion of the daughters in this poem finds full expression in the repulsive vacuity of Robert Artisson. It is proper for the revelation to include 'something which is as unforeseen, as completely organised, even as unique' as this fourteenth-century minor devil and his slave of passion. But our initial shock of surprise gives way to a shock of recognition. Aside from his oblique Yeatsian ancestry (the boar without bristles in his malevolent aspect; the 'shape' of the Second Coming, with 'gaze blank and pitiless as the sun, . . . moving its slow thighs'), Artisson was ready to take his place in this poem. Yeats himself had earlier suggested that he might be one of the Sidhe;[16] and Dame Alice Kyteler was virtually a human daughter of Herodias, for she was one of those witches who, according to popular belief, were called together at night by 'a spirit named Herodias'.[17] Her traffic with Artisson renders the human complicity in the barbaric dance of time, the abandonment of independence and dignity as man approaches the nadir of the historical cycle. Even the items of her sacrifice (according to Holinshed, 'nine red cocks and nine peacocks eies')[18] were as though destined to take their place in the poem. The scream of a peacock or the crowing of a cock has often, in Yeats's work, heralded a new cycle or the entrance into eternity. But the speaker of his poem does not hear a living bird's annunciation. He sees the dismembered dead: mute testimony of time's outrage.

In 'Dove or Swan' Yeats would define a civilisation as 'a struggle to keep self-control'. It is 'like some great tragic person, some Niobe who must display an almost superhuman will or the cry will not touch our sympathy. The loss of control over thought comes towards the end;

first a sinking in upon the moral being, then the last surrender, the irrational cry, revelation – the scream of Juno's peacock'.[19] The narrator of 'Rosa Alchemica' similarly envisioned the end of his civilisation and reflected that vision in his own soul. But because his will was weak, and because the dark forces of the abyss were correspondingly weak though decoratively elaborated, his cry barely touched our sympathy. After many more turns of Yeats's winding stair – after much controlled assimilation of those forces from beyond the ego – the speaker of 'Nineteen Hundred and Nineteen' can have a stronger will and clearer perception of himself. Hence his own ethical dialectic, and no external Michael Robartes, can lead him on toward vision. Though far from 'superhuman', he can gaze upon the complex image which the 'troubled mirror' shows him and not sink unmanned into the half-deceit of any consolation. . . .

SOURCE: extract from ch. X, 'Resurrected Gods', in *Swan and Shadow* (Chapel Hill, N.C., 1964), pp. 222–32.

NOTES

[Reorganised and renumbered from the original – Ed.]

1. Walter Pater, *Greek Studies* (London, 1910), p. 193 (cf. also pp. 220, 225, 251); Thucydides, *History of the Peloponnesian War*, I vi.

2. *Plays and Controversies* (London, 1923), pp. *v–vi*.

3. See *The Collected Works of C. G. Jung* (New York, 1953–). v, p. 249ff.

4. *Collected Plays* (London, 1952), p. 152.

5. Bespaloff, *On the Iliad*, trans. Mary McCarthy (New York, 1947), p. 105.

6. Nietzsche, *The Birth of Tragedy*, in *The Complete Works of Friedrich Nietzsche*, ed. Oscar Levy, 18 vols (Edinburgh and London, 1909–24), p. 61.

7. W. M. Flinders Petrie, *The Revolutions of Civilisation* (London, 1911), pp. 4–5.

8. *Autobiographies* (London, 1955), p. 332.

9. A. N. Jeffares, *W. B. Yeats: Man and Poet* (London, 1949), p. 225. Symons's poem dates from 1897; Yeats's 'The Hosting of the Sidhe' was published in 1893, and 'The Secret Rose' in 1896.

10. *The Wind Among the Reeds* (London, 1899), p. 65.

11. *The King of the Great Clock Tower* (New York, 1935), p. 21. Yeats misremembers Heine's description as being of Salome: see *Atta Troll*, XIX.

12. Jacob Grimm, *Deutsche Mythologie*, 4th edn (Berlin, 1876), I, pp. 234–7, 526; II, pp. 735, 778, 882ff.; III, pp. 282, 420. Grimm is also cited by Thomas Wright in Richard de Ledrede, *A Contemporary Narrative of the Proceedings Against Dame Alice Kyteler*, ed. Thomas Wright (London, 1843), p. *iv*. Grimm

assimilates Herodias, Diana and other goddesses. Charles Leland, in *Aradia, or the Gospel of Witches* (London, 1899), pp. 102–3, speaks of the association but questions the derivation from the Herodias of the New Testament.

13. See a report of the dance in a magazine which Yeats read and to which he contributed: G[eorge] N[orman], ' "Electra" and "Salome" ', *The Mask*, I (April 1908), p. 24b. Cf. also Yeats's memory of 'some Herodias of our theatre, dancing seemingly alone in her narrow moving luminous circle': *Autobiographies*, p. 321.

14. *A Vision*, rev. edn (London, 1962), p. 273.

15. Walter Pater, *The Renaissance*, (1873; reissued London, 1910), pp. 115–16.

16. Augusta Gregory, *Visions and Beliefs in the West of Ireland* (London and New York, 1920), I, p. 272.

17. Richard de Ledrede, *A Contemporary Narrative* . . ., p. *iii*. According to Jeffares (op. cit., p. 328), Yeats read of this case in Carrigan's *History of the Diocese of Ossory* and St John D. Seymour's *Irish Witchcraft and Demonology* (Baltimore, Md, 1913); and also (p. 226) read the British Museum MS. which gives an account of the case. It seems probable that he consulted Wright's edition of that MS., which Seymour mentions: *Irish Witchcraft* . . . , p. 25.

18. Raphael Holinshed's *Chronicle of Ireland* (1587), p. 69, cited in Ledrede, *A Contemporary Narrative* . . . , p. 46, and also in Seymour, *Irish Witchcraft* . . . , p. 29.

19. *A Vision*, p. 268.

G. S. Fraser Yeats's Byzantium (1960)

. . . ['Byzantium' (1930)] is a poem about the relationships between life, death and art. Or more strictly it is a poem about what at once attracted and repelled Yeats in life, about what he at once hoped and feared from death, and about what he aspired to in his own art. That, at least, is the main large clue I can give to the poem, though it is a clue that will not mean very much until it has been drastically expanded. There is a higher level than the level I have suggested, or a more abstract one, at which one can also truthfully say that the poem is about the tension in Yeats's mind between the ideas of the One and the Many, the Eternal and the Temporal, the Permanent and the Mutable, Wisdom and Action, considered as polar opposites. But such a generalisation helps even less than my first one until we bring it to bear concretely on the poem. Which, I suggest, let us now proceed to do.

But before we start taking the poem stanza by stanza, note that it is a sequel, using many of the same symbols, to an earlier poem, 'Sailing to Byzantium' [1927]. In that earlier poem, Yeats writes, as he often writes, as a passionate man and a great poet confronting old age and death. The world of sensual delight –

> ... The young
> In one another's arms, birds in the trees
> – Those dying generations – at their song,
> ...

– that world is, he says in the earlier poem, no country for an old man. We should not accept decrepitude passively, but the soul should sing louder for every tatter in its mortal dress. So Yeats has set sail for the holy city of Byzantium and he wants its sages to be the singing-masters of his soul. Byzantium, in this earlier poem, is pretty obviously a symbol of the permanence of art, even after the artist is dead, set against the mutability of life.

And when Yeats says in this earlier poem that he wants, after death, to be transformed into a golden singing bird, singing to the lords and ladies of Byzantium of what is past, or passing, or to come, part of what he means, at a very prosaic level, is simply that after his death he will have a kind of immortality in his poems, which will always appeal to choice spirits through their beautiful workmanship and the time-transcending universality of their themes. I say this is *part* of what he means, because if it were all of what he means, 'Sailing to Byzantium' would simply be a rather precious and fanciful variation on a very trite poetic commonplace. It would be, at the best, an ingenious minor poem. If it is more than that, it is because Yeats has an imaginative apprehension of what his fanciful notion rests on. The great lines in the poem, the lines that morally transform it, are not about mosaics or sages or golden birds: they are these lines:

> ...
> Consume my heart away; sick with desire
> And fastened to a dying animal
> It knows not what it is; ...
> ...

'Sailing to Byzantium' is, in fact, ultimately not a poem about a rather precious fancy, but about the state of mind, a very painful state, from which the false consolation of such a fancy could spring. I don't think, in fact, that the proper final response to 'Sailing to Byzantium' is that Byzantium is the right destination for either Yeats or us; and in fact Yeats's last poems are anything but poems of mere mechanical artifice; they are very much poems of the heart sick with desire and fastened to a dying animal, poems of what, very late, he was to call 'lust and rage'; poems of what he calls, in 'Byzantium' itself, the fury and the mire of human veins. More broadly, I think, it helps in considering 'Sailing to Byzantium' and 'Byzantium' to remember the constant tug, inside Yeats, in two directions: towards the idea of a state of being transcending life, often imagined as a kind of artificial paradise which we create for ourselves, after death, out of the images of the beautiful things we have admired here; and again towards actual physical life at all levels, the level even of 'a blind man battering blind men'.

Byzantium, in the poem before us, gets comparatively little from, and gives comparatively little to, our idea of the historic Byzantium. I don't mean that Yeats gets anything wrong; every detail is right, from the glittering domes to the dolphins which were depicted on mosaic floors – not on walls (which were reserved for human personages) nor on ceilings (which were reserved for divine or supernatural beings). The very puzzling phrase, even, about 'flames begotten of flame' refers at one level, quite prosaically, to the bits of glittering glass used to pin the square marble chips of mosaic together; they glittered like flame, and the glass-blower's flame had created them. But Byzantium in the poem is, of course, mainly a symbol for timeless or persistent order of some sort, set against an outer flux; it stands for something which at once transcends and torments man. It is enough if the Byzantium of the poem gets from the Byzantium of history an air of remoteness, of ancientness, of dignity, an air of being the noble and undecaying centre of something, the Empire sprawling around and prodded at by barbarians, in more or less permanent decay. There is the idea also, perhaps – which modern historians, I believe, are very sceptical about, but which was the accepted idea when Yeats was a young man – of Byzantine civilisation (compared, say, to the raw, changing civilisation of the Franks) as static, mummified, even fossilised.

Yet the Byzantium of the poem, though inherently symbolic, is not merely symbolic; it is presented, it is there, we explore it like a city in a dream. And because it is an explorable complex image Yeats is able to do more than to state the debate between life and art, between the passion of the sick heart fastened to the dying animal and the prestige of the artifice of eternity, in a rather abstract way: I think he *is* rather abstract in the earlier poem, 'Sailing to Byzantium'; but here, in this poem, he gives flesh to the conflict, he acts it out.

Let us take the first stanza now:

> The unpurged images of day recede;
> The Emperor's drunken soldiery are abed;
> Night resonance recedes, night-walkers' song
> After great cathedral gong;
> A starlit or a moonlit dome disdains
> All that man is,
> All mere complexities,
> The fury and the mire of human veins.

The first line is very powerful and concentrated. It plants one of the key words of the poem, the word 'image', and it introduces one of the key notions of the poem, the notion of the poet's task as that of the simplification, the purification, of experience. The word 'image' is a very familiar word in Yeats's poetry and prose. He thought of images –

> These masterful images because complete
> Grew in pure mind, but out of what began?
> . . .
>
> ['The Circus Animals' Desertion']

– as what his poems were made of, were elemented out of: he meant something like an archetypal symbol, a symbol pregnant with large undefined significance. But if we contrast 'the unpurged images' here with 'grew in pure mind' in the later poem, and if we remember how the later poem goes on –

> . . .
> Grew in pure mind, but out of what began?
> A mound of refuse or the sweepings of a street,
> . . .

– we get the force of 'unpurged' here, I think.

Poetry starts, to put it that way, with rather violent or messy emotions; high tragedy, according to Aristotle, purges us of these. The soldiers and the night-walkers – I take the night-walkers to be prostitutes – now in bed, or disappearing, are part of this violence or messiness. They also stand for life, for the action that springs from anger or lust, as contrasted with the wisdom that is a property of the dead. Fury, later in the stanza, goes with the soldiery, I think, and mire with the night-walking whores. The great dome of St Sophia despises them, but we are to think of the great dome of the sky too, and 'starlit' should remind us of Yeats's preoccupation with astrology –

> . . .
> As the outrageous stars incline
> By opposition, square, and trine,
> . . .

– and 'moonlit' should remind us of the phases of the moon in *A Vision*: the moon presiding over birth and over the changes of human history, the goddess of mutability. What disdains (or distains) all that man is, is, as it were, a set of springs of fate larger and simpler than himself. His destiny is plotted out ahead, his free will is an illusion. As for the emphasis on 'complexities', remember the powerful use of the opposite word in 'Vacillation' [section VII]:

> *The Soul.* Seek out reality, leave things that seem.
> *The Heart.* What, be a singer born and lack a theme?
> *The Soul.* Isaiah's coal, what more can man desire?
> *The Heart.* Struck dumb in the simplicity of fire!
> . . .

The fire is important, for what happens later on in 'Byzantium'. It is the highest element, coping the universe, higher than air, purer than air, infinitely less gross than earth and water:

> . . .
> *The Soul.* Look on that fire. Salvation walks within.
> *The Heart.* What theme had Homer but original sin?

So the great dome of St Sophia looks down, one might say, on man and his doings like God or the Fates: the symbol of a transcendental, anti-humanistic culture or religion, essentially hostile to one aspect, at least, of Yeats's own genius. The three key words, repeated throughout the poem, 'mire', 'fury / furies', 'complexities / complexity' – and the other key word 'blood' that comes in the third stanza – are not words with a merely negative weighting. They are the Many against the One, the Immanent against the Transcendental. How positively some of them might be weighted we can see in 'Crazy Jane Talks with the Bishop':

'. . .
But Love has pitched his mansion in
The place of excrement;
For nothing can be sole, or whole
That has not been rent.'

Or in 'Her Vision in the Wood':

. . .
Or but to find if withered vein ran blood,
I tore my body that its wine might cover
Whatever could recall the lip of lover.

. . .
That thing all blood and mire, that beast-torn wrack,
Half turned and fixed a glazing eye on mine,
. . .
That they had brought no fabulous symbol there
But my heart's victim and its torturer.

Now, the second stanza of 'Byzantium':

Before me floats an image, man or shade,
Shade more than man, more image than a shade;
For Hades' bobbin bound in mummy-cloth
May unwind the winding path;
A mouth that has no moisture and no breath
Breathless mouths may summon;
I hail the superhuman;
I call it death-in-life and life-in-death.

The plain grammar of that is that before Yeats there floats an image that might be the image of a man or a ghost; but the fact that it is there, that it is a present poetic image, is more certain than whether it is an image of something shadowy or substantial. 'Shade' has, I think, a full range from the sense 'ghost' to our memory of the shadows on Plato's cave; the real man may be the soul, the invisible man, and the physical man, that we call real, may be the cast shadow. The image, the projection of this ambiguity into art, is what we must cling to. The very obscure lines about 'Hades' bobbin bound in mummy-cloth' that 'may unwind the winding path' are a reference, Miss Kathleen Raine tells me, to what occultists call 'the dreaming back'. The winding path is our path forward in life, the successive experiences we wind round us till, when we die, they are wrapped round us like a mummy-cloth; our first task when we die is to unwind them, to live our lives backward, in reflection. 'For wisdom is a property of the dead'; here we act out our rôle and do not understand it; there we understand it retrospectively without being able to alter it. The mouth that has no moisture and no breath may be that of a severed head, as in the Mabinogion – and Friar Bacon's brazen head is a very late distortion of the same old tradition – through which 'the breathless mouths' of departed spirits may speak. The superhuman, as in great tragedy, is the point of intersection between life and death. The last line is an allusion to the cryptic, much-quoted utterance of Heracleitus: they – the spirits, the gods, the supernatural powers, our own real beings on the other side – live our lives and die our deaths.

The next stanza gets to the pivoting subject, which is great works of art:

> Miracle, bird or golden handiwork,
> More miracle than bird or handiwork,
> Planted on the star-lit golden bough,
> Can like the cocks of Hades crow,
> Or, by the moon embittered, scorn aloud
> In glory of changeless metal
> Common bird or petal
> And all complexities of mire or blood.

This is the golden mechanical bird, into which, in 'Sailing to Byzantium', Yeats wanted to be transformed: it is his poems, in which he has his immortality. And the three key words of the first line give us, with marvellous compression, our three prevailing views since classical times of the nature of a work of art. For the Platonist, the golden bird is a 'miracle'; it depends on supernatural inspiration. For the Aristotelian, it is a 'bird'; it is a work of art because it is an imitation of nature. For more prosaic, or less profound, minds it is a 'golden handiwork' – what the critic should attend to is the worth of the material and the care of the craftsman. The word 'miracle' gets Yeats's favouring emphasis here, just as the word 'image' in the previous stanza gets a more favouring emphasis than 'man' or 'shade'. It is not by accident that the cocks of Hades perch on a star-lit golden bough. The stars stand for inexorable fate again; the cocks of Hades are an emblem of Hermes in his rôle of psychopermpos, or conductor of souls to the underworld. Yeats has an early story in which an old man crows like a cock when a woman is dying, the signal for her departure to the other world. And the golden bough is not only a bit of Byzantine decor, but Frazer's and Virgil's golden bough, the magic wand that admits us to the underworld. That is one thing, then, that a great work of art can do: summon and conduct us to the world of spirits. But if the cocks of Hades are embittered by the moon – the moon of Yeats's own system in *A Vision*, the moon of the phases of the moon, the goddess who presides over birth, change and mutability – then what they do is scorn the temporal, mock at the cycle of births. One might think of a writer like Dante for the exploration of the spiritual, the supernatural world; and of a writer like Swift for the scorning of 'common bird or petal'. Yeats is defining two types of sublime art; this apparently fantastic stanza has an iron logic.

Then the penultimate stanza:

> At midnight on the Emperor's pavement flit
> Flames that no faggot feeds, nor steel has lit,
> Nor storm disturbs, flames begotten of flame,
> Where blood-begotten spirits come
> And all complexities of fury leave,
> Dying into a dance,
> An agony of trance,
> An agony of flame that cannot singe a sleeve.

This, as Constantine Trypanis has pointed out to me, is at one level a perfectly literal description of a mosaic floor, with a representation on it of the sea and dolphins. 'Blood-begotten spirits' refers, he thinks, partly to the fact that only animals, like dolphins, not men nor supernatural creatures, would be represented on the floor: it would be irreverent to tread on kings, angels or gods. The flames that no faggot feeds nor steel has lit are the bits of glinting glass – begotten of flame, the glass-blower's flame – that glitter in between the small marble squares of the mosaic. No storm disturbs them, because the sea on the floor is only a represented sea. There is the idea of art as imitation here, and of the real sea, with real uncontrollable dolphins not far away; and of the flux of images as it were held static, and purged, by art. But the rhythm makes the thing say, of course, ever so much more than this. The time is midnight, the dead pregnant moment between two days, the moment when we can expect revelations. Something is revealed to us. What? We can think of fire as the highest element, the clothing of purified spirits: 'Look on that fire, salvation walks within!' We can think of Mr Eliot's refining fire in which you must move in measure, as a dancer.

And then the last great stanza:

> Astraddle on the dolphin's mire and blood,
> Spirit after spirit! The smithies break the flood,
> The golden smithies of the Emperor!
> Marbles of the dancing floor
> Break bitter furies of complexity,
> Those images that yet
> Fresh images beget,
> That dolphin-torn, that gong-tormented sea

Astraddle on the dolphin's mire and blood: the spirits ride, that is to say, the body; and here, I think, we have no neo-Platonic hierarchical mysticism but Plato's own simple and intensely dramatic dualism: the Platonic idea of self-control, the man driving a chariot with two horses, the will, like an athlete, holding in check 'the mob of the senses', the bodily passions. There is something athletic about Plato, something we do not get in the neo-Platonists: a feeling that he who does control the body may safely exult in it. And remembering Arion crowned, and all the stories about dolphins rescuing poets, we get the idea of life in the body as, after all, not something to be abhorred but a necessary stage in the spirit's journeyings. The flood is the great sea of being, the Heracleitan flux, and the smithies who break it, what are they? Partly great artists; partly also what Sacheverell Sitwell once called 'the canons of giant art'. They impose on the flux order, form, significance. The marbles of the dancing floor break bitter furies of complexity. But then there is a change. Literally, for the grammar, the marbles also break

> . . .
> Those images that yet
> Fresh images beget,
> That dolphin-torn, that gong-tormented sea.

But the triumphantly mounting rhythm will not let us take it like that. The effect, as Miss Raine has pointed out to me, is rather like that of Blake's 'Tiger', where images and rhythm similarly work against logic. Blake seems to be making the rather inane remark that it must be a good god who makes lambs and a bad god who makes tigers; in fact, the images and the rhythm make us exult in the splendour of the god who makes tigers. Here similarly we are told that the representation of the flux, on the marble floor, controls the flux. But it is the real flux, with all its terror and fertility, not the represented one, that we are suddenly presented with: it is as if the sea of Marmara was suddenly overflowing the mosaic sea on the marble floor, real dolphins bouncing above the mosaic dolphins. The gong is the great cathedral gong in the first stanza; it is only a real sea, not a marble sea, that its beatings could torment or disturb. The images that can beget fresh images are, once again, the unpurged images, the images of life. We remember where we heard about 'begetting' before, in 'Sailing to Byzantium':

> . . .
> The salmon-falls, the mackerel-crowded seas,
> Fish, flesh, or fowl, commend all summer long
> Whatever is begotten, born, and dies.
> . . .

Let me summarise now what I think Yeats is doing in this poem, or what is happening to him. Yeats was a man of marked antithetical mind: he liked to set things against each other, a man's outward personality, for instance, and his real inner nature; harshness and scorn and the tenderness they may hide; a style of life he admired and the historical necessity he saw destroying it; and so on – but also very much, all the life and the work, life and art. He gets the extraordinary dramatic concentration of his poems from this antithetic play, and he also gets their mode of development; he has only to say something positive to begin, immediately and ironically, to question it: a tender song will have a mocking refrain, and a mocking song will have a tender one. When he is really at his greatest he seems to me, however, to get beyond the antithetic mode to a unitary vision:

> . . .
> O chesnut-tree, great-rooted blossomer,
> Are you the leaf, the blossom or the bole?
> O body swayed to music, O brightening glance,
> How can we know the dancer from the dance?
>
> ['Among School Children']

We are making delicate distinctions. The *expression* there remains antithetical; but the suggestion is that the antithesis has become pointless. Here the antithesis is as forceful as it could be between the marbles of the dancing floor and the images that yet fresh images beget; it is wrought to the highest possible point of dramatic tension. But the stating of an antithesis *with* the utmost possible tension – I owe this observation to my friend, Miss Raine – does in some sense resolve it. This is a great poem; working on it, what has astonished me is how its Dionysian impact is combined with an almost mathematical exactitude in the development of an argument. Not a word does not pull its weight. John Wain once suggested to me that the poem is trickery: 'a stylised reverie' with no real intellectual content. I hope I have made the reader feel that this is not true.

SOURCE: essay, 'Yeats's Byzantium', in *Critical Quarterly*, II, 3 (1960), pp. 254–61.

Frank Kermode On 'Among School Children' and the Byzantium Poems (1957)

. . . I come now, having commented on some of Yeats's other dancers, to the poem in which the Dancer makes her most remarkable appearance. 'Among School Children' is the work of a mind which is itself a system of symbolic correspondences, self-exciting, difficult because the particularities are not shared by the reader – but his interests are not properly in the mind but in the product, which is the sort of poetry that instantly registers itself as of the best. What I have to say of the poem should not be read as an attempt to provide another explication of it, or to provide a psychological contribution to the understanding of the poet. I have . . . a rather narrow interest in its images, and that is what I propose to pursue.

The 'sixty-year-old smiling public man' of the poem is caught in the act of approving, because he has ventured out of his *genre*, of a way of educating children which, as we have seen, is completely inimical to his profoundest convictions. The tone is of self-mockery, gentle and indeed somewhat mincing, with a hint of unambitious irony – 'in the best modern way', we can pick up this note without prior information, but it is at any rate interesting to know that the children are engaged in the wrong labour, the antithesis of the heroic labour of the looking-glass. The old man, because he is old and a *public* man, does not protest, but sees himself as amusingly humiliated, not too seriously betrayed, putting up with the shapelessness and commoness that life has visited upon him. But children of the kind he sees before him remind him of the great image of a lady who was all they could not hope to be, a daughter of imagination, not of memory; a daughter of the swan, the perfect emblem of the soul, and like Leda the sign of an annunciation of paganism and heroic poetry, for which the soul is well-lost. But she too is old; he thinks of her present image: 'Did Quattrocento finger fashion it?' For even in old age she has that quality of the speaking body, the intransigent vision, perhaps, of Mantegna. And he himself had had beauty, though he had spent it in his isolation and intellectual effort, and become shapeless and common, the old scarecrow of the later poems. The fifth stanza develops this theme, the destruction of the body by Adam's curse, which for Yeats is the curse of labour. It is a reworking of some lines from *At The Hawk's Well*, of ten years earlier:

> . . .
> A mother that saw her son
> Doubled over a speckled shin,
> Cross-grained with ninety years,
> Would cry, 'How little worth
> Were all my hopes and fears
> And the hard pain of his birth!'

This old man has lain in wait for fifty years, but he 'is one whom the dancers cheat'; 'wisdom', conclude the singers, 'must lead a bitter life', and he who pursues it prizes the dry stones of a well and the leafless tree above a comfortable door and an old hearth, children and the indolent meadows. This is the plight of the old man in the schoolroom, to be with the scarecrow thinkers and teachers and poets, out of life; the scarecrow is the emblem of such a man, because he is an absurd, rigid diagram of living flesh that would break the heart of the woman who suffered the pang of his birth.

But there are other heartbreakers, though these do not change with time, but 'keep a marble or a bronze repose'. 'Marble and bronze' is a recurrent minor motive in Yeats. It occurs in simple form in 'The Living Beauty' (1919), where there is an antithetical relationship between it and that which is truly 'alive' – alive in the normal sense, and possessing that speaking body which includes the soul.

> I bade, because the wick and oil are spent
> And frozen are the channels of the blood,

> My discontented heart to draw content
> From beauty that is cast out of a mould
> In bronze, or that in dazzling marble appears,
> Appears, but when we have gone is gone again,
> Being more indifferent to our solitude
> Than 'twere an apparition. O heart, we are old;
> The living beauty is for younger men:
> We cannot pay its tribute of wild tears.

These masterly verses have the seeds of much later poetry. The purpose of art, in the life of the poet, is to mitigate isolation by providing the Image which is the daily victory. 'I suffered continual remorse, and only became content when my abstractions had composed themselves into picture and dramatisation . . .' But the relief is impermanent; the poet discovers that 'he has found, after the manner of his kind, / Mere images'. There is a tormenting contrast between the images (signified by the bronze and marble statuettes) and the living beauty. And out of this contrast grows the need for a poetic image which will resemble the living beauty rather than the marble or bronze. No static image will now serve; there must be movement, the different sort of life that a dancer has by comparison with the most perfect object of art. Here we see, in strictly poetic terms, a change comparable to that wrought by Pound in the abandonment of Imagism, and the development of a dynamic image-theory. The Image is to be all movement, yet with a kind of stillness. She lacks separable intellectual content, her meanings, as the intellect receives them, must constantly be changing. She has the impassive, characterless face of Salome, so that there is nothing but the dance, and she and the dance are inconceivable apart, indivisible as body and soul, meaning and form, ought to be. The Dancer, in fact is, in Yeats's favourite expression, 'self-begotten', independent of labour; as such she differs totally from the artist who seeks her. She can exist only in the predestined dancing-place, where, free from Adam's curse, beauty is born of itself, without the labour of childbirth or the labour of art; where art means wholly what it *is*. The tree also means what it is, and its beauty is a function of its whole being, achieved without cost, causing no ugliness in an artist. This is one of the senses of the magnificent concluding stanza:

> Labour is blossoming or dancing where
> The body is not bruised to pleasure soul,
> Nor beauty born out of its own despair,

Nor blear-eyed wisdom out of midnight oil.
O chestnut-tree, great-rooted blossomer,
Are you the leaf, the blossom or the bole?
O body swayed to music, O brightening glance,
How can we know the dancer from the dance?

'A savoir que la danseuse *n'est pas une femme qui danse*, pour ces motifs juxtaposés qu'elle *n'est pas une femme*, mais un métaphore résumant un des aspects élémentaires de notre forme, glaive, coupe, fleur, etc., et *qu'elle ne danse pas*, suggérant, par le prodige de raccourcis ou d'élans, avec une écriture corporelle ce qu'il faudrait des paragraphes en prose dialoguée autant que descriptive, pour exprimer, dans la rédaction: *poème dégagé de tout appareil du scribe*.' This is Mallarmé's accurate prediction of Yeats's poem.[1]

'Among School Children' might well be treated as the central statement of the whole complex position of isolation and the Image. Later there were many fine poems that dealt with the nature of the sacrifice, and of the fugitive victory; like 'Vacillation', which asks the question 'What is joy?' and answers it with an image, of a sort to be achieved only by choosing the way of Homer and shunning salvation; or like the 'Dialogue of Self and Soul', or the simple statements of 'The Choice':

The intellect of man is forced to choose
Perfection of the life, or of the work,
And if it take the second must refuse
A heavenly mansion, raging in the dark.

When all that story's finished, what's the news?
In luck or out the toil has left its mark:
That old perplexity an empty purse,
Or the day's vanity, the night's remorse.

There are poems, too, which give the problem a more specifically religious turn. The paradise in which labour and beauty are one, where beauty is self-begotten and costs nothing, is the artificial paradise of a poet deeply disturbed by the cost in labour. The ambiguities of hatred and love for 'marble and bronze' inform not only those poems in which Yeats praises the active aristocratic life and its courtesies, but also the Byzantium poems, which also celebrate the paradisal end of the dilemma. In this paradise life, all those delighting manifestations of growth and change in which the scarecrow has forfeited his part, give way to a new condition in which marble and bronze are the true life and inhabit a changeless world, beyond time and intellect (become, indeed, the image truly conceived, without human considerations of cost). The artist himself may be imagined, therefore, a changeless thing of beauty, purged of shapelessness and commonness induced by labour, himself a self-begotten and self-delighting marble or bronze. 'It is even possible that being is only possessed completely by the dead'; we return to the ambiguous life or death of the Image. Those who generate and die, perpetually imperfect in their world of becoming, have praise only for that world; the old man has no part in it, praising only the withered tree and the dry well, hoping only for escape into the world of complete being, the world of the self-begotten. 'The artifice of eternity', like 'the body of this death', is a reversible term.

'Sailing to Byzantium' could scarcely be regarded as less than a profoundly considered poem; yet Yeats was willing to accept the criticism of the acute Sturge Moore that the antithesis of the birds of the dying generations and the golden bird was imperfect; and this consideration was one of the causes of the second poem, 'Byzantium'.

> Your 'Sailing to Byzantium' [wrote Moore], magnificent as the first three stanzas are, lets me down in the fourth, as such a goldsmith's bird is as much nature as man's body, especially if it only sings like Homer and Shakespeare of what is past or passing or to come to Lords and Ladies.

Yeats sent him a copy of 'Byzantium' so that he should have an idea of what was needed for the symbolic cover design of his new book (at this time he was going to call it not *The Winding Stair* but *Byzantium*) and added that Moore's criticism was the origin of the new poem – it had shown the poet that 'the idea needed exposition'. Only a little earlier, by the way, Moore had provided Yeats with a copy of Flecker's 'A Queen's Song', which has a certain relevance to 'Byzantium', being a treatment of the topic of living beauty *versus* bronze and marble, or in this instance, gold:

> Had I the power
> To Midas given of old
> To touch a flower
> And leave its petal gold
> I then might touch thy face,
> Delightful boy,
> And leave a metal grace
> A graven joy.

Thus would I slay –
Ah! desperate device! –
The vital day
That trembles in thine eyes,
And let the red lips close
Which sang so well
And drive away the rose
To leave a shell.

We have already seen why Yeats was so interested in Byzantine art; it gave him that sense of an image totally estranged from specifically human considerations (and particularly from discursive intellect) with meaning and form identical, the vessel of the spectator's passion, which led him to develop the Dancer image. These lines of Flecker point also towards that life-in-death, death-in-life, which characterises the perfect being of art. The absolute difference, as of different orders of reality, between the Image and what is, in the usual sense, alive, was the crucial point upon which the first Byzantium poem had, on Moore's view, failed; it was so important to the poet that he did his work again, making the distinction more absolute, seeking some more perfect image to convey the quality, out of nature and life and becoming, of the apotheosized marble and bronze. The bird must absolutely be a bird of artifice; the entire force of the poem for Yeats depended upon this – otherwise he would scarcely have bothered about Moore's characteristic, and of course intelligent, quibble. Professor A. N. Jeffares has shown how full are the opening lines of 'Sailing to Byzantium' of peculiarly powerful suggestions of natural life, the life of generation; the salmon carries obvious suggestions of sexual vigour, and, it might be added, of that achieved physical beauty Yeats so much admired, immense power and utter singleness of purpose, in the business of generating and dying. Of course the golden bird must be the antithesis of this, as well as the heavenly counterpart of old scarecrows. It prophesies, speaks out as the foolish and passionate need not; it uses the language of courtesy in a world where all the nature-enforced discriminations of spirit and body, life and death, being and becoming, are meaningless. 'Marbles of the dancing floor / Break bitter furies of complexity'. And it is this world that Byzantium symbolises. Mr Jeffares says the bird is different in the second poem because 'here it is explicitly contrasted with natural birds, to their disadvantage'. In fact the same contrast is intended in the earlier poem; the new degree of explicitness is what Moore's criticism forced upon the poet. The focus of attention is no longer on the poignancy of the contrast between nature and art in these special senses; nature now becomes 'mere complexities, / The fury and the mire', and the strategy of the poem is, clearly, to establish the immense paradoxical vitality of the dead, more alive than the living; still, but richer in movement than the endless agitation of becoming.

And this is precisely the concept of the dead face and the dancer, the mind moving like a top, which I am calling the central icon of Yeats and of the whole tradition. Byzantium is where this is the normal condition, where all is image and there are no contrasts and no costs, inevitable concomitants of the apparition of absolute being in the sphere of becoming. We can harm the poem by too exclusive an attention to its eschatology, and it is salutary to read it simply as a marvellously contrived emblem of what Yeats took the work of art to be. There is no essential contradiction between the readings. The reconciling force is Imagination, the creator of the symbol by which men 'dream and so create / Translunar Paradise'. Or, to use the completely appropriate language of Blake: 'This world of Imagination is the world of Eternity; it is the divine bosom into which we shall all go after the death of the Vegetated body. This World of Imagination is Infinite & Eternal, whereas the world of Generation, or Vegetation, is Finite & Temporal. . . . The Human Imagination . . . appear'd to Me . . . throwing off the Temporal that the Eternal might be Establish'd. . . . In Eternity one Thing never Changes into another Thing. Each Identity is Eternal.' There is no better gloss on Yeats's poem, a poem impossible outside the tradition of the Romantic Image and its corollary, the doctrine of necessary isolation and suffering in the artist. . . .

SOURCE: extract from ch. 4., 'The Dancer', in *The Romantic Image* (London, 1957), pp. 82–9.

NOTE

1. [Ed.] The passage from Mallarmé reads, translated: 'I mean that the ballerina *is not a girl* dancing; that, considering the juxtaposition of those group motifs, *she is not a girl*, but rather a metaphor which symbolises some elemental aspect of earthly form: sword, cup, flower, etc., and that *she does not dance* but rather, with miraculous lunges and abbreviations, writing with her body, she *suggests* things which the written work could *express* only in several

paragraphs of dialogue or descriptive prose. Her poem is written without the writer's tools.' *Mallarmé: Selected Prose Poems, Essays and Letters*, translated with an introduction by Bradford Cook (Baltimore, Md., 1956), p. 62.

Harold Bloom On 'A Dialogue of Self and Soul' (1970)

. . . The Higher Criticism of Yeats, when it is more fully developed, will have to engage the radical issue of his subjectivity, particularly as it is expressed in his myth of the *antithetical* man. A beginning has been made, by Whitaker and Priscilla Shaw in particular, but the subject is immense and crucial, for in the end Yeats will stand or fall by it.[1] Before he was forty, Yeats had concluded that

> . . . in the end the creative energy of men depends upon their believing that they have, within themselves, something immortal and imperishable, and that all else is but as an image in a looking-glass. So long as that belief is not a formal thing, a man will create out of a joyful energy, seeking little for any external test of an impulse that may be sacred.[2]

This is a pure and beautiful solipsism, with something of the Paterian splendor of Stevens's Hoon (who is himself not quite a solipsist, since he is in the act of *finding*, even if it be only of himself, more truly and more strange). Nothing in the Self's wonderful declaration at the close of 'A Dialogue of Self and Soul' goes beyond re-affirmation of this ecstatic and reductive solipsism, since the source to which every event in action or in thought is followed will turn out to be the self: 'Measure the lot; forgive myself the lot!' We are moved by the reciprocal blessings that follow, and yet we might be a touch uneasy also, for the self happily is blessing the self. Everything is, after all, 'but as an image in a looking glass', and so we but look upon ourselves.

Buber remarks, with too transcendentally bitter a wit, that the spirit withers *gloriously* in the air of monologue. His oxymoron is accurate, but his own emphasis is too much on the withering. Yeats's title might well have been 'Two Monologues of Self and Soul', for in fact where is there dialogue in this glorious poem? That is hardly a fault, as we are dealing with a poem *qua* poem. There are, for me, no faults to be discerned in this poem, for like 'Vacillation' and 'The Man and the Echo' it is a poem of total self-revelation, and Yeats is never stronger than when he is totally exposed.

The Soul takes the lead, despite the necessary priority of the Self in the title, and the triumph of the Self's solitary declaration in the poem's second part. For the poem's genetic impulse belongs to the Soul; Yeats has been very near the gates of death (having just experienced his first severe illness since childhood) and he turns to consider the Last Things in a very different spirit than that of *A Vision*. His moral character or *primary* half summons his dominant personality or *antithetical*, questing half, to a judgement. The 'winding ancient stair' is Dantesque and Blakean, both purgatorial and a Jacob's ladder for a new struggle of naming. The time approaches dark of the moon:

> . . .
> Fix every wandering thought upon
> That quarter where all thought is done:
> Who can distinguish darkness from the soul?

The Soul's difficult question is not in the poem's first published version. There is no answer in the poem, and the Soul expects none. Nor does the Self attempt an answer, but only muses upon a ceremonial sword, as Oisin might have done. If the Self will not regard the Soul, it is because the blade is emblematical not only of love and war, but of the joyful and solipsistic creative energy that reduces all else to an image in a looking-glass. Sato's sword is yet more solipsistic as an emblem:

> . . .   still as it was,
> Still razor-keen, still like a looking-glass
> Unspotted by the centuries;
> . . .

The soul, still anxious for dialogue, rightly sees its antagonist now as the obsessed imagination, and appeals for both imagination and intellect to focus on 'ancestral night', that the purgatorial cycles of death and birth may be ended. There is no reply, as the obsessed Self continues its sustained brooding. This reverie is purposeful, and the questing Self seeks and finds emblems of day to set against the purgatorial tower in order to claim justification for the 'crime' of rebirth. Giving the Self up for lost, the Soul is permitted the blessing of monologue:

> Such fullness in that quarter overflows
> And falls into the basin of the mind
> That man is stricken deaf and dumb and blind
> For intellect no longer knows
> *Is* from the *Ought*, or *Knower* from the *Known* –
> That is to say, ascends to Heaven;
> Only the dead can be forgiven;
> But when I think of that my tongue's a stone.

The Soul is describing a state of being perilously close to Phase I of the Great Wheel. The cost of complete objectivity is everything that makes us human, as we become absorbed by supernatural context. Ascending to Heaven is the same as yielding to 'complete passivity, complete plasticity'. The Soul (and this is the poem's necessary limitation) is a Yeatsian initiate, or at least has read *A Vision* carefully. Only the dead can be forgiven, for only the dead can undergo the complex Yeatsian purgatorial process. The Soul speaks for many readers of *A Vision* in flinching from the process. But the difference is that the Soul yields to the process; its language indeed is not drawn from Phase I but from *A Vision*'s general definition of the Four Faculties, where Creative Mind and Body of Fate are the Knower and the Known, and Will and Mask are the Is and the Ought.[3] The final speech of the Soul in the poem is thus reduced to the voice of anonymous process, and appropriately ends upon the image of a stone.

The most neglected of truths about the 'Dialogue's famous declaration of autonomy by the Self, is that the Self ignores Yeats's account of the laws of process as completely as the Soul accepts them. The poem's largest irony is that the Soul is an esoteric Yeatsian, and the Self a natural man. Where Yeats, in the Epilogue to *A Vision*, insisted: 'No living man can drink from the whole wine', the Self begins by observing: 'A living man is blind and drinks his drop.' Where the Soul insists upon a darkness, from which it cannot even distinguish itself, and worships a plenitude of supernatural influx so full 'that man is stricken deaf and dumb and blind', the Self confesses its blindness but lives in vision, the vision, of self-confrontation and self-forgiveness. What the Self fights free of is everything in Yeats that has mythologised at its expense.

What the Self offers instead is to divest itself of everything except the life it has lived, which it would live again, not in the purgatorial and supernatural way of *A Vision*'s dreamings-back, but naturally, with all the pain of Self necessarily entailed. This is a more openly autobiographical Yeats than the great shaper of the *Autobiographies:*

> . . .
> Endure that toil of growing up;
> The ignominy of boyhood; the distress
> Of boyhood changing into man;
> The unfinished man and his pain
> Brought face to face with his own clumsiness.

Painful enough; more painful is what the next stanza describes, the involuntary acceptance by the finished man of the caricature of himself his enemies have provided. The *Last Poems* has an undistinguished and disgruntled piece called 'Are You Content?'. Like the 'I am content' that so powerfully opens the two final stanzas of the 'Dialogue', this recalls a legend of the days just before Shelley's death. His double comes upon the poet and demands: 'How long do you mean to be content?' Yeats too now confronts his double, his own Soul, and bitterly answers the same question with 'Forever!':

> I am content to live it all again
> And yet again, if it be life to pitch
> Into the frog-spawn of a blind man's ditch,
> A blind man battering blind men;
> . . .

Rhetorically, this is at a successful extreme, even for Yeats. Dialectically, it is a Gnostic rather than a naturalistic statement (though modified by 'if it be life'). Yeats is too shrewd to keep his vision of life's bitterness so general, and pitches us with him 'into that most fecund ditch of all', the self-maiming pride of a defeated Romantic love:

> . . .
> The folly that man does
> Or must suffer, if he woos
> A proud woman not kindred of his soul.

This is part, though only part, of the High Romantic pride of the last stanza, the pride of being 'such as I'. The great original of the injunction to cast out remorse, and so Yeats's direct ancestress here is again the audacious Cyntha of Shelley's *The Revolt of Islam*:

Reproach not thine own soul, but know thyself,
Nor hate another's crime, nor loathe thine own.
It is the dark idolatry of self,
Which, when our thoughts and actions once are gone
Demands that man shall weep, and bleed, and groan;
O vacant expiation! Be at rest. –
The past is Death's, the future is thine own.

Yeats does not take precisely this advice, since for him 'our thoughts and actions once are gone'; and yet return, to be followed to their source in Self. Yeats has his own 'dark idolatry of Self', to replace the Christian variety which he has joined Cyntha in casting out. The sweetness that flows into his breast is very close to the sublime variety the 'eagle look' of Maud Gonne had induced in him ('So great a sweetness flows / I shake from head to foot') and is a kind of triumph of the Self over its own capacity for loss, remembering what is fit for a man and poet of Phase 17, whose Body of Fate is 'loss'. The categories of *A Vision*, which oppressed and captured the Soul, re-enter the Self's realm of the 'Dialogue' only as a reminder of how lonely the Yeatsian ecstasy must be. The blessing given and taken at the close is hardly a sanctification of the commonplace, as it might have been for Wordsworth, but rather a more intense and less humanly admirable late version of the Sublime mode. That does not make it less attractive, or less magnificent as a poem.

SOURCE: extract from *Yeats* (New York and London, 1970), pp. 372–7.

NOTES

[Renumbered from the original – Ed.]

1. Besides Thomas Whitaker, *Swan and Shadow* (Chapel Hill, N.C., 1964), consult the lucid discussion in Priscilla Shaw, *Rilke, Valéry and Yeats: The Domain of Self* (New Brunswick, 1964).
2. *Explorations* (London, 1962), p. 151.
3. *A Vision*, rev. edn. (London, 1962), p. 73.

SELECT BIBLIOGRAPHY

For publication details of books and articles excerpted in this selection – all of which are highly recommended for further reading – see the Source note at the conclusion of each piece. For comments on many of the items below, see the Introduction.

George Bornstein, *Transformations of Romanticism in Yeats, Eliot and Stevens* (Chicago, 1976).

Elizabeth Cullingford, *Yeats, Ireland and Fascism* (London and Basingstoke, 1981).

Denis Donoghue, *Yeats* (London, 1971).

Denis Donoghue and J. R. Mulryne (eds), *An Honoured Guest* (London, 1965).

Richard Ellmann, *Yeats: The Man and the Masks* (London, 1949; 2nd edn, 1961).

Edward Engelberg, *The Vast Design* (Toronto, 1964).

Richard Finneran, 'W. B. Yeats', in *Anglo-Irish Literature: A Review of Research* (New York, 1976).

Ian Fletcher, 'Yeats and Lissadell', in D. E. S. Maxwell and S. B. Bushrui (eds), *W. B. Yeats, 1856–1965* (Ibadan, 1965).

Northrop Frye, 'The Rising of the Moon: A Study of *A Vision*', in Donoghue and Mulryne (eds) – see above.

James Hall and Martin Steinman (eds), *The Permanence of Yeats* (New York, 1950).

G. M. Harper (ed.), *Yeats and the Occult* (London, 1976).

Daniel Hoffman, *Barbarous Knowledge: Myth in the Poetry of Yeats, Graves and Muir* (New York and London, 1967).

Joseph Hone, *W. B. Yeats* (London, 1943; 2nd edn, 1962).

A. N. Jeffares, *W. B. Yeats: Man and Poet* (London, 1949; 2nd edn, 1962).

A. N. Jeffares (ed.), *Yeats: The Critical Heritage* (London, 1977).

Robert Langbaum, *The Mysteries of Identity* (New York and London, 1977).

Giorgio Melchiori, *The Whole Mystery of Art* (London, 1960).

James Olney, *The Rhizome and the Flower* (Berkeley, Cal., 1982).

Jon Stallworthy, *Between the Lines: Yeats's Poetry in the Making* (Oxford, 1963).

Jon Stallworthy (ed.), *Yeats: Last Poems*, 'Casebook' series (London and Basingstoke, 1968).

Donald T. Torchiana, ' "Among School Children" and the Education of the Irish Spirit', in A. N. Jeffares and K. G. W. Cross (eds), *In Excited Reverie* (London, 1965).

Donald T. Torchiana, *W. B. Yeats and Georgian Ireland* (Evanston, Ill., 1966).

LIST OF CONTRIBUTORS

W. H. AUDEN (1907–73): British-born poet, dramatist and critic; Professor of Poetry at Oxford, 1956–61. Committed to Marxism in the thirties, he abandoned left-wing politics after moving to America in 1939. His most important short pieces are to be found in his *Collected Shorter Poems, 1930–1944*, (1966).

R. P. BLACKMUR (1904–65): American poet and critic whose critical works include *Language as Gesture* (1952) and *Form and Value in Modern Poetry* (1957). His collected poetry was published in 1978.

HAROLD BLOOM: American critic, Professor in the Humanities, Yale University. He has written extensively on the English romantic poets, advancing a new theory of poetic influence; his publications include *The Anxiety of Influence* (1973) and *A Map of Misreading* (1975).

CLEANTH BROOKS: American scholar and critic, Gray Professor of Rhetoric Emeritus of Yale University; his books include *The Well Wrought Urn* (1947) and *William Faulkner: The Yoknapatawpha Country* (1963).

T. S. ELIOT (1888–1965): American-born poet, dramatist and critic; he became a British subject in 1927. One of the foremost poets and critics of the twentieth century, author of *The Waste Land* and *Four Quartets* and (in criticism) *After Strange Gods* (1934), *On Poetry and Poets* (1957) and *To Criticise the Critic* (1965).

RICHARD ELLMANN: American scholar and critic, Goldsmiths Professor of English Literature, Oxford, since 1970, and Woodruff Professor, Emory University. His numerous works include the definitive biography of James Joyce (1959; 2nd edn, 1982) and *Yeats: The Man and the Masks* (1949; 2nd edn, 1961).

G. S. FRASER (1915–80): British poet and critic; he taught in the University of Leicester; his literary criticism includes *The Modern Writer and His World* (1957) and *Essays on Twentieth-Century Poetry* (1977), and he edited the Casebook on Keats's *Odes*.

DANIEL HARRIS: American critic and editor, currently affiliated with Rutgers University; his interests include Gerard Manley Hopkins and the modernist dramatic monologue.

T. R. HENN (1901–74): Irish critic and poet; he taught at Cambridge; his publications include the edited edition of Synge's work and *The Bible as Literature* (1970).

HUGH KENNER: American critic, Andrew Mellon Professor in Humanities, Johns Hopkins University; his books include *The Invisible Poet: T. S. Eliot* (1959), *The Pound Era* (1972) and studies of Joyce and Beckett.

FRANK KERMODE: British scholar and critic, King Edward VII Professor of English Literature at Cambridge (1974–82), and Professor of English at Harvard University. His numerous works on Renaissance and modern literature include *Romantic Image* (1957), *The Sense of an Ending* (1967) and *The Genesis of Secrecy* (1979); and he is the editor of the Casebook on *King Lear*.

F. R. LEAVIS (1895–1978): influential British literary critic, founding editor of *Scrutiny*; he taught at Cambridge. His publications include *New Bearings in English Poetry* (1932), *Revaluation* (1936), *The Great Tradition* (1948), *D. H. Lawrence: Novelist* (1955), *English Literature in Our Time and the University* (1969) and *The Living Principle* (1975).

GEORGE ORWELL (1903–50): British novelist and essayist; his most famous works are *Animal Farm* (1945) and *Nineteen Eighty-Four* (1949).

THOMAS PARKINSON: American poet, dramatist and critic; Professor of English, University of California at Berkeley; his publications include the edited correspondence of Hart Crane and Ivor Winters (1978).

DONALD STAUFFER (1902–52): American critic, formerly Professor of English at Princeton University; his publications include *The Art of Biography in the Eighteenth Century* (1941) and *A World of Images* (1949).

C. K. STEAD: New Zealand poet, novelist and critic, Professor of English, University of Auckland; his publications include *The New Poetic: Yeats to Eliot* (1964) and the Casebook on *Measure for Measure*.

ALLEN TATE (1899–1979): American poet, novelist and critic; he taught at several universities and latterly at Minnesota; his critical works include *On the Limits of Poetry* (1948), *The Man of Letters in the Modern World* (1956) and *Essays of Four Decades* (1969). His *Collected Poems* were published in 1977.

THOMAS R. WHITAKER: American critic, Professor of English at Yale University; his publications include *Fields of Play in Modern Drama* (1977).

EDMUND WILSON (1895–1972): American writer; his distinguished and prolific oeuvre includes poems, plays, fiction, criticism and such well-known works as *To the Finland Station* (1940) and *Patriotic Gore* (1962).

YVOR WINTERS (1900–68): American poet and critic, Professor of English at Stanford University, 1948–66. He advocated a return to classical principles and attacked the romantic tradition in *In Defense of Reason* (1947); his other publications include *Maule's Curse: Seven Studies in . . . American Obscurantism* (1938), *The Function of Criticism* (1957), *On Modern Poets* (1959) and *Forms of Discovery* (1967). His *Collected Poetry* was published in 1978.

ACKNOWLEDGEMENTS

The editors and publishers wish to thank the following who have given permission for the use of copyright material:

W. H. Auden, essay 'The Public vs the late William Butler Yeats' in *Partisan Review*, IV, No. 3 (Spring 1939), by permission of the editor; Harold Bloom, extract from *Yeats* (1970), by permission of Oxford University Press Inc.; Cleanth Brooks, extract from *Modern Poetry and the Tradition* (1939), by permission of The University of North Carolina Press; T. S. Eliot, extracts from *On Poetry and Poets* (1957), by permission of Faber and Faber Ltd; Richard Ellmann, Introduction and extracts from *The Identity of Yeats* (1968), by permission of Faber and Faber Ltd; G. S. Fraser, extract from 'Byzantium', essay in *Critical Quarterly*, II (Autumn 1960), by permission of Mrs Eileen Fraser; Daniel Harris, extract from *Yeats, Coole Park and Ballylee* (1974), by permission of The Johns Hopkins University Press; T. R. Henn, extract from *The Lonely Tower* (1965), by permission of Methuen & Company; Hugh Kenner, extract from article 'The Sacred Book of the Arts' (1958), by permission of the author; Frank Kermode, extract from *Romantic Image* (1957), by permission of Routledge & Kegan Paul Ltd; F. R. Leavis, extract from *New Bearings in English Poetry* (1950), by permission of the Author's Literary Estate and Chatto and Windus Ltd; George Orwell, extract from *Collected Essays, Journalism and Letters*, volume II (1968), edited by Sonia Orwell and Ian Angus, by permission of the Estate of George Orwell and Martin Secker & Warburg Ltd; Thomas Parkinson, extract from *W. B. Yeats: The Later Poetry* (1964), by permission of the University of California Press; C. K. Stead, extract from *The New Poetic* (1964), by permission of the author; Allen Tate, extract from *On the Limits of Poetry* (1948), by permission of the Ohio University Press; Thomas R. Whitaker, extracts from *Swan and Shadow: Yeats' Dialogue with History* (1964), by permission of The University of North Carolina Press; Edmund Wilson, extract from *Axel's Castle: A Study in the Imaginative Literature of 1870–1930* (1959), by permission of Charles Scribner's Sons; Yvor Winters, extract from *The Poetry of W. B. Yeats* (1960), by permission of the Ohio University Press; W. B. Yeats, extract from *Essays and Introductions* (1961), *Autobiographies* (1955), *Explorations* (1962), *Letters on Poetry* (second edition 1964), and *The Letters of W. B. Yeats* (1954), by permission of A. P. Watt Ltd on behalf of Anne Yeats and Michael Yeats.

Every effort has been made to trace all the copyright holders but if any have been inadvertently overlooked the publishers will be pleased to make the necessary arrangements at the first opportunity.

INDEX

This index includes significant references only. Names mentioned in passing are not included. Page numbers in **bold type** denote essays or extracts in this Casebook. Works by Yeats cited in the text are listed alphabetically under his name.